THE GREATEST TRUE CRIME STORIES EVER TOLD

THE GREATEST TRUE CRIME STORIES EVER TOLD

Tales of Murder and Mayhem Ripped from the Front Page

EDITED BY TOM McCARTHY

LYONS
PRESS

Guilford, Connecticut

An imprint of Globe Pequot, the trade division of
The Rowman & Littlefield Publishing Group, Inc.
4501 Forbes Blvd., Ste. 200
Lanham, MD 20706
www.rowman.com

Distributed by NATIONAL BOOK NETWORK

British Library Cataloguing in Publication Information available

Library of Congress Cataloging-in-Publication Data
Names: McCarthy, Tom, 1952– editor.
Title: The greatest true crime stories ever told : tales of murder and mayhem ripped from the front
    page / edited by Tom McCarthy.
Description: Guilford, Connecticut : Lyons Press, [2021] | Includes bibliographical references.
Identifiers: LCCN 2021016522 | ISBN 9781493056705 (paperback ; alk. paper)
Subjects: LCSH: Murder—Case studies. | Crime—Case studies.
Classification: LCC HV6513 .G695 2021 | DDC 364.152/3—dc23
LC record available at https://lccn.loc.gov/2021016522

♾™ The paper used in this publication meets the minimum requirements of American National
Standard for Information Sciences—Permanence of Paper for Printed Library Materials, ANSI/
NISO Z39.48-1992.

CONTENTS

CONTENTS

INTRODUCTION

IF READING TRUE CRIME IS A GUILTY PLEASURE, THIS COLLECTION OF stunning heists and unspeakable murders from the front pages of history will leave no doubt about the verdict.

Guilty as charged.

Let's get this out of the way first, before you proceed too far into this eminently readable collection of stories about unimaginable murders, breathtaking and daring robberies, and an Arctic chase so fraught with danger, courage, and human endurance you'll be looking for a parka and thick gloves before you've finished.

Rule number one: Don't admit you love true crime stories.

You read them quietly and alone, when friends and family are otherwise occupied. You don't talk about what you've read over dinner or among friends or at work. Yet you can't wait to be alone with your latest true crime book.

What is it about true crime stories? Why are they so wildly popular? True crime is fascinating because it offers a glimpse of a darkness we don't converse with in our daily lives. True crime is best read, not participated in. Yet we're drawn to it because we want to understand the motivations and the minds that can, in the case of the infamous Lizzie Borden, actually dismember one's father and stepmother, then calmly deny doing so as their still-warm bodies lay bleeding in the family's prominent Fall River home.

True crime aficionados, and there are too many to count, have voracious appetites for more. They cannot get enough. They can drink in the horror, fascinated, but seem inoculated against it. True crime stories to a true believer are like shots of adrenaline, providing thrills not unlike jumping out of an airplane, with or without a parachute. They enjoy the fear and vicarious thrills but know they can simply put the book down if it gets to be too much.

And, of course, pick it up again later and finish the story.

We read true crime because we want to wonder how we would have reacted if we witnessed a marauding gang of bank robbers shoot to death a young teller and try to get away. Would we have saddled up and given chase? The citizens of Northfield, Minnesota, did—without hesitation and with admirable results.

Three unsuspecting men's lives were cut short at the hands of their lovers in Gangland Chicago. Did they deserve their fates? Did the women who killed them so icily deserve to hang for their crimes?

A mysterious and murderous trapper is hunted like an animal across unforgiving Arctic mountains in subzero temperatures, the prey's near-superhuman endurance testing the finely honed survival instincts of Royal Canadian Mounted Police. He nearly got away and in the process drew sympathetic headlines around the word.

A body in a trunk alerts police to a mysterious murder, but by the time they are on the trail, the suspect is halfway around the world. How do they get him back to the United States to stand trial, and, more perplexing, how do they get him to admit he did it?

These are some of the enticing and unsettling stories in this collection, and they can be read safely and quietly from the comfort of your favorite chair, free from prying eyes, and with no need to explain to others who might not understand your fascination with the darker human instinct that led to such perfidy and chaos. And that's perfectly fine.

Here also is a first-person account of the infamous Lufthansa robbery that netted millions, the story of a beguiling society bank robber so confident that he broke into the same New York City bank twice to pull off the biggest haul in history, and the tale of a devastated father who seeks to have his son's murderers pay for their crime.

Here are not only the suspects, obvious or not, but also the detectives who wanted to put them in prison and were willing to put their own lives at risk to do so. Did the perpetrators get away with their perfidies? Did the rule of law prevail in the end? Were the right people caught and prosecuted?

Readers will have to decide for themselves.

Read quietly, safely.

You will not be disappointed, and no one has to know.

ONE

Murderess Row

Jon Seidel

The men were dead, and their deaths had not been gentle, that was certain. Should the women responsible hang?

CHICAGO CONFRONTED A MURDER SPREE IN THE MID-1920S THAT would be characterized by the *Daily News* as "women's finest hunting season on record here." Killer beauty was a factor not only in the newspaper coverage but also in the criminal courts. Jurors struggled with the idea of holding women responsible for murder and even sending them to the gallows.

The story of three women in particular captured the mood of the moment. Two inspired a play that would reinforce, for generations, Chicago's reputation as a town full of jazz, beauty—and blood.

DUMPY

Upsetting all precedents in the criminal courts of Cook County, a jury this afternoon not only found a woman guilty of murder, but sentenced her to death, together with her co-conspirator, Peter Crudelle. The jury found that Crudelle, aided by Mrs. Isabelle Nitti—now Mrs. Crudelle—had killed Frank Nitti with a hammer.

—*CHICAGO DAILY NEWS*, JULY 9, 1923

FRANK NITTI HAD BEEN MISSING NINE MONTHS WHEN THE BODY appeared in a catch basin just outside Chicago.

From the waist up, it was mostly a skeleton. The flesh had disappeared from the face. It wore a pair of trousers and a shoe on its left foot. The other shoe would be found in the murky water below.

The body bobbed in the water near the northeast corner of Thirty-Ninth and Ridgeland in Stickney—that is, until a man working for the town of Berwyn finally pulled up his hip boots and climbed into the water on May 9, 1923. He helped four other men—including an undertaker—yank it out using a rubber mat with a rope tied to each corner.

They laid the body on the grass. Then the Berwyn worker jumped back into the catch basin, baling water in a search for clues. He cut his own finger along the way. Ultimately, he found the body's lower jaw and other bones amid the muck.

"Look! There is a ring on this," another man called out.

The worker had been holding a bone he'd discovered above the rim of the catch basin. He dipped it back into the water to clean it and called for the undertaker or the police chief. Both had left. So the worker dropped the bone and the ring into the pocket of his overalls for safekeeping.

Authorities would later conclude the body's skull had been fractured "by a blunt octagonal instrument about one and a quarter inches in diameter."

The mystery of Frank Nitti's disappearance followed a fight between the Italian truck farmer and one of his older children, Mike.

Mike wanted $500 from his father to go get married. Frank Nitti refused to turn it over. He even slapped his son, a witness said. Mike had been working in the city instead of on the farm, and Frank Nitti allegedly told him, "Only bums work in Chicago."

Eventually, Mike turned on his father. He knocked the old man down and kicked and beat his father until his father was nearly unconscious. When the beating ended, Frank Nitti stood up, holding his stomach, and faced his son with tears in his eyes and blood on his face.

"You have got me," he said before slinking away.

Two weeks passed. Then came July 29, 1922. Frank Nitti's wife, Sabella Nitti, later insisted she had been preparing to put her younger children to bed around nine o'clock at night. That's when her husband announced he was headed out to the field. He wanted to make sure no vandals burned the oats.

That was the last time she saw him. Coincidentally, their son Mike disappeared at the same time—and wouldn't return for a week.

By the time the body appeared in the catch basin, Sabella had a new husband. She had married Peter Crudelle, a hired hand on the farm. And their relationship raised suspicion.

Sabella would go on to be remembered by the *Daily News* as a "dumpy, ugly Italian woman." And such opinions wound up mattering big-time. Sabella's perceived lack of beauty—and the pretty faces of those who would join her on Murderess Row in the 1920s—clouded everything that happened next.

In Sabella's case, so would a language barrier, as authorities tried to navigate between English and Italian.

Months before the body appeared in the catch basin, Sabella and Crudelle had been hauled into the office of the Cook County state's attorney, along with Sabella's son Charlie. A jury would later be told that, in a crucial moment, a prosecutor asked Charlie in Italian, "Who killed your father?"

"My mother and Peter Crudelle," Charlie answered.

The prosecutor turned to Sabella and asked, "Did you kill your husband?"

In a moment of apparent confusion, Sabella said, "Whatever Charlie said, that is true."

But when the jury finally had a chance to hear "whatever Charlie said," he told them, "On the twenty-ninth of July, my father left—I don't know where he went."

Police and prosecutors insisted on a different story. Charlie allegedly said his father had been sleeping under a wagon when Crudelle grabbed a hammer and snuck up on the farmer; that Charlie pushed Crudelle in an attempt to save his father's life, causing Crudelle to drop the hammer; that Sabella picked it up and handed it back to Crudelle so he could finish the job; and that Crudelle and his mother lifted his father's body into the wagon, hitched a horse to it, and hauled the body to a drainage canal.

Deputy Cook County sheriff Paul Dasso said he actually took Charlie and Crudelle back to the farm to walk through, step by step, how Crudelle had supposedly disposed of the body. The sheriff hitched a horse to a wagon and, during the reenactment, Crudelle drove. Charlie gave directions.

Once the men pulled the wagon as close to the drainage canal as possible, Dasso said Charlie explained how Crudelle had lifted the body and carried it toward a bridge. Charlie also allegedly said he did not actually see Crudelle dump his father's body in the canal. But he said he heard the splash.

Lawyers would later point out that the catch basin where Frank Nitti's body was supposedly found was a mile away, and its only drain was six or seven inches in diameter. "It would be impossible for a human body to pass through."

Meanwhile, Dasso said Crudelle muttered one English word during his reenactment: "Bullshit."

It wasn't until the badly decayed body was found in the catch basin that authorities finally made their arrests for Frank Nitti's murder—Peter Crudelle, Sabella Nitti, and Charlie were all indicted.

Two dubious factors led to the body's identification as Frank Nitti. First, the shoes. A male relative who once worked for him said he had asked Frank Nitti for a pair of shoes in April 1922. Frank Nitti bought him a pair of tan shoes. The man, Sabella's nephew, said he wore them for two or three days but eventually gave them back because they were too big. He insisted that Frank Nitti wore them until he disappeared three months later. The shoes were typical tan shoes with no distinguishing marks.

The worker viewed the body found in the catch basin in May 1923 and insisted those were the same shoes.

Then there was the ring. Frank Nitti's other son, James, insisted it had once belonged to him. He said it had a red stone, but he'd broken it and thrown the ring into the front yard. He said his father picked it up, flattened its prongs, and began to wear it.

When the body was found, Dasso went out to arrest Sabella, Crudelle, and Charlie.

With his pistol in his hand, Dasso tried the front door of their home. It was bolted shut.

"You open that door or I will kick it in," Dasso insisted, according to the court records.

The sheriff heard the latch open, so he pushed open the door. Inside he saw Crudelle and Sabella Nitti as well as her children. Dasso declared that Frank Nitti's body had been found, and he was there to make an arrest.

Sabella began to break down, Dasso said later. He said she turned to one of her daughters and said, "Goodbye now. I am going to be gone for a long time." Sabella, Charlie, and Crudelle climbed into a patrol wagon, and the police drove them to a police station in nearby Cicero.

— ◆ —

The language barrier continued to frustrate throughout the trial. Meanwhile, Sabella found herself being represented by Eugene Moran, an attorney who she would later insist she had never hired.

Judge Joseph David berated Moran repeatedly. At one point, after James Nitti described Sabella's alleged admission in the office of the state's attorney, the judge cut off the testimony, sent the jury away, and began to lecture the lawyer.

"Now listen," the judge said. "If you don't know how to protect the rights of parties, I will protect them."

The jury heard from a woman named Anna Volpe, a Nitti family acquaintance, who said that Frank Nitti fired Crudelle in June 1922 after he realized Crudelle and Sabella had been "guilty of immoral conduct."

Volpe said Sabella sent one of her sons with five dollars to give to Crudelle. She also alleged that Sabella insisted she wanted to marry Crudelle and was sick of her husband.

She claimed she heard Sabella say, "I don't want the husband anymore. I don't want to see him anymore. I don't want him."

She allegedly said, "My husband stinks."

The judge at one point called attempts to translate Volpe's testimony "disgraceful." But it continued. And jurors were also told that Sabella dismissed Volpe at one point by saying, "Go on, because I am going to bed and sleep with Pete."

Sabella's attorney asked Volpe whether Frank Nitti ever wore jewelry.

"He wore a ring without a stone, and it was all hammered down," Volpe said.

A prosecutor followed up, showing Volpe the ring found with the body in the catch basin. "Have you ever seen that ring before?"

"For two years he wore it always on the third finger of the left hand," Volpe declared.

Through the interpreter, Volpe added, "Look close, and you will see there is dough in there. He used to knead his own bread."

"Show us the dough in the ring," the defense attorney insisted.

"Look," Volpe said in English. "Dry bread. Look. See. See."

"That is dry bread," the defense attorney conceded.

But Moran pressed on after Volpe said she had recognized the corpse pulled from the catch basin.

Moran: "Did you see his eyes?"

Volpe: "I could not see the eyes."

Moran: "Did you see any hair?"

Volpe: "No."

Moran: "Did you see any skin on his face?"

Volpe: "No."

Moran: "Did you see any ears?"

Volpe: "I saw blows on his head, two of them."

Moran: "Did you see any ears?"

Volpe: "I did not look close enough to see those."

Moran: "Did you see any skin on this part of the body?"

Volpe: "Yes, I saw his whole body."

Moran: "Did he have any underwear on?"

Volpe: "They were consumed, yes, they were all consumed."

Moran: "Decomposed, you mean?"

Volpe: "Yes."

Moran: "Did you recognize the shoes?"

Volpe: "Yes, I saw the shoes."

Moran: "Did you recognize the shoes to be those of Frank Nitti?"

Volpe: "I saw the shoes, but I did not recognize them because I had not seen them before."

———

When Sabella finally took the stand, she was asked about her earlier interview with prosecutors, in September 1922. She insisted she "didn't understand; there were so many people." And she said somebody warned her not to go, saying, "They will kill you."

"At that time, Mrs. Nitti, did you say that whatever Charlie said was right?" the attorneys pressed.

"No, no, no," Sabella insisted.

When her attorney showed her the hammer alleged to be the murder weapon, she acknowledged she had seen it before—at the Volpe home.

"It was never at my house," she said. "I know all of the tools at my farm."

Finally, her attorney asked directly whether she and Crudelle had murdered Frank Nitti.

"If I had seen Pete Crudelle strike my husband on the head with that hammer, I would have killed Pete Crudelle before he would have killed my husband," Sabella said.

———

Prosecutors eventually dropped the case against Charlie. But the jury found Sabella Nitti and Peter Crudelle guilty in July 1923. In doing so, it handed down a sentence that upset "all precedents in the criminal courts of Cook County," according to the *Daily News*.

Crudelle was to hang. So was Sabella—a woman.

An interpreter tried to translate the jury's "guilty" verdict. But Sabella simply shrugged her shoulders. When photographers tried to take a picture of "the only woman ever sentenced to death in Cook County," Sabella turned the other way.

It soon became clear that Sabella didn't understand.

The judge avoided giving her an explanation. Her attorney said he "simply couldn't." And in the jail, authorities said they wished not to destroy her "protecting shield of ignorance."

So the next day, authorities finally tracked down someone to explain things to her through the iron grate at the jail.

"Ask her if she understood what the jury said," Moran told the interpreter.

Sabella, occasionally rubbing her hands against the pink gingham dress she wore in the jail, shook her head.

The defense attorney shuddered. "Tell her she has been condemned to hang by the neck until dead," he said.

The interpreter's voice choked. He said the words. Then there was a pause.

"God help me!" Sabella finally screamed, falling to her knees.

But there was more. The interpreter pressed on, determined to end the awful ordeal.

"Did you know that the same verdict had been passed on Peter?" he asked.

"No, no," Nitti gasped, swaying back and forth on her knees as she began to wail. Finally, she called for her "baby"—Charlie—who was standing nearby.

"Oh my baby!" she said. "Come here and help me!"

Charlie didn't budge. Sabella lost all control. The jailers tossed cold water in Sabella's face.

The next day, Sabella began to beat her head against the bars of her cell until she was bloody. Then she tried to choke herself. Finally stopped by the guards, she began to refuse her food.

Her defense attorney assured reporters her hanging would never be carried out.

"Even though she is ugly and without sex appeal, someone will intercede to avert the carrying out of this horrible sentence," Moran said, according to the *Daily News*. "We are not going to set a precedent here as hangers of women."

<hr>

Meanwhile, the jurors had trouble of their own. Their wives were not happy with them for sending a woman to the gallows.

The jury foreman reportedly told a court official, "My wife is in hysterics," and he spent twenty minutes meeting with the judge.

"I don't know what to do," he said. "She is so wrought up over this verdict that nothing will pacify her. She threatens to leave me if Mrs. Nitti hangs."

The *Daily News* tried to track his wife down but couldn't find her. A reporter decided to interview the couple's nine-year-old daughter instead.

"Papa and Mama love each other a lot," the girl said. "Last night was the first time Papa ever made Mama cry. Papa said it was his duty to have that woman hung by the neck and then Mama cried worse. Now she's gone away, but I won't tell where. She told me not to."

Then the paper reached out to other jurors' wives.

"I am much distressed that my husband voted to take a human life," one said. "Of course, I would not leave him on that account, but I feel very badly about it. I have wept a good deal over it."

Another approved of her husband's judgment.

"If Mrs. Nitti helped to do such a deed, why should she be shielded?" she said.

Still another said she'd be especially angry "if I thought he changed his opinion because he believed that he might thereby please me."

The *Daily News* even spoke to one juror's mother.

"Women should suffer the same penalty as men for the same crimes," the woman said, adding that her son was "perfectly right. I know he would follow the dictates of his conscience in any event, and that is what I wish him always to do."

⁓

When it came time to formally hand down the sentence, Judge David told Sabella's defense attorney, "I am powerless. There can be no doubt as to the guilt of this woman. She committed a horrible crime; the state's proof was unmistakable; the jury could not do otherwise than find her guilty.... I am personally opposed to capital punishment, but the law gives me no right to set aside the jury's verdict. I can only impose the sentence that the jury has decreed."

The *Daily News* said Sabella and her silent new husband "stared anxiously about them as the strange lawyers and stranger judge went through their inexplicable ritual of words. They understood nothing, except, perhaps, that something was being attempted in their behalf."

The judge asked, "Have the defendants anything to say as to why sentence should not be passed?"

Sabella and Crudelle stared blankly until the judge asked that the question be interpreted. Crudelle began repeating, "I don't understand. I don't understand."

Rather than explain further, the judge formally set their hanging for October 12. Sabella "moaned like an animal," the *Daily News* said. Deputies began to lead her away, walking her past an elevator shaft.

Sabella suddenly threw herself headfirst toward the shaft. The bailiffs stopped her just in time.

⁓

The slightest glimmer of hope finally appeared for Sabella in August. Judge David agreed that month to let six newly appointed Italian attorneys take up her case and explain why the verdict should be tossed—even though he insisted they had almost no hope of success.

"There is not one chance in one hundred that anything can be introduced which will induce me to set aside the verdict," the judge said. "I believe Mrs. Nitti was legally tried. Neither do I believe that I can be induced to grant a stay of execution. I shall not permit myself to be swayed by sentimental considerations."

Later that month, the new team of lawyers made their case. Mostly, they insisted the man who had defended Sabella at trial had been incompetent. As promised, the judge shot them down.

"There is no law that permits a judge to discharge counsel for the defense," he said. "And this is especially true in a case such as this, where the attorney was selected and retained by the defendants themselves. It is the experience of this court that ninety percent of the lawyers in all criminal cases are incompetent."

After the hearing, the *Daily News* wrote, "Only a commutation from Governor Small or a stay from a higher court can now save Mrs. Nitti from the hangman's noose."

That's exactly what happened. A few weeks before her scheduled execution with Crudelle, the Illinois Supreme Court handed down a stay of execution. Less than an hour later, one of Sabella's new lawyers stood outside her jailhouse window, sharing a few soft words of Italian.

They brought shrieks of joy.

"Thank you, God. You answered my prayer," Sabella cried.

The lawyer thrust his hand through the bars of the window, and she kissed it.

———⌒◦⌒———

In their briefs to the supreme court, Sabella's new lawyers tore into Moran, Sabella's original defense attorney.

"These ignorant foreigners went to their trial and their doom without counsel," the lawyers wrote. And, because prosecutors took advantage "of the stupidity and incompetency" of the man who tried to do the job, they also "took an unfair and unwarranted advantage" at trial. They concluded that Sabella and Crudelle "would have been far better off without any counsel."

Then the new lawyers pointed to examples in the record, like when Judge David warned the defense attorney, "I shall have to ask some lawyer to step in here and assist you in the defense."

Moran said simply, "Your Honor, I think I have practiced law long enough to know how to try a case."

But the judge told him, "You may have practiced law for a dozen years or for a thousand years, but it is not proper for you to bring out questions that are detrimental to your client."

The state's high court finally handed down its opinion in April 1924.

"The fact that the defendants were ignorant, illiterate foreigners, unacquainted with law or court procedure in this or any other country, and unable to speak and understand the English language, requires that we take into consideration the gross incompetency and stupidity of counsel appearing for them," the supreme court said in its ruling.

"It is quite clear from an examination of the record that defendants' interests would have been much better served with no counsel at all than with the one they had."

The court said the lawyer's "stupidity" alone was not enough to overturn the convictions. But there was more.

The court made note of the fight between Frank Nitti and his son Mike, writing that "the trouble between Mike and his father occurred just two weeks before his father disappeared, and the evidence shows that Mike disappeared the same night and was gone for a week. This evidence was relevant and should have been admitted."

The man who witnessed the fight said Mike had threatened to kill him if he testified.

As for Sabella's so-called confession at the state attorney's office, the court wrote that evidence of what happened there is "in such rambling fashion that it is difficult to determine the exact circumstances under which they were made." And, they said, "Mrs. Nitti was crying and moaning while Charles was telling his story, and there is no proof that she heard or understood what he said."

With that evidence eliminated, the court said there was nothing to tie Crudelle to the murder, and there was nothing to prove he had been "guilty of immoral conduct" with Sabella.

The court also seemed dissatisfied with the identification of the body found in the catch basin, complaining that no one had said whether Frank Nitti's hair and weight matched the corpse's.

"Before the dread sentence of death is finally passed on this man and woman on evidence as uncertain and unsatisfactory as that on which this conviction stands, there ought to be a further investigation with competent counsel representing the accused," the court wrote. "Safety and justice require that this cause be submitted to another jury. The judgments are reversed, and the cause is remanded to the criminal court of Cook County."

Sabella heard the news from reporters, but she did not immediately understand what had happened. Once assured she was to have a new trial, she took it to mean her freedom was certain.

She wept. And she prayed.

Months later, prosecutors would find their case permanently crippled.

"I never killed my husband," Sabella insisted. "I never did."

The "Chic" Divorcée

Mrs. Belva Gaertner, chic divorcée, sobbed out a story at the Wabash Avenue police station this morning of a gin-engendered hiatus in her memory during which, the police say, she shot and killed Walter R. Law, an automobile salesman, as they were returning together early to-day in her automobile from a round of the cabarets.

—*Chicago Daily News*, March 12, 1924

The Nash sedan sat suspiciously in the darkness in the middle of a road on Chicago's South Side in March 1924.

The engine seemed slightly warm. No one was around. It was the middle of the night.

Officer Morris Quinn spotted the automobile on Forrestville Avenue, just north of Fiftieth, around 1:30 a.m. His partner was not far, but Quinn decided to take a closer look on his own. The officer walked along the wet, slushy roadway until he neared one side of the car, but it was too dark to see inside. So he moved to the other side and lifted his flashlight.

The car was full of blood. Quinn saw a man, dressed in a brown overcoat, lying over the steering wheel. Red droplets continued to fall from the man's right cheek, where Quinn saw a bullet hole.

On the floor of the car was a gun and a bottle of gin.

Quinn fired his own weapon twice in the air to get his partner's attention, then he called the station. His partner surveyed the neighborhood and found someone who had heard two shots—likely Quinn's. Meanwhile, another officer had arrived and called back to the station to run the car's license number. It took only a few minutes to learn the registered owner of the bloody sedan.

Belva Gaertner of the 4800 block of Forrestville Avenue.

The police soon found the former cabaret singer in her apartment. Gaertner had a long nose and a crooked smile. That night, she also stank of booze and had undressed for the evening. But at the officers' request, she showed off the outfit she had worn out on the town: a green dress, a white hat, a pair of white satin slippers, and a brown karakul coat covered in blood.

With that, a spectacle had begun that would be recounted for generations in the musical *Chicago*. The original play was written by *Chicago Tribune* reporter Maurine Watkins.

Gaertner admitted she owned a Nash sedan. And she said she had used it earlier to visit the Gingham Inn at Sixty-Eighth and Cottage Grove with a man named Walter Law. She said she thought she had left the car "up the street."

Then she began to tell police—and soon, prosecutors—varying versions of how the night had played out.

"Oh, Mr. Attorney," Gaertner at one point told a prosecutor, "I can't remember anything—not if I have to hang for it."

Gaertner explained that Law, a married car salesman with a three-year-old son, had come to her home the night before. The two had known each other since December 1923, and they sometimes went out two or three times a week.

Before they left for the Gingham on March 11, 1924, Gaertner said she grabbed a gun out of her dresser drawer and handed it to Law for fear of being robbed. On the way to the Gingham, they stopped for a fifth of gin near Fifty-Fifth and Cottage Grove.

When they got to the Gingham, Law escorted Gaertner inside and then left her alone while he put the car away and washed his hands.

By the time he returned, he saw Gaertner dancing with a man known as "Curley."

That man later told a coroner's jury his name was B. Brown—"floor man" at the Gingham. He said he had already seen Gaertner and Law "a few times" there. And on the night in question, while Law went to the bathroom to wash his hands, he said he asked Gaertner if she wanted to dance. She agreed, and they danced until Law came out of the bathroom.

When Law returned, Curley said he motioned for Law to take over the dance.

"[Law] liked me, and we seemed to be friends," Curley said later.

He also said Gaertner and Law drank ginger ale that night and didn't seem drunk. That suspicious testimony "caused a smile," the *Daily News* wrote later.

When Gaertner and Law sat down at their table, Gaertner said Law began to talk about the gun.

"He said to me there is nine shots in this gun," Gaertner said. "We will toss a coin to see who shoots first and alternate shots. You shoot at me and I at you and then toss a coin to see who fires the ninth shot."

Gaertner said she didn't understand what he was talking about, and they quickly laughed off the drunken conversation.

The night went on. Gaertner said she didn't know how long they stayed, but it was "long enough to drink enough gin that I don't remember leaving the place at all."

Still, in another version of the story given to police and recounted in the *Daily News*, Gaertner said that "on our way to my home, we began talking about 'stick-up men.'" She said, "I told Law we were taking an awful risk going home so late. Think of it. What if some bandit stopped and robbed us and maybe tried to get rough with me, what would we do?" She said, "I'll bet I'm a better shooter than you are."

Law told her she was wrong. He laughed out loud and patted her on the shoulder. "I'm a wonderful marksman; I never miss," he said.

This time, Gaertner said it was she who jokingly suggested the game of Russian roulette with the gun.

"And then—oh, I don't know just what did happen," Gaertner said. "I was too drunk."

Regardless of how it happened, Gaertner said she suddenly remembered a shock—a great noise. They were inside her car. She felt blood on her hands, and she saw more of it running down Law's face. Unsure of what had happened, she tried her best to get Law's heavy body off the steering wheel—hoping she could drive the car to a doctor. But Law wouldn't budge.

Eventually Gaertner tried talking to Law, hoping to rouse him. It was no use. Finally, she got out of the car and went home.

"I undressed but couldn't sleep," Gaertner said. She said she "was dressing to go and see if Mr. Law wouldn't talk to me when the police came."

When it came time to go to the police station, the officers asked Gaertner to get dressed. She nearly forgot her jewelry. On her way out of the apartment, she put on six or seven rings and a watch.

Later, at the station, an officer noticed that the watch was covered in blood. It had stopped at 1:15.

———

Law's death left at least two people reeling. Gaertner's former husband, William, apparently thought they had been working toward a reconciliation—and a third marriage. The first had been annulled when he realized she had been divorced from her previous husband for less than a year. The second union didn't last either. But in March 1924, he said he wanted to try again.

"I'm through with her now forever," William Gaertner insisted.

But he soon sent his attorney to represent her and declared he would stand by her to the end.

Meanwhile, in a small frame house in the 3200 block of Ellis, neighbors comforted Law's wife, Freda. The beauty of Law's widow arguably topped Gaertner's. But by the time her photograph appeared in the *Daily News*, her face had been filled with the grief and betrayal of a woman whose husband had just been murdered while out with another woman. She held the couple's three-year-old son, who looked toward the camera with innocent, but curious, eyes.

"Walter died at his work," Freda Law insisted, putting her denial on full display. "He had sold Mrs. Gaertner that car, and he was demonstrating to her how to drive it. He did that with almost all his customers.

"I never heard of the Gaertner woman until I read about Walter's death in the papers," she continued. "I do not believe she killed him. The bullet that caused his death came from the outside and probably never was meant for him. . . . Walter was always devoted to me. I never suspected him of doing anything that might give me cause to be jealous, and I don't suspect him now."

Law's father also insisted on the explanation given by his daughter-in-law: "Walter died at his work."

During the inquest into her husband's death, Freda Law said she last saw her husband alive in the morning before he left for work. She said he called around six o'clock to see if she wanted to do anything that evening.

"I said I was going to stay home and sew," Freda Law said.

Walter Law told his wife he then planned to stay at the office for a while. Freda said that was not unusual.

However, she said her husband did not drink. She said he didn't carry guns.

And she said he had never mentioned Belva Gaertner's name.

———

Another story emerged during the coroner's inquest. A colleague of Law's named Paul Goodwin said Law had talked about taking out more insurance shortly before his death. Goodwin said he had asked why.

"Miss Gaertner threatened to shoot me," Law allegedly told him.

Goodwin said Law had then laughed the whole thing off. Still, Goodwin said he had heard about a violent incident two weeks earlier. Law had allegedly been visiting Gaertner and went to leave when she suddenly locked the door, threw the key under the bed, and threatened him with a knife.

Despite all the talking she had done, Gaertner refused to testify at the inquest. She waited until the next morning, at the jail, to deny Goodwin's testimony between bites of a sugar roll.

The *Daily News* wrote that Gaertner had gone through a transformation since police had discovered her at her Forrestville apartment.

"Cosmetics, a comb, and a night's rest had done their work," the newspaper wrote, "and Mrs. Gaertner was a picture of self-possession, a woman of the world."

"I'm feeling very well," Gaertner told reporters as she posed for a photograph. "Naturally, I should prefer to receive you all in my own apartment; jails are such horrid places. But one must make the best of such things."

As for Goodwin's story, she said, it was "simply ridiculous."

"I never threatened Law," she said. "True enough, I was fond of him."

Even as Freda Law prepared for the burial of her cheating husband, Gaertner told the press that Law was "not worth killing." She predicted that a "broad-minded jury of worldly men" would never convict her.

While visiting with Gaertner, a *Daily News* reporter noticed another inmate standing nearby—Sabella Nitti, who had yet to be freed and still faced the gallows for killing her husband.

Sabella, the newspaper said, "looked on curiously and gave a friendly 'good morning' nod to the new arrival."

Gaertner's case quickly took a backseat to more sensational murders. But when she finally went to trial that June, the *Daily News* wrote that Gaertner looked "younger and fresher since her incarceration—hardly like the same woman the police found cowering in her apartment, her clothing covered with the blood of the young married man who had been her companion during the fateful evening.

"A smart white blouse, neat patent-leather pumps, and a small satin hat with a rhinestone ornament completed her attire today," the *Daily News* noted. "She wore white kid gloves, as if for a matinee."

Freda Law, the newspaper said, was "younger and prettier than the woman whom Walter Law chose for his cabaret companion." Still, it said, she was "slim and pathetic in her black garments."

Meanwhile, a prosecutor found himself complaining about a nuisance in the courtroom: cameras. They began to click as Gaertner took her seat for jury selection.

"The cameras are not disturbing me nor the defendant nor the men called for jury service as far as I can see," the judge said. "Proceed with the questioning."

Another prosecutor named Harry Pritzker asked potential jurors, "Would you be willing to mete out the same punishment to a woman that you would to a man?"

Gaertner leaned forward, absorbed in what is typically a tedious process. Her attorneys tried to do away with jurors who preferred the Volstead Act to boozy women, and prosecutors tried to rid the panel of jurors who would go easy on a woman.

However, Gaertner's lawyers apparently won the case right there. Prosecutors would go on to lay out the entire incriminating story—how Gaertner's clothing was found covered with blood after a night of drinking in which Law wound up dead in her car.

But the jury still acquitted her.

The defense attorneys didn't even put on a case. People who had waited an entire day to see if Gaertner would testify wound up being disappointed. She just sat there, chin in hand, staring at a piece of evidence brought into the courtroom by prosecutors—the slippers she had worn the night Law died.

Prosecutors were not even bold enough to ask for the death penalty.

The Prettiest Woman Ever Tried for Murder in Chicago

Mrs. Beulah Annan, termed by her questioners "a modern Salome," sat quietly this morning in the matron's room at the South Clark Street police station and greeted visitors with an imperturbable glance from under long lashes drooping over half-closed eyes.

—*Chicago Daily News*, April 4, 1924

Beulah Annan wore her red hair in a bob. She spoke with a velvety southern drawl. And while her paramour lay dying on the floor with a bullet in his back, the press said she danced for hours to a jazzy tune about the girl "who never could be true."

Three weeks after police found Walter Law dead in Belva Gaertner's car, Beulah Annan took over the headlines with a tale of betrayal, murder, and stunning good looks. The *Daily News* labeled Annan "the prettiest woman ever tried for murder in Chicago," and she gave the *Tribune's* Maurine Watkins the other half of her blockbuster play.

Reporters discovered the daughter of a Kentucky farmer at the South Clark police station early in April 1924. By then, her long lashes had drooped over half-closed eyes that had lost "every trace of fire that must have illuminated them," a reporter wrote. She tried to explain how a laundromat coworker named Harry Kalstedt had wound up dead on April 3, 1924, in her apartment in the 800 block of East Forty-Sixth.

The tale was sensational. But like Gaertner's, the more she told it, the more it changed. And it evolved into a tale of self-defense.

"I don't think I ever loved anybody very much," Annan said, according to the *Daily News*. "You know how it is—you keep looking and looking all the time for someone you can really love."

Annan remained on her hunt for love despite being married to a garage mechanic named Albert Annan. He had been away, at work, when Annan said Kalstedt came by with two quarts of wine. She said she had the day off, and they planned to spend the afternoon together.

They drank the wine, she said. All of it. And then they began to fight as they listened to records.

"I taunted Harry with the fact that he had been in jail once," Annan said. "And he said something nasty back to me. Seems like we just wanted to make each other mad—and to hurt each other. I finally called him a name."

She called him a "jailbird," the press said.

"You won't call me a name like that," Kalstedt declared.

Kalstedt suddenly began to rush toward the bedroom, Annan said. There could have only been one reason. A gun was there, in plain sight. Though Annan had kept it under a pillow, she said the pillow had been turned back, revealing the weapon.

"I ran," Annan said. "And as he reached out to pick the gun up off the bed, I reached around him and grabbed it. Then I shot. They say I shot him in the back, but it must have been sort of under the arm."

Kalstedt looked at the beautiful woman. "Anne," he said, "you've shot me."

"No, Harry," Annan said, trying to comfort the man as she put her arms around him. "You're all right. You're not shot."

Then he fell against a wall.

The singer on the jazz record crooned about "Hula Lou—the kind of girl who never could be true." The record ended as Kalstedt took what Annan thought were his last breaths. The needle began to scratch. Outside, Annan heard children shouting. Beyond that, silence reigned.

Annan went to the bathroom to wash the crimson blood from her magnolia-white hands. She also took a washcloth and tried to wipe the blood off Harry's face.

"I washed it off," she said, "and kissed him."

Then Annan walked back over to the record player. And she started it again.

"I couldn't stand the silence," she said.

Annan allegedly played her records for hours while Kalstedt lay on the floor. Her explanation: "I was in a mad ecstasy."

Annan may have thought Kalstedt died immediately. But the shooting likely took place around two o'clock in the morning, and a doctor would testify that Kalstedt died later in the afternoon.

That would have meant Kalstedt laid there alive, for hours, while Annan danced.

Annan eventually came to her senses. She said she called her husband around five o'clock in the morning, but she insisted, "I don't see how it could have been that long. I just kept going back and forth between the living room and the bedroom, where Harry's body lay, and playing the phonograph."

When she reached Albert Annan at the garage where he worked in the 9100 block of Baltimore, she told him, "Come home. I've shot a man. He's been trying to make love to me."

Albert came home. He believed his wife's story, but he insisted they call the police.

When the detectives arrived, some of them doffed their caps at the sight of Annan. Albert told them he had shot Kalstedt, but the men took it for simple chivalry. Annan said, "That's just my husband. I did it. He's just trying to protect me."

Annan later insisted she spoke that night to a prosecutor named Roy Woods. She said they spoke while she stood beside her kitchen sink, and he convinced her to give a confession she would later take back.

"He said if I would tell him all about it he would help me," she said.

Annan powdered her nose during the coroner's inquest and refused to testify. Albert listened to the testimony—about his wife's confession to the shooting and to multiple acts of infidelity—and twisted his hands. When it ended, he gave Annan money to take back to the jail.

Annan told reporters she would have rather been in Kalstedt's place.

"Thinking it all over, I think I would rather have been shot myself," Annan said. "Of course, it all happened so quickly, I didn't have time to think then."

At this point, Annan hadn't even been given her jail uniform. She still wore her silk stockings and new shoes while sitting beside other inmates Belva Gaertner and Sabella Nitti.

Annan's trial began just as Chicago was learning about one of the most heinous crimes in its history—the brutal killing of fourteen-year-old Robert Franks.

"Killed boy kidnapped for ransom," the *Daily News* headline blared on May 22, 1924. Below it, in smaller print, were the words "Get jury to try Beulah."

Prosecutors again found themselves fighting sympathy toward women among potential jurors. They asked the candidates, "Will the sex of the defendant have anything to do with your decision as to punishment if the defendant is proved guilty?"

They even went so far as to ask, "Do you think that if the defendant had a pretty face it would influence you in your deliberations of this case?"

Annan looked pale when she arrived in the courtroom. She looked neither at Albert nor her mother—both were in the gallery. She sat with her eyes closed through most of the questioning, but the *Daily News* said they flew open when she heard these words from the prosecutor: "There are three forms of punishment for murder. One of them is the death penalty."

Prosecutors said they would let the jury choose the punishment.

Two days later, as police speculated that Bobby Franks's killer might have committed suicide, Annan's trial seemed to take on less significance. Still, she managed to put on a show for the ages when she testified. The *Daily News* declared that "no more dramatic story ever was told from the witness stand."

The courtroom was packed when Annan, wearing a "simple frock of blue" with a white collar, refused to repeat the confession she had given the month before. "Her voice was soft, her manner demure," the *Daily News* said.

"She seemed in every way to deserve her distinction as the most beautiful woman ever tried for murder in Cook County," the newspaper gushed.

Cameramen cast their lights on Annan, disorienting her for a moment as she began to tell the story. She said Kalstedt was already drunk when he knocked on her door, asking for money to buy some wine. Though he asked for six dollars, she gave him only one.

She later said Kalstedt returned with a package of wine and offered to let her have some, taking off his hat and overcoat.

"Have a drink?" he asked.

Annan said she told him, "No, I couldn't have a drink, because he'd already had too much."

"Just have one drink and then I'll go," he allegedly pressed, turning on the record player. "Come on, let's go into the other room."

"No," Annan said she insisted. "My husband's liable to come home."

Still, she admitted she began to drink with him. He sat down on the couch, and she sat beside him.

"Try to pull yourself together. My husband's liable to come home," Annan said.

"What the hell do I care?" Kalstedt asked. "Come on and come across. Quit stalling. You know you're not afraid of your husband."

That was when Annan deployed what appeared to be her ultimate defense against the chilling thought of an execution.

"I told him," she whispered. "I told him he must leave me alone. And then I told him why."

Annan hesitated on the witness stand. She looked downcast, her cheeks delicately flushed. Everyone in the courtroom held their breath. Finally, she lifted her eyes to the jury.

"I told him I was going to have a baby," she said.

Kalstedt didn't buy it.

"Another woman told me that once and got me to marry her," he said. "I also did five years once, because a woman wouldn't come across when I wanted her to."

"My husband will come in and kill you and maybe both of us," Annan said.

Suddenly, Annan said, Kalstedt rose from the couch, made a comment about a gun, and began to make his way to the bedroom. Annan followed.

"He reached for the gun, but I was nearer," she said. "He kept coming toward me."

Annan said she pushed him away, putting her left hand on his right shoulder.

"Then I shot him," she said.

"The Victrola was still going round and round, though it wasn't playing," Annan said. "I went to the Victrola, then back to the bedroom and sat beside him. I tried to see whether he was dead or not. I don't know how long I sat there or what I did. I couldn't seem to do what I wanted to."

She said she finally got the phone and called a number she thought was her husband's. But it didn't work. And she kept calling it. Finally, she said, a man on the line told her to "refer to your directory." She remembered she had a piece of paper with his number on it and called him.

Annan denied playing "Hula Lou" while Kalstedt lay on the ground. The bloody record had been introduced as evidence earlier in the trial.

"No, no," she said. "I went to the phonograph and shut it off. That's how the blood got on the record. But I didn't play [it]. How could I?"

⸺

When closing arguments began, a prosecutor fought his principal battle—with Annan's beauty.

"You've seen that face," he said. "Surely it is a fair presumption that no man before Kalstedt had dared tell her to go to hell. It is a fair presumption that she was made bitterly angry."

But it wasn't enough. The jury acquitted Annan.

A few days later, Annan ran off "in the country somewhere" with her husband, according to the *Daily News*. They hoped to forget about her trial and rest.

But Annan soon announced she'd be leaving Albert. He had gone broke paying for her defense.

The *Daily News* would note that "the stork didn't get Beulah's courtroom order. He never called."

"I'm through with men," she told reporters after leaving the courtroom. "I'll never marry again."

Annan married again in 1927. She eloped with the owner of a Chestnut Street garage. It didn't last. A year later, she died in a Chicago sanitarium under an assumed name. Her mother accompanied her body back to Kentucky for the funeral.

The *Daily News* said that, in her final days, Annan had reconciled with her father.

The minister who spoke at her funeral said Annan "was sorry she had not lived a better life."

And, he said, "God was merciful in giving her a chance to repent."

TWO

The Preller Murder Case

Thomas Furlong

The murderer was at large in a foreign country. He had committed the perfect crime. Or so he thought.

THE PRELLER MURDER OCCURRED IN THE SUMMER OF 1885, IN ONE OF the rooms of the Southern Hotel, St. Louis, Missouri. Clarence Preller was a young Englishman, as was his slayer, Hugh M. Brookes. The discovery of the body, the apprehension of the murderer, and his trial and execution attracted the attention of the civilized world. The true story of the conviction of the perpetrator of this foul crime has never before been published.

Hugh M. Brookes was a native of Hyde Park, a suburb of London, England. His father and mother were respectable people and schoolteachers by profession. The young man was about twenty-five or twenty-six years of age when he committed this crime. He had never done anything but go to school; consequently, he was well educated. The last school he attended was a law school. He ran away from this institution after stealing a lot of property that belonged to fellow students. The plunder he secured consisted mostly of ornaments and bric-a-brac, which he pawned in Liverpool, England, to secure enough money with which to purchase a first-class ticket on a ship heading to Boston, Massachusetts. After boarding the vessel, he made the acquaintance of Clarence Preller.

Preller was a trusted employee of a large export establishment of London. His duties required him to travel nearly all over the world, or, at least, to visit the principal cities of the world. He was a young man, being about thirty years of age, and finding fellow countryman Brookes an agreeable companion, took very kindly to him.

Brookes represented himself as being a titled nobleman who had just finished his course at college and was making a pleasure tour of America. He called himself Maxwell.

During the voyage from Liverpool to Boston, Preller told Maxwell, as I will call him hereafter, that after he had attended to a matter of business for his firm at Boston, he had to go to Toronto, Canada, where he would be detained but a day or two. Then he would leave Toronto for St. Louis, Missouri, where he also had some business to do for his firm, which would require but a short time, and that from there he would go through to San Francisco, California, and sail from there on the first steamship to Auckland, New Zealand. Maxwell told him that he believed he would go from Boston to St. Louis, where he (Maxwell) would await the arrival of Preller from Toronto, then accompany him to Auckland just for the trip. This proposition pleased Preller.

They arrived safely in Boston, where they remained two or three days together and where Maxwell learned that Preller had in his possession seven hundred-dollar bills. After Preller had finished his business in Boston, they settled their bills at the Adams House, where they had stopped, went to the depot together, and separated, Preller going to Toronto and Maxwell to St. Louis. They had agreed that Maxwell was to stop at the Southern Hotel in St. Louis, there to await Preller. Maxwell arrived at that hotel and engaged a room, where Preller joined him a couple of days later. I think it was Saturday when he arrived, and they occupied the same apartments.

On the following Sunday, after they had eaten their dinner and returned to their room, Preller complained of suffering from stomach trouble. Maxwell claimed to have some knowledge of medicine and administered an overdose of morphia, hypodermically. A short time after administering the drug, and when he saw that Preller was beginning to breathe his last, he poured more than half the contents of a four-ounce bottle of chloroform into Preller's almost lifeless lips. When Preller was dead, Maxwell stripped the body and placed a suit of his own underwear on him. Maxwell was small in stature, being only about five feet five inches in height, while Preller was much larger and about six feet tall. Maxwell's clothing was marked with the name of Hugh M. Brookes and was entirely too small for the body of Preller.

In removing the underwear, Maxwell used a candle snuffer, which is very much like a pair of scissors, only the cutting surface is a half circle. He cut the undergarments the full length of the limbs so that he could easily strip them off. Then he managed to pull his own garments onto the body. He emptied out the trunk belonging to Preller and pressed the body into it. He had to almost double it into a circle to get it into the trunk, but he succeeded. Then, strapping and locking the trunk, he put his own as well as Preller's effects into his own trunk and retired for the night.

The next morning, after breakfast, he called at the cashier's office, settled his bill, and stated to the clerk that his friend Preller had been obliged to make a short run out of town, would be back to the hotel in two or three days, and desired that the room be held for him, as his trunk and effects would remain there until he called for them. Maxwell explained that he had to leave that morning and expected his friend Preller to join him later.

He instructed the head porter to bring his large trunk down into the corridor. The one he had ordered brought down contained the dead body, but, to his consternation, the porter brought down the one in which his and Preller's effects had been packed. He became very much alarmed and had his trunk taken to Union Station and checked to San Francisco, buying a ticket for that place. He departed over the Frisco Road and arrived in San Francisco, where he remained one night, and the following day bought a ticket for Auckland, New Zealand, and sailed that afternoon.

The weather was quite warm in St. Louis, and after a few days decomposition set in on the corpse in the trunk. The odor from the room attracted the attention of the servants. They reported to the office, the room was entered, and the body was found. The police were notified at once. A good description of Maxwell was furnished by the hotel people, and telegrams were sent in all directions, giving this description and requesting Maxwell's arrest.

Captain Leas, chief of police of San Francisco, received one of these telegrams, started his detectives investigating, and succeeded in learning that the murderer had sailed for Auckland some three or four days before he had received the telegraphic description of him from St. Louis. On learning this, Chief Leas cabled the proper authorities of Auckland a full description of Maxwell and even the number of the stateroom he occupied on the ship. Of course, Captain Leas's telegram reached Auckland several days before the ship arrived.

When the ship arrived at Auckland, the police sent out two of their detectives with the pilot who was to guide the steamer on which Maxwell had taken passage into port. They arrested him as soon as they boarded the ship, and when the vessel landed, they immediately notified the St. Louis authorities, in accordance with Captain Leas's instructions. After obtaining proper extradition papers, the chief of police of St. Louis sent two of his detectives to Auckland to bring Maxwell back to St. Louis. They went to Auckland by way of San Francisco, found Maxwell in jail there, and brought him back to St. Louis. It was a long and expensive trip and cost the city of St. Louis a great deal of money.

On arriving in St. Louis, the prisoner was locked up without bail on the charge of murdering Preller. He immediately employed two lawyers to defend him. After having consulted with his lawyers, Maxwell became jubilant—so much so that he became obnoxious to his fellow prisoners. He was naturally inclined to be overbearing and seemed to hold himself aloof from the other prisoners. He was rather inclined to braggadocio and attracted a lot of attention. The daily papers devoted a great deal of space to him, which he seemed to enjoy immensely. In fact, the notoriety appeared to be very pleasing to him.

A few days after Maxwell had been lodged in jail in St. Louis, Ashley C. Clover, circuit attorney of St. Louis, in company with Marshall F. McDonald, assistant circuit attorney, drove out to this author's residence one night. I was then chief special agent for the Missouri Pacific Railroad Company, and both Mr. Clover and Mr. McDonald were personal friends of mine.

Mr. Clover stated that the object of their visit was in reference to the Maxwell case. He went on to explain that although the arrest and returning of Maxwell from Auckland to St. Louis had cost the city of St. Louis a great deal of money, and the case had become one of international importance, he did not believe that the officers of the St. Louis Police Department had made any efforts to get at the real facts in the case. So far they had not found enough evidence to procure a conviction in case the defendant went on the stand and testified that the giving of too much chloroform to Preller was an accident. Mr. Clover said that he wanted the real facts in the case. "For," he said, "while there is scarcely any doubt that Maxwell caused the death of Preller by an overdose of chloroform, he may have done it innocently, and if such is the case, under our laws, he could not be convicted of the murder and ought not to be, in my opinion.

"But, on the contrary, if he dosed him purposely and feloniously with forethought and malice, he ought to be convicted. If he did it innocently, and I could be assured of that, I would be pleased to ask the jury to acquit him, but, as I said before, if he is guilty it would be my duty as circuit attorney to insist on his conviction. And now, Tom, I want you to get the facts in this case for me."

To this I replied, "Mr. Clover, I really do not know anything about this case except what I have read in the newspapers, and, of course, you know as well as I do that a man cannot base much of an opinion on a case of this kind on newspaper accounts, and, therefore, I wish you would give me a little time to think the matter over. I fully approve of the sentiments that you have expressed in connection with the case and will be glad, indeed, to do all in my power to assist you."

Both gentlemen said they wished that I would take the matter under advisement until the following evening at eight o'clock, at which time they would again call at my house to talk the matter over with me.

The following evening at the appointed time, they called and were both apparently anxious to learn what I thought I could do in the way of obtaining the facts pertaining to the case.

After the usual greeting, and when both had been seated, I said, "Gentlemen, I have been thinking about the case in question and have become satisfied that there are but two people who know the whole facts connected with the case and the facts that you now desire to know. One of these persons is now in jail, and the other is dead. In my opinion Maxwell is the only living person who knows the facts, and, therefore, he is the only person from whom these facts can be obtained. I believe I can get those facts from him, but I want you gentlemen to understand that I am in the employ of the Missouri Pacific Railroad Company, and, of course, they are paying me for all my time, but if I were not in their employ, I could not do this myself on account of my being so well known. For that reason it would be necessary for me to select a competent operative to do this work under my instructions. I shall be glad to do this, or anything else that I can do to assist you in unraveling this case, with the understanding that I am not to receive any compensation for what I may do myself, but I shall expect you gentlemen to pay the operative that I may use in this work the same amount of salary that we are paying him and his actual expenses. As I said before, I will do all that I can but will neither expect nor receive any remuneration for my services."

"Tom," replied Mr. Clover, "there is no fund provided by the city for the employment of outside talent for such work as this in question, but I expect to pay the expense out of my own pocket, and I shall insist on paying you for your services in connection with this matter."

I answered, "I will receive nothing for any work that I may do in the matter."

At this point in the conversation, Mr. McDonald, who had been sitting quietly, listening to Mr. Clover and myself, said, "Tom, how do you expect to obtain the facts in this case? That's what I would like to know."

"Mr. McDonald," I responded, "I feel that it would be easier for me to go ahead and do this work than it would be for me to undertake to tell you how I propose to do it."

Mr. Clover then said, "Tom, I am going to place this matter in your hands. I want you to go ahead and get this thing started as soon as possible, as the defendant's attorneys are clamoring for a speedy trial, and I do not wish to keep them waiting any longer than I can help. You do this work in your own way, and I will pay the bills."

I said, "All right."

The next day I telegraphed to Philadelphia to an operative in my employ there. He was an entire stranger in St. Louis. I wired him to come at once and not to stop at my office but to come direct to my house on his arrival in the city, which he did.

His name was John McCulloch. He was about thirty-five years of age, about five feet ten inches in height, and weighed about two hundred pounds. He was well built, had a sandy complexion, and was rather a good-looking fellow. He was wearing side whiskers, or burnsides, as they were called, and a blond mustache and looked very much like an Englishman. He was honest and of sober habits but a little thick-headed, or, in other words, dull of comprehension. In instructing him it was necessary to explain each detail fully, and sometimes it would seem as if it were necessary to take a hammer and pound the instructions into his head, but when he once understood thoroughly what you wanted him to do, he would carry out instructions to the letter.

Right here it might be well to take the reader into my confidence. I had decided to get my operative (McCulloch) into jail, where he could meet Maxwell, without the knowledge of the local police officers.

After explaining the nature of the case to him, I instructed him to procure the leading daily papers of St. Louis, dating back to the time of the murder, and to read every line that had been published relative to the case. This he did, and it took him about three weeks. I met him each evening during that time and rehearsed with him what I wanted him to do, from the time he was arrested, and how he should act after his arrest and incarceration.

Early in February 1886, I succeeded in getting possession of a few blank checks from the office of D. S. H. Smith, who was local treasurer of the Missouri Pacific Railroad Company in St. Louis. Being chief special agent of the road, I had occasion to visit the local treasurer's office frequently, and being well known, not only to the local treasurer but to all of his office force as well, I had no difficulty in obtaining the blank checks without the knowledge of Dr. Smith, as the local treasurer was called by most of the people who knew him, or any of his clerks.

My chief clerk was a good penman and was familiar with the signature of Dr. D. S. H. Smith. I had him practice for some time imitating Dr. Smith's signature and found that he could imitate it so clearly that it would have been accepted as genuine by any bank teller. While I wanted a fairly good imitation of the signature, I did not want it to be so good that it would be received at the bank. After practicing for a time, he succeeded in making a signature that I thought would answer my purpose. I had him fill out one of the blank checks for the amount of $1,188.10. I then gave this check to McCulloch with instructions to present it to the paying teller of the Mechanics Bank, which was then on Fourth Street. He was to present this check at 9:45 sharp the following morning. I had received a check, a day or two before this, that bore the signature of Dr. Smith and had purposely held this out and was waiting across the street from the bank when I saw McCulloch, whom I will hereafter call Frank

Dingfelter, as this was the name he assumed and the name to which the check had been made payable.

On entering the bank, Dingfelter went to the window of the paying teller, Mr. Warner, and presented the check. Warner examined the check very carefully and, by reason of its being for so large an amount and Dingfelter being an entire stranger to him (I, having allowed Dingfelter time enough to have reached the paying teller's window, entered the bank with my check in my hand), held the check that Dingfelter had presented, and when he saw me he excitedly motioned to me to come to his window. When I reached the window, Warner commanded me, in an excited manner, to arrest that man, pointing to Dingfelter.

I said, "What do you want him arrested for?"

Warner, holding up the check, said, "Why, he has presented a large fake check for nearly twelve hundred dollars bearing the name of Dr. Smith. Why, you know Dr. Smith's signature?"

I replied, "Yes, here is one of Dr. Smith's checks. I know this is genuine, for I saw the doctor sign it."

He compared the fake check with mine, and I said to Mr. Warner, "While I am not an expert on handwriting, I do not believe that Dr. Smith wrote that signature."

Mr. Warner exclaimed, "I am positive he did not!"

Then, turning to Mr. Dingfelter, I asked, "Where did you get this check?"

"I got it from Dr. Smith" was his reply.

"Does Dr. Smith know you?" I asked.

In rather a gruff manner, he answered, "Yes, he knows me."

"Will you go with me and see Dr. Smith?" I asked.

"Well, I do not know whether I will or not. I don't know who you are," he replied.

At this I laid my hand on his shoulder and said, "You will either accompany me to Dr. Smith's office or I will send for a patrol wagon, take you to police headquarters, and have you locked up."

"Are you an officer?" he asked.

To which I replied, "Yes, I am the chief special agent of the Missouri Pacific Railroad Company."

"Oh, well," said he, "that is different. I will go with you and see Dr. Smith."

It was drizzling rain the morning of this occurrence. It was quite chilly, and the streets and sidewalks were wet and slippery and dirty, as the streets of St. Louis were not kept as clean at that time as they are now. I took the fake check, and Dingfelter and myself started for Dr. Smith's office, which at that time was in the Missouri Pacific general office building on the corner of Sixth and Locust Streets. We walked west on Pine from Fourth. When we reached the corner of Sixth and Pine Streets, I gave Dingfelter a signal, which had been prearranged. This signal was for him to hit me a good stiff punch, as the fighters call it. There was a large, clumsy patrolman, wearing a raincoat, standing under an awning near the corner saloon. I was walking on the left-hand side of Dingfelter, and when I gave him the signal, he cut loose with his right hand, which landed just over my right eye and a little to the side. I had instructed him to hit me hard, and if he succeeded in knocking me down and I became groggy from the blow, he was to stumble and fall himself so as to give the big, clumsy police officer time to reach us. The officer was standing about ten feet from us when Dingfelter struck me, but I knew how slow he was, and I wanted to be sure to give him an opportunity of getting hold of Dingfelter. I went down all right and, in fact, was a little dazed from the effects of the blow. Dingfelter stumbled and fell, and the policeman made a dash (such as a heavily loaded ice wagon going uphill would make) and succeeded in reaching him, not, however, until he had arisen, and I also had got to my feet. He got to Dingfelter about the same time I did. The latter made a good fight and tore off most of the uniform of the policeman and my coat, vest, and collar. All of us went down in the street and rolled around in the mud. Our ears and faces were filled with mud before we finally succeeded in subduing Dingfelter, but I am satisfied if he had tried his best he could have gotten away from both of us, as he was a powerful man.

My office was on Eighth Street, just north of Pine, and this fight occurred just two blocks from my office, so after we had subdued Dingfelter, I suggested that we take him there so as to give us an opportunity of washing ourselves while we were waiting for a patrol wagon to take the prisoner to police headquarters. This we did, and on arriving at my office, we turned the prisoner over to my chief clerk and one of my operatives, who happened to be there, while the policeman and myself began digging the mud out of our ears and washing our faces. After washing, I found that my right eye was very much discolored, and where my face had come in contact with the pavement there were a number of small cuts and scratches, which were somewhat inflamed, and I really had a sore face.

The operative who I have mentioned before, whose name was Phillips, on seeing my face said to me, "Why, you sure ought to go and see a doctor at once. Your eye is in bad shape, and you need medical attention immediately. Let me go up to police headquarters with this fellow. I can attend to the matter for you."

I thanked him and said that I wished he would do so. I told him what had occurred at the bank and instructed him to make a complaint against Dingfelter accordingly. In due time the patrol wagon arrived, and the police officer and Phillips escorted Mr. Dingfelter to police headquarters. At this time Hughie O'Neil was chief of detectives, and Major Lawrence Harrigan was chief of police for the city of St. Louis.

As soon as Dingfelter was hustled into the detectives' office in the Four Courts, Chief O'Neil and a squad of his men immediately set about searching him. They found in one of his inside pockets a letter, addressed, sealed, and stamped, but apparently which Dingfelter had forgotten to mail. It was directed to San Francisco. They also found about seventy-five or one hundred dollars and some other articles, all of which were taken from him and placed in the police department archives for safekeeping. The letter was eagerly opened and read. This letter was quite lengthy and was just such a letter as one crook would write to another. There was then, and had been for some time previous, a gang of bank swindlers working the cities of the Pacific Coast, and the newspapers had been printing a great deal about the operations of this gang several weeks prior to the time of which I write, and for this reason the detectives of St. Louis were led to believe by the finding of the letter that they had struck something that might lead to the capture of the bank swindlers. The contents of the letter appeared in the afternoon papers. Some of these papers censured me for having failed to discover this letter.

After reading the comments of the papers regarding this letter, I would have considered myself very stupid, indeed, for having missed the letter were it not for the fact that I knew that I had not had an opportunity to search Mr. Dingfelter up to the time he assaulted me and the officer on Pine Street, and then I also knew it had taken me about two hours to compose and dictate that same letter.

Dingfelter was locked up, of course, and the time was set for his preliminary hearing, to be held several days later. In the meantime, the St. Louis papers were devoting lots of space to Dingfelter and his alleged crime—a relief to the newspaper readers, as they had begun to grow tired of reading day after day about Maxwell and what his attorneys expected to do for him. From the time of Dingfelter's arrest up to the time of Maxwell's trial, the newspapers scarcely mentioned the latter's name. Some of them occasionally mentioned my name in rather a joking manner, because I had been stupid enough to miss that letter. When Dingfelter was called for his preliminary hearing, he was promptly remanded to jail to await the action of the grand jury.

He was besieged by lawyers who were anxious to defend him, but he declined their offers, telling them when the time came he had lawyers selected to defend him and steadfastly refused to divulge their names. The second day after his arrest, Dingfelter was allowed to mingle with the other prisoners in what was called the "bull ring." An allotted time is given to the prisoners each day in this place for exercise. Maxwell noticed that almost immediately after his arrest, the newspapers were giving Dingfelter all the notoriety and had dropped himself, so he hastened to make the acquaintance of one so notorious when they met in the "bull ring." This was the only opportunity of meeting him, and from the first time that Maxwell saw Dingfelter, he never lost an opportunity of talking with him, and he stuck to Dingfelter like the proverbial fly to the horse.

The first time Maxwell approached Dingfelter, he rushed up to him and said, "You are Dingfelter, I believe." Dingfelter replied that he was, and Maxwell then said, "They seem to have a strong case against you."

"You will have to excuse me, sir. I don't want to be considered impolite," Dingfelter replied, "but I must decline to talk to anyone in this place about my case, as you call it. I don't believe it would be a good thing for me or any other person to talk about a charge that is pending against them in a place of this kind. I shall be glad to talk with you on any other subject, however, but I trust that you will hereafter refrain from asking me any questions regarding the charge now pending against me in court, and then, I don't know you."

Maxwell hastily said, "Oh, I am Maxwell. I am the fellow who is charged with the murder of that man Preller, who was killed in the Southern Hotel and whose body was found in a trunk. I was arrested at Auckland, New Zealand, and brought back here to St. Louis to stand trial, but I have been assured by my attorneys that I will be acquitted. They have no proof against me, and just as soon as I can get a trial, why, of course, I will go free."

"So you are Maxwell," said Dingfelter. "I have been reading in the papers about you, and if you will pardon me for saying it, it seems to me that you have already been talking too much about your case. If you are not guilty of the crime with which you stand charged, why, you ought to be acquitted, and I hope you will be."

After this first interview between Maxwell and Dingfelter, he and many other prisoners looked on Dingfelter as being a wise and unusually smart prisoner. Dingfelter was in jail forty-seven days, and during all that time, Maxwell never let an opportunity pass without talking to him. I received daily reports from my operative, a task that I found very difficult, and it became more difficult by reason of the Southwestern Railroad strike, which broke out on March 4, 1886, and continued during Dingfelter's stay in the St. Louis jail. Being chief special agent for the Gould system, my time was occupied in protecting the railroad company's property and in apprehending people who were continually committing illegal acts. I was occupied almost day and night in this work.

From Dingfelter's daily reports, I learned that Maxwell had admitted that he had killed Preller for the purpose of obtaining seven hundred-dollar bills that he knew Preller to have, as he had shown him the money in the Adams House at Boston before they separated there. He also had pawned the plunder for the money that had brought him to America, and he said that he had made Preller believe that he was connected with the titled family of Maxwell, that his right name was Hugh M. Brookes, and that he would like to place himself under the guidance and advice of an able crook, as he believed Dingfelter to be, when he gained his liberty, as he was sure he would, in the near future.

He told Dingfelter in detail how he had killed Preller by administering an overdose of morphia, hypodermically; of how, after dinner on the fatal Sunday, Preller had complained of a pain in his stomach; that he, Maxwell, saw that was his opportunity for carrying out the plan he had already formed for taking Preller's life in order to secure the money; that he had provided himself with a large quantity of morphia and the hypodermic syringe; and that he had also procured four ounces of chloroform for the purpose of administering it to Preller immediately before death to prevent the body from becoming rigid, as it does immediately after death, "as," said Maxwell in his explanation to Dingfelter, "I had to conceal his long body in the trunk, which was so much shorter, and I did not want to cut off his limbs, fearing that the trace of the blood would betray me."

On receiving Dingfelter's report relative to the use of the morphia in the murder, I at once reported the fact to Mr. Clover and Mr. McDonald, who immediately arranged with two of the most prominent doctors in St. Louis to examine the body of Preller for traces of the morphia. Mr. Clover and Mr. McDonald, the doctors, an official of Bellefontaine Cemetery, and I went to the cemetery where Preller's body had been buried and exhumed the body, and the doctors made the necessary examination, keeping what they discovered to themselves, and they did not divulge anything about it until called on to testify at Maxwell's trial, when they said that the traces of the hypodermic syringe were plainly visible on the arm and that traces of morphia were found.

When Maxwell was arrested, a quantity of morphia and a hypodermic syringe were found among his effects, but up to this discovery neither had been considered in connection with the murder, as it had been taken for granted that Preller's death had been caused by chloroform. Of course, the exhuming of the body and the arrangement that had been made were known to no one but Mr. Clover and Mr. McDonald, the two doctors, the cemetery official, and myself, and it was treated as a profound secret.

Meanwhile, after Dingfelter had been in jail and had obtained the information we wanted from Maxwell, I decided that it was unnecessary to keep him there longer, so I arranged to have Dingfelter released on bail, which had been fixed at $3,500. I had ex-Judge Henry D. Laughlin, of St. Louis, sign Dingfelter's bond. I did this without Judge Laughlin's knowledge that I even knew who Dingfelter was. On his release I immediately sent him to New York, where he entered into correspondence with friends of Maxwell's. Just before being released, he asked Maxwell if he could keep a secret, and Maxwell said that he could, whereupon Dingfelter said, "I expect to leave this place soon."

"How are you going to get out?" asked Maxwell.

"Ah," said Dingfelter, "that is none of your business. You said you could keep a secret, and the first thing you are doing is to pry into my business by asking how I am going to get out. After I am gone from here, of course, you will know it, but if you do not know how I propose to get out, it will be impossible for you to tell anyone about it. For that reason it is better that you should not know anything further than what I have already said."

Maxwell apologized and promised not to be so inquisitive again. Dingfelter then said, "Now, Maxwell, after I am on the outside and away from this place, if I can do anything for you, I shall be glad to do it."

"You can do a whole lot for me," Maxwell answered, "by getting two of your friends to come here when my trial is called and have them testify that they met Preller and myself in Boston; that they accompanied us to the depot when we were leaving Boston; that at the depot I proposed that the party take a parting drink; that Preller, these two men, and myself went to a café, that I ordered two bottles of champagne, and that when I paid for it I displayed a roll of seven hundred-dollar bills; that I explained that I wanted to change one of these hundred-dollar bills so that I might have some smaller change to pay expenses on my way to St. Louis. If they will testify to this, it will account for the six hundred-dollar bills I took from Preller."

Dingfelter asked, "Are you sure that your lawyers will not get these friends of mine into trouble or let the police get next to them if I can get them to come?"

Maxwell assured Dingfelter that his friends would be perfectly safe in coming to St. Louis and that the police would not get next to them, providing, of course, that the parties were not already known to the police. He took a card bearing his name from his pocket and tore it in two halves, giving one half to Dingfelter and retaining the other himself, saying, "Be sure and give these witnesses half of the card, which will serve to identify them to my attorneys when they arrive here, as that half of the card will match the half that I will retain; the edges of the torn card will match and will answer the purpose of an introduction."

It was about five o'clock in the evening when Dingfelter was released from jail on bond, and at that hour the courts in the building had adjourned for the day, and the newspaper correspondents and all others except the few attachés who were on duty had left the building. Thus Dingfelter left the jail unobserved. On his release from the jail, he came to my house by a circuitous route, where he remained until a late hour that night, when he left to take a train for New York. I instructed him to open a correspondence with Maxwell on his arrival in New York so as to get positive instructions from Maxwell as to what the witnesses were to testify to when they appeared on the stand in his defense. He carried out these instructions to the letter. His letters reached Maxwell through his attorneys, and Maxwell's letters reached him through the same source, and in due time, all the letters were sent to me with his report.

They kept up this correspondence at intervals until Maxwell's trial was called. I told Dingfelter to appear in St. Louis on the morning of the trial, which he did. On arriving here he went to a private lodging house, and being a stranger in the city, his presence was unknown to any person but himself and the circuit attorneys, Clover and McDonald.

When his trial was called, Maxwell took the stand in his own defense and testified that he had administered chloroform to his friend Preller on the fatal evening at the Southern Hotel for the purpose of allaying the pain that he was suffering from, as both Mr. Clover and Mr. McDonald had predicted he would testify. Maxwell went on to state that Preller's suffering was caused by an acute attack of stricture, from which he had been suffering more or less for some time.

On hearing this testimony from Maxwell, it was decided to again exhume the body of Preller so that the two doctors could make another examination of the remains and either corroborate or disprove Maxwell's testimony, as this was one of the most vital points in the trial. When the body was exhumed, the doctors removed the organs, taking them to their laboratory, where the examination was made, and they later came into court and testified that their examination had shown beyond a doubt that Preller had never suffered from stricture.

Frank Dingfelter was among the first witnesses called by the prosecution. In answer to his name, he entered the courtroom from the private office of the circuit attorney, and after being duly sworn in, took his seat on the witness stand. After sitting down he turned his face toward Attorney McDonald, who was conducting the prosecution for the state. Maxwell got a full view of Dingfelter for the first time since he had seen him in the jail. From where I was sitting, I could get a good view of Maxwell's countenance.

I was watching him closely, and when he saw Dingfelter he recognized him instantly. He turned ashy pale and nearly fainted and would have fallen out of his chair were it not that he was partly supported by one of his attorneys who was sitting beside him. He hurriedly communicated to his attorney that he had recognized Dingfelter, whereupon the attorneys for the defense became very much excited. Dingfelter was asked by Attorney McDonald the following questions:

Question: What is your name? Answer: John F. McCulloch.

Q. Where were you born? A. Wilmington, Delaware.

Q. How old are you? A. Thirty years.

Q. What is your business? A. Detective.

Q. By whom are you employed? A. Thomas Furlong.

Q. Do you know the defendant in this case [pointing to Maxwell]? A. Yes, sir.

Q. Where did you first become acquainted with him? A. In the city jail.

Q. Were you a prisoner in the jail? A. Yes, sir.

Q. What were you charged with? A. I believe it was forgery.

Q. When and where were you arrested? A. I was arrested at the Mechanics Bank on the corner of Fourth and Pine Streets, this city, by Thomas Furlong, who was afterward assisted by a police officer whose name I do not know.

Q. Why did Furlong arrest you? A. He was commanded to do so by the paying teller of the Mechanics Bank.

Q. Why did the teller cause your arrest? A. Because I presented a check bearing what purported to be the signature of D. S. H. Smith, local treasurer of the Missouri Pacific Railroad Company. The paying teller told Furlong, in my presence, that the signature was a forgery.

Q. Did you know it to be a forgery? A. I did not.

Q. Where did you get this check? A. Mr. Furlong gave me the check and instructed me to present it at the bank, as I did, and told me that he would be at the bank when I presented it.

Q. Was Mr. Furlong there? A. Yes, he came into the bank while I was at the teller's window. That was when Mr. Warner, as I believe the teller's name is, told him to arrest me.

Q. Then you do not know whether the check was a forgery or not? A. No, sir. I was only obeying the instructions of my employer, Mr. Furlong. I guess he can tell you all about that check.

The courtroom was crowded, and as soon as Dingfelter stated that he was a detective, one of the city detectives rushed out of the court, pell-mell, to the office of the chief of police, which was in the opposite end of the building, and informed the chief of what had occurred. The chief rushed into the courtroom, and from that time on, consternation seemed to prevail among all the authorities around the Four Courts building.

Dingfelter was kept on the witness stand for about two days, and during his entire direct testimony, nearly every question asked him by the prosecuting attorney was objected to by the attorneys for the defense. After McCulloch, as I will call him by his right name hereafter, had been excused from the witness stand, I was called. After being duly sworn in and asked the preliminary questions, I was told by the prosecuting attorney to state to the court and jury how I had been approached by Mr. Clover and himself and what I had done in connection with the case.

I gave a detailed account of my work from the start up to that moment, being interrupted occasionally by an objection from the defendant's counsel. When I had finished my direct testimony, all of which has already been related, the counsel for the defense began to cross-examine me. My cross-examination consumed nearly a day and a half.

The defendant's counsel first wanted to know how long I had been in the detective business. I answered that I had first become engaged in the business in September 1862. The attorney said, "Then you have had a great deal of experience?" I answered that I had, and then he said, "Where did you get this check?," exhibiting the check in question. I asked permission to examine the check, which was granted by the court, and after looking at it carefully, I answered, "This is one of the blank checks that I took from Dr. Smith's office in the manner already described."

Question: Then you stole this check from Dr. Smith's office? Answer: I took that blank check from Dr. Smith's office without his knowledge or consent.

Q. Who filled out this check and signed Dr. Smith's name to it? A. That check was filled out by one of my employees. I stood alongside of him while he filled it out. He did it under my instructions, and if he had refused to do it I would have discharged him and he knew it; and if the law has been violated in any way, I am responsible for it.

The attorney for the defense insisted that I give the name of the person who filled out the check, but the court overruled the question on the ground that I had assumed the responsibility. The counsel for the defense then said, "You know that you were violating the law by having this check made out as you did, did you not?"

I replied, "Under certain conditions, it might have been a violation of the law."

Counsel for the defense asked, "You know that it was a forgery and forgery is a crime under the law?" My answer was the same as before, that it would have been forgery under certain conditions. But he insisted on me answering him with a direct "yes" or "no." At this, prosecuting attorney McDonald appealed to the court, stating that the witness could not answer the question with a direct "yes" or "no" unless permitted to explain what the certain conditions referred to were. The court permitted me to explain under what conditions the making of the check would not be considered forgery, to which I replied that inasmuch as that intent is the essence of crime, and that as there was no intent to obtain money or other valuables by means of this check on my part, who was responsible for the making of it, and that I was at the bank on the morning that McCulloch presented the check for the purpose of preventing the teller from cashing the check, if he, perchance, had not noticed that the signature of Dr. Smith was not genuine, and for the further reason that I had promptly apprehended the man who had presented the check at the bank for having done so. This was all a matter of court record.

Here I wish to say that almost every person in the courtroom, after hearing my testimony as to my obtaining the blank checks and causing one to be filled out and presented at the bank, were of the opinion that I had gotten myself into serious trouble. Many clung to that opinion until they heard my explanation, and the competent court attorneys saw at a glance that I was safe when I explained that intent was what constituted a crime.

I have been asked many, many times since the arrest of McCulloch and my tussle with him why I caused him to knock me down and to strip the policeman and myself, leaving us in almost a nude condition, which compelled me to go around several days with my right eye and one side of my face discolored—as some of them said, "in mourning"—and my answer has always been that I had decided everything I did in connection with the case was absolutely necessary so that I might obtain the true facts of the case, which were very essential for the proper prosecution of the perpetrator of this heinous crime, as he was the only living person who knew the real facts.

I knew that Maxwell was enjoying the notoriety the newspapers were giving him, and I also knew that the public was growing tired of reading about him and, therefore, believed that if I could paint my operative as a more desperate criminal for the time being, the notoriety he would obtain through the papers would have the effect of attracting Maxwell's attention to him so that he might bask in the light that was being attracted to McCulloch. And, as it turned out, my predictions proved true. I deemed it necessary to have McCulloch slug me and make the fight that he did with the police officer and myself in order to allay any suspicion that might arise in the mind of the chief of police or any of his men.

The chief was an alert and experienced officer, and if he suspected for a moment that McCulloch was not what he represented himself to be, or that he was connected with me, he would have undoubtedly exposed our scheme and thereby destroyed our efforts, which were for the honest purpose of serving the ends of justice.

Both McCulloch and myself were acting parts, and from the result it seems that the parts were acted well. I could have gotten the blank check from Dr. Smith, I have no doubt, merely by asking for it, but he, of course, would have wanted an explanation from me, and if I had explained why I wanted it, he would have been obliged to state the facts on the witness stand when called before the grand jury, and this would have been fatal to my scheme. Had I told my operative Phillips, who lodged the first complaint against McCulloch, or Dingfelter, as he called himself, he would have been compelled, under oath, to have stated the truth. This, too, would have been fatal. My keeping the matter a secret resulted in every person telling the truth, or what they believed to be the truth. I myself appeared neither at police headquarters nor at the preliminary hearing, nor before the grand jury, and was not called on to testify until Maxwell was on trial.

Marshall F. McDonald was sitting alone in his office one day, about a month after Dingfelter had been in jail and had made such good progress with Maxwell, when William Marion Reedy, better known then as Billy Reedy, entered his office. Reedy was, at that time, a reporter for the *Globe-Democrat* and very popular. He knew every official around the Four Courts and, in fact, every man in St. Louis who was worth knowing. He was a warm friend and great admirer of Mr. McDonald, and on entering his office and noting that he was alone, he said, "Mac, why don't you select the right kind of a fellow and have him locked up in jail with Maxwell? He might succeed in getting the facts as to Preller's murder from him."

Mr. McDonald was startled to hear this suggestion from Mr. Reedy, but, being a man of steady nerves, he managed to conceal his surprise. He told Reedy that he did not believe that anything could be accomplished by locking a man up in jail for that purpose. "For," said Mac, "there are nearly four hundred prisoners in that jail, and a man might be there for months before he could get to Maxwell, and then it is quite likely that his attorneys have already advised him not to talk to any person about his case."

Reedy said, "It occurred to me that it might be a good thing to do, and I therefore made the suggestion to you for what it is worth, but, as you do not think it worthwhile to try it, just let it go."

He left the office, and just as soon as McDonald could don his hat and coat and leave his office unobserved, he hastened to me. I saw at a glance that he was excited and believed something unusual had happened. I greeted him and asked him to be seated and then said, "Mac, what is the matter?"

He extended his long right arm and exclaimed, "Why, the whole thing is up!"

"What's up?" I asked. "Mac, what do you mean?"

"Why, Billy Reedy came into my office a little while ago and suggested that I pick out the right kind of a fellow and have him locked up in jail so that he might work on Maxwell," he said.

"Is that all Reedy said?" I asked.

He then went on and detailed as nearly as he could recollect just what Reedy had said. I asked him what he had said to Reedy, and he told me. I then said, "Do you think that Reedy noticed your excitement when he made the suggestion to you?"

"No, he could not have," he replied. "I was not excited. I never get excited."

"You were excited when you came in here, and if Billy Reedy noticed it when he made that suggestion, it might set him to thinking, and inasmuch as you did not take kindly to the suggestion, he might possibly make the suggestion to Chief Harrigan," I said.

"Oh, no," replied Mac. "Billy would not make any suggestions to the chief. He is my friend, and I appreciate the feeling that prompted him to make the suggestion, but confound it, I wish he had not thought of it."

I said, "Mac, we know that Billy Reedy is a bright young fellow, a great news gatherer, and a loyal friend of yours. I do not believe he will say anything more about it, and now I think the best thing to do is to quietly await developments."

My advice was followed, and I do not believe that William Marion Reedy, who is now proprietor and editor of the *St. Louis Mirror*, has ever known just how much that friendly suggestion of his worried his friend

Marshall F. McDonald. I have told in my story how McCulloch remained in jail and got the facts from Maxwell, and our scheme was not spoiled by Mr. Reedy's suggestion, for he never repeated it to any other person.

The testimony at the trial was overwhelmingly against Maxwell, and the jury before whom this case was tried quickly returned a verdict of guilty of murder in the first degree, and Hugh M. Brookes, alias Maxwell, was hung for one of the most cold-blooded murders of the age.

The St. Louis Police Department had an exhibit in the Educational Building during the Louisiana Purchase Exposition, St. Louis, which consisted of photographs and police records of criminals, burglars, tools, and various weapons. This exhibit also had the noose with which Brookes, alias Maxwell, was hung and his photograph and the picture of the two St. Louis officers who brought him back from Auckland, New Zealand. There were thousands of people who viewed this exhibit, and I deem it proper to tell the public that the police department had positively nothing to do with obtaining the evidence that convicted Maxwell. They had really nothing to do with his arrest other than sending out his description.

He was arrested through the efforts of Captain Leas, chief of police of San Francisco, California. His conviction was due to my efforts and the work of my operative, McCulloch, and to Mr. Clover and Mr. McDonald. Mr. Clover paid the expenses from his own pocket, and Mr. McDonald deserved a great deal more credit than he was accorded for the masterful way in which he handled the prosecution, but not one of these names were mentioned in the exhibit at the World's Fair. Mr. Clover paid about $600 out of his own personal funds for the expenses incurred in obtaining the evidence, and I got a black eye and a swollen jaw as my compensation.

THREE

They Took Everything

Jason Ryan

Losing a son to violence can do strange things to a father.

IT'S NOT A GOOD SIGN WHEN A POLICE OFFICER SHOWS UP AT YOUR FRONT door. It's even worse when it's the chief who's knocking.

Francis Keala did not have to go far to reach the home of Charles Marsland. The neat, single-story house on Poipu Drive was just a mile from Keala's own home in the tranquil Honolulu neighborhood of Hawaii Kai. The chief had been there many times on account of his friendship with Marsland. Their boys went to school together and were close friends as well. The men shared a boat, which they used to take the boys swimming, diving, and fishing. Police Chief Keala and Marsland, a lawyer for the city of Honolulu, worked together plenty too, any time the department faced a legal problem. The men were so close that Marsland had asked Keala to be his son's godfather.

But unlike past visits, today's house call would not be a happy one. Marsland would soon greet Keala at the door and suffer through the worst day of his life. The man had already endured some doozies. During World War II, Marsland had commanded an infantry landing craft in the Pacific theater, participating in the invasion of the Philippines as American forces sought to regain control of the islands from the Japanese. After the war, in Boston, the young lawyer went through a bitter divorce that resulted in his return to Hawaii and his family being split in two. About the same time as his island homecoming, Marsland's father died.

Yet none of this heartache and tragedy was sufficient preparation for the morning of April 17, 1975, when Marsland answered the door to hear the most heartbreaking news a parent can hear: his child was dead. Through sobs, Chief Keala revealed the news that Marsland's nineteen-year-old son, Chuckers, had been found lifeless that morning in Waimānalo, a rural area on the other side of the Koolau Mountains, about ten miles away from the Marsland home. Chuckers had been shot multiple times in the head and chest and left on the side of a desolate road.

"As soon as I saw Francis, I knew something was terribly wrong, because he was crying," Marsland later wrote. "When he told me that Chuckie was gone, something inside me died too."

A motorist had discovered Chuckers's body that morning at daybreak, near the Waimānalo intersection of Hihimanu and Nonokio Streets—back roads, off the main highway that circled the island, running through farmland that abutted the Koolau Mountains. Because of this out-of-the-way location, as well as the probability that Chuckers was killed very early in the morning, it was unlikely anyone had witnessed the murder save the killer or killers. Nearby residents had, however, heard multiple gunshots.

Whoever killed Chuckers certainly wanted him dead. An autopsy performed later that day confirmed Chuckers had been shot twice in the chest with a shotgun at close range, with pellets entering his heart. If that had not been enough to kill him, at least four gunshot wounds to his head were. They had been delivered into his face from a handgun fired at point-blank range.

Chuckers had been well-dressed, sporting garb typical of the 1970s disco scene. He wore a blue leisure suit with a blue-and-white long-sleeve button-down shirt underneath. On his feet were blue socks and white boots. Around his throat was a puka shell necklace, and in his pockets were packs of gum and cigarettes as well as some loose change and a paycheck. Two gold rings were on his fingers. Such attire was appropriate for his job as a doorman, or bouncer, at one of Waikiki's most popular nightclubs, the Infinity. Chuckers had worked a shift there until the club's closing at four in the morning. Two hours later he was found dead.

Like his father, Chuckers was tall and lean, standing six feet two inches tall and weighing 177 pounds. He had recently moved out of his father's home in Hawaii Kai, where he had lived for nearly eight years following his parents' divorce in Boston. Marsland said he returned to Hawaii with his eleven-year-old boy because he wanted his son to feel "the sand beneath his toes." To Marsland's satisfaction, Chuckers embraced life by the sea and was fond of water sports. Also living at the Marsland home was Marsland's girlfriend, Polly Grigg.

For high school Marsland sent Chuckers to his alma mater, Punahou School. Protestant missionaries to Hawaii founded the private school in

1841 to educate their children. A decade later the school opened to all races and religions. Since then Punahou School had developed into one of the most well-regarded schools in Hawaii if not the United States. Alumni of the school include President Barack Obama, golfer Michelle Wie, actress Kelly Preston, eBay founder Pierre Omidyar, and Hiram Bingham III, a US senator and explorer of the Incan city of Machu Picchu.

Chuckers's enrollment at Punahou School, from which he graduated in 1973, was not the only sign of an upper-crust life in Hawaii. Marsland was a member of the Outrigger Canoe Club. There, during the summer, Chuckers would practice canoeing during the week in preparation for weekend races. He could also use the club to surf, riding across the same shoreline as famed Hawaiian surfer and Olympic swimmer Duke Kahanamoku, who was once also a club member. When Chuckers was old enough to drive, Marsland bought his son a Chrysler convertible to match his own. Now Chuckers could cruise Oahu himself.

On learning of Chuckers's death that April morning, one of Marsland's first calls was to Chuckers's girlfriend, Cathy Clisby, who was at the couple's apartment in Waikiki. When she was told of her boyfriend's murder, Clisby began crying and screaming, "Chuck's dead!"

Friends and family streamed to the Marsland home that day to offer condolences, clogging Poipu Drive with cars. Among the visitors was Chuckers's friend Eric Naone, who had just seen his buddy early that morning as the Infinity nightclub was preparing to close and Chuckers was finishing his shift. Naone offered to help at the Marsland home by moving some of the other guests' cars. He greeted Mr. Marsland in the garage. To Naone, Marsland looked visibly depressed.

Marsland confirmed the observation with his words: "They took everything away from me," the grieving father told Naone.

As in much of the rest of the United States, Hawaii's violent crime rate had been climbing. The 1970s was easily the most murderous decade in modern Hawaiian history, and in 1975 homicide detectives in Honolulu had much more than the murder of Chuckers Marsland to consider. Just halfway through the year, the Honolulu Police Department was overwhelmed with twenty-eight murder cases, half of them unsolved. This midyear murder count was greater than any full-year total in the 1960s.

Almost immediately the trail went cold. Days passed, then weeks, without an arrest for the killing of Chuckers Marsland. In the aftermath of his death, on April 17, 1975, the police searched Chuckers's apartment, questioned his coworkers, and interviewed his friends. Despite these efforts, the police received few clues in the murder.

Coworkers told police that Chuckers seemed fidgety as he finished his shift at the Infinity. His colleagues thought it strange when he asked them for their pau drink, which was the free alcoholic beverage an employee earned from the club at the end of the night. Something was obviously bothering Chuckers, but he confided this anxiety to no one.

The police made notes of the men and women Chuckers spoke with in his last hours, knowing that his work in a nightclub often brought him into contact with patrons who were members of the Hawaiian underworld. They also found the murder victim's car parked in Waikiki, making it likely Chuckers had gotten into another automobile that took him around to the other side of the island, where he was killed. The assumption, then, was that Chuckers knew his killers. Otherwise why would he enter the car unless forced to do so? But this was guesswork, and that wasn't enough to make a solid case.

The lack of progress began to exasperate Charles Marsland. As he told his son's friend Eric Naone, Chuckers was "everything" to him, his only son, his namesake, and the only consolation for Marsland's failed marriage in Massachusetts. When Marsland had split with his wife a decade or so earlier, each parent had taken custody of a child. Marsland kept the boy; his ex-wife, Jane, was to raise the younger girl, Laurie Jane.

Charles Marsland had originally gone to Massachusetts to attend college. The only child of deep-sea diver and underwater demolition expert Charles F. Marsland and schoolteacher Sadie Marsland, he had been born in Honolulu on April 11, 1923. One of his grandfathers, who emigrated to Hawaii from Norway, worked on Oahu's Ewa plantation in the late nineteenth century and also served as a member of King Kalākaua's royal guard. Marsland was fiercely proud of his family's history on the islands and their status as a kamaaina family. According to a friend, Marsland "bristled at any questioning of his local credentials."

Like his son after him, Marsland attended the prestigious Punahou School for high school—swimming, running track, and playing football. He was handsome and well-dressed—characteristics that would remain consistent his whole life. During his senior year in 1940, the school year-book, the *Oahuan,* remarked that Marsland "has made quite a reputation for himself as a dancer deluxe and a number-one good sport. Charlie's amiable grin has been a contributing factor in making him quite a popular fellow."

After a stint at the University of Hawaii, Marsland enrolled in Tufts College in Medford, Massachusetts. There he also joined the Navy Reserve Officers Training Corps, becoming a crack rifle shot. On account of this military training, Marsland would not get to enjoy campus life in New England for long.

At the end of Marsland's first semester, Japanese planes bombed Pearl Harbor in Hawaii, prompting the United States to enter World War II. Marsland eventually found himself back in the Pacific, though he was not home in Hawaii but sailing the ocean to help invade the Philippines. Lieutenant Marsland served as an executive officer, or second in com-mand, on a ship carrying infantry before becoming a commanding officer himself. Photos from his voyage show his often bare-chested crew as they island-hopped the Pacific after coming through the Panama Canal.

At war's end Marsland remained in the Pacific with the navy, work-ing as a discipline and prison administration officer based at Pearl Har-bor. About seven years after first starting college, Marsland then returned to Tufts and graduated in 1949. Next came enrollment at Northeastern University School of Law in Boston, where he graduated three years later. Within a year he was hired as a legal assistant in the office of the attor-ney general of Massachusetts. By 1953, Marsland was named an assistant attorney general, investigating and prosecuting cases involving gambling, organized crime, and murder. He found the work thrilling, especially when his office coordinated massive stings.

By 1953, he had married, his bride the former Jayne Watts, a tal-ented entertainer who became one of Boston's first female television personalities, working as a popular weathergirl for WBZ-TV under the name Jane Day. Judging by Day's reputation, Marsland had done well for himself. His wife was not only a widely described beauty but also cheerful and clever. Among her calling cards was her famous "thought for the day," which accompanied her daily weather forecast. Another was her ability to write important weather information on a glass wall for her viewers—using both hands at the same time. People loved her, and fans lined up at events sponsored by department stores to meet her and obtain her autograph.

"No announcer," one newspaper columnist wrote, "can make the advent of awful weather sound sunnier than Jane Day."

Within a few years of marriage, the young couple moved to the South Shore community of Hingham, just south of Boston, and began a family. Their son, Charles F. "Chuckers" Marsland III, was born in 1955. A daughter, Laurie Jane, was born two years later. Despite the demands of small children, the Marslands kept an active social calendar, helping promote and partaking in local dances, plays, fashion shows, and charitable events.

At this point in his life, Marsland was ascendant. He had survived the war and reintegrated into society, securing work as a prominent prosecutor in his new home of Massachusetts. He had married a stunning and charming wife who was adored by thousands of television fans. He had become a father to a baby boy and girl. Next up, of course, was a political run.

In 1958, Marsland resigned his position in the attorney general's office and began work in private practice. He set his sights on becoming district attorney for Plymouth County, hoping to unseat the incumbent, a fellow Republican. But Marsland fell short, earning about 42 percent of the vote in the Republican primary.

A bigger disappointment would follow, as his marriage broke up. It is unclear what prompted Marsland and his wife to split, though some of Marsland's acquaintances cite infidelity as the cause and that Marsland claimed to have punched his wife's lover.

Returning to Hawaii with Chuckers in 1967, Marsland hardly ever spoke of his family life in Boston. Given the sensitivity of the situation, few friends dared to ask him much about the particulars behind his departure. They knew, though, that Marsland's relationship with his daughter suffered during this turn of events and that father and daughter spoke infrequently after their separation, despite Marsland's attempts to contact her. Friends of Marsland say that this estrangement caused him great sorrow. Upon the death of Chuckers, he had in effect lost both of his children.

Shortly after arriving back in Honolulu, Marsland began dating Polly Grigg, an interior designer who worked for Sheraton Hotels. Elegant and accomplished, Grigg was eventually named a vice president with design responsibilities for Sheraton Hotels across Asia and the Pacific. Grigg had moved to Hawaii after her husband died from injuries sustained in World War II. Like Marsland, she had a son from her marriage.

In 1971, Marsland the lawyer became deputy corporation counsel for the city and county of Honolulu, handling civil legal issues and lawsuits. Oftentimes this work involved the Honolulu Police Department, requiring Marsland to defend police officers from complaints of brutality and to ensure the department's compliance with federal requirements to better integrate and promote women in the police force.

All the while, Marsland's son, Chuckers, was maturing into a man.

By all accounts Marsland doted on his son, wanting the best for him. Yet, like many parents, he struggled to be consistent with discipline. At times Marsland was observed to be overly strict with Chuckers. In other instances Marsland was more a friend than father, acting in a manner one might expect with no mother in the house.

"He was a good, caring dad … liked to kid around with his son, maybe kind of pushed the envelope a little bit and maybe say some off-color things, but nothing mean or really nasty," said Mark Keala, a friend and classmate to Chuckers and a son of the Honolulu police chief. "He didn't come across as being like a real hard-ass to Chuck."

When Chuckers was a teenager, Marsland enrolled him in Erhard Seminars Training, a self-actualization course popular in the 1970s. Self-control was a significant focus of the seminars, so much so that participants were not allowed to leave a session to use the bathroom.

For most of his teen years, Chuckers bounced around Oahu playing sports, joining pickup basketball games, or racing in the ocean at the

Outrigger Canoe Club. Chuckers's own friends describe him as a little bit of a misfit, never exceedingly popular or smart but nonetheless cheerful enough to always keep company with a small group of buddies. Such friends were willing to tolerate Chuckers's major flaw: a tendency to exaggerate and boast.

"As he got older, he wanted to try and fit in more and more. He would embellish a lot of things, relationships, people that he knew, and so forth," said a friend.

"Typically you roll your eyes, because you know that's kind of who Chuck was, a little over the top . . . wanted people to know him, wanted people to like him," continued Keala. "When he would tell his stories, you know, in high school, his stories were always a little bit bigger and a little bit wilder than the story would actually turn out to be. That was kind of his nature."

At home it was much of the same. Grigg confided to a friend that she felt Marsland had spoiled Chuckers and that the boy incessantly bragged about his well-to-do mother in Boston. Grigg said Chuckers was "just so full of himself you could hardly listen to him when he got to be a teenager."

Toward the end of high school, Chuckers's body filled out. Mentally, too, he had seemed to mature, at least from the perspective of his proud father.

"From an awkward, raw-boned teenager," Charles Marsland wrote in a letter, "he had developed a poise, maturity, and grace far beyond his years. He spent a part of each day in either the gym or the water, and his shoulders and chest matured from raw strength to being incredibly powerful."

Suddenly Chuckers was less inclined to tolerate slights from others, fighting back when he was pushed around during athletic contests. As his buddy Jon Andersen recalled, Chucky became somewhat of a "wise guy," no longer willing to be picked on or intimidated. An acquaintance of Chuckers's from Waikiki's late-night scene gave the same assessment, claiming Chuckers "changed from a real nice guy to a tough-guy type. He was a hard-as-nails, shove-around type of guy," said the acquaintance.

Among those who could no longer boss Chuckers around was his father. The two were said to quarrel more often as Chuckers got older. By age nineteen, Chuckers's desire for independence was so strong that he moved out of his father's house and started living with his girlfriend, Cathy Clisby, and her roommate, Alexander Pedi.

Clisby, who was originally from Canada, had moved to Honolulu with a girlfriend after finishing high school in Washington State. She found work in Honolulu restaurants and bars, eventually becoming a cocktail waitress in Waikiki. It was through her job that she met Chuckers, though she knew him as Chuck. It was not long before they began sharing an apartment at the southern end of Waikiki, close to Diamond Head, just a few blocks from the beach.

"I adored him. He was a great guy," said Clisby. "Very, very personable."

The two spent lots of time together, often dining for breakfast early in the morning after finishing work at separate nightclubs. Then they would head home to sleep.

"Him and Cathy were sweethearts. Both tall, super looking. . . . They were a couple madly in love," said Pedi.

The couple was serious enough to discuss moving together to California, where Chuckers had been offered an athletics scholarship to Pepperdine University. In high school Chuckers had been a star volleyball player, helping Punahou capture its first state title in 1972.

"He had a lot of potential," said his high school coach, Chris McLachlin. "He was a great leaper and had all the talent to be an outstanding college volleyball player."

Before enrolling at Pepperdine, Chuckers began taking classes at the University of Hawaii and nearby Chaminade University. He also took a night job at the disco, seeming in no hurry to leave for California. Instead he was happy to live and work in Waikiki, where he could enjoy the nightlife, relax on the beach, and spend time with his girlfriend.

Chuckers's position as a doorman at the Infinity disco sometimes demanded a tougher and more vigilant disposition. How else to manage drunks and customers who wanted to fight on the dance floor? And with lines out the door and three hundred people inside listening to live music, the management appreciated an employee who could resolve a problem quickly.

"He liked the situations where he had to manhandle some badasses at Infinity," said Pedi. "He loved being a doorman over there. He liked to flex his muscles."

As a doorman and host, Chuckers was charged with seating and supervising guests. His boss, manager Paul Bowskill, said Chuckers was always punctual, well-mannered, and hardworking. He liked to smile, he recalled, and was sometimes mischievous.

At this time, Bowskill said, the Infinity was one of a handful of popular Waikiki nightclubs. In the 1970s, Waikiki was the best place in Honolulu to find entertainment, for locals and tourists alike. Whether in search of music, a movie, a good restaurant, or a good time, Waikiki was it. As Pedi recalled, "It was a cowboy show. It was disco at its finest. You had the nightclubs. I was a regular John Travolta. I was out there boogying and getting what I could get. Had money in my pocket, wearing a tuxedo and having a good time. It was great; it was wild. Drugs rampant, huge. Cocaine. Pot. Thai stick was out there for a while. There was all kinds of stuff. Hash oil, oh my god. . . . We all had our dashikis and our razor-blade chains around our necks. Bell-bottoms and our jumpsuits."

But not everyone shared such enthusiasm for the entertainment district. As writer William Helton reported in 1971, "Here lies Waikiki, four hundred and fifty acres of concrete and humanity crunched between an Army fort, a park, a canal, and the ocean. . . . It mixes in all the ingredients of an urban eyesore in the middle of a paradise: Easy money for thugs and prostitutes, a festering jungle for dope addicts and pushers, traffic madness, parking frustrations, and gallons of noise."

Supplying much of this noise were the nightclubs. Just down the street from the Infinity was the Polynesian Palace, where the Hawaiian hunk Don Ho crooned his hit "Tiny Bubbles" to two sets of sold-out shows six nights a week, packing more than five hundred people inside for each show. Described by *People* magazine as a "swarthily handsome" combination of Wayne Newton, Don Rickles, and Charles Bronson, Ho's biggest fans were his "grandmas"—blue-haired women who could not resist the heartthrob and his naughty sense of humor. These older fans stormed the stage after each show to receive an open-mouthed kiss from the lusty singer.

The action could be just as lively backstage. Ho's dressing room in the Polynesian Palace was a popular hangout for friends and acquaintances of the singer, not to mention a necessary stop for many politicians and Hollywood celebrities. One of Ho's friends, John Defries, said that "second to the State Capitol, Don's dressing room attracted all types. The place was a beacon, and he was a consummate host."

Among the regular visitors were a number of Hawaiian gangsters, including Eric Naone and Ronnie Ching. Both men were fixtures of Waikiki's late-night scene, and both were muscular and intimidating. Naone, an unemployed Vietnam veteran who claimed to have hopes of becoming a police officer, was so strong he was reputed to lift and press a homemade barbell consisting of manhole covers welded to each end of an iron rod. His personality was alleged to be as cold and hard as the metal he lifted.

"Eric Naone was not a pleasant individual. If you was on the wrong side of Eric Naone, look out. He was frightening," said Christopher Evans, a Honolulu lawyer who defended Naone. "He was one of the entourage for Don Ho. He was a muscle guy, he was the arm, he was protection. You just didn't want to be on the wrong end of Eric Naone, believe me."

Naone and Ching would wander Waikiki under cover of darkness, patronizing various nightclubs, usually dressed in heavy leather coats. One of their regular stops was the Infinity, where they'd stop to chat with their friend Chuckers Marsland. Of the two gangsters, Naone was a closer friend to Chuckers. They played softball together on weekends and hung out at bars. On a few occasions, Naone, who was a few years older than his buddy, was invited to eat at the Marsland home with Chuckers and his father.

Having a friend as strong and fierce as Naone was convenient for Chuckers in his work as a doorman. When certain guests would become boisterous at the Infinity, Chuckers would not hesitate to drop Naone's name. Naone did not mind and was glad to back up a friend, especially since Chuckers had been threatened by a Samoan clubgoer who had previously tangled with Naone.

That altercation had started when a gang of five or six Samoans jumped Naone. Following the assault, Naone swore revenge. To facilitate the payback, he and some friends had a sit-down with the Samoans in which Naone proposed fighting them again, two at a time, until he had run through the whole gang. The Samoans supposedly refused.

Not to be denied retribution, Naone kept tabs on the Samoans, eventually finding them one evening at the Infinity nightclub. By Naone's own admission, when a Samoan named Nico approached Naone and asked for a match, Naone said nothing. Instead of a match, he launched a flying karate kick, hitting Nico in the lower stomach and sending him staggering backward. Nico left the club without retaliating, at least not that night. Such was the rough-and-tumble landscape in Waikiki for street toughs.

On another occasion Naone, Ching, and another man entered the Infinity and motioned for Chuckers to join them in the bathroom. A few minutes later, they reemerged, and Chuckers's buddies quickly left the club. Noticing the strange interaction, Chuckers's manager, Bowskill, asked what was going on. Chuckers promptly unbuttoned his coat, revealing three handguns tucked into his belt. The gangsters had asked him to hold them, perhaps because police were nearby.

Bowskill expressed disapproval and told Chuckers to inform his father about the incident. It was common knowledge among the club employees that Chuckers's father was a prominent attorney for the city and familiar with many members of the police force. Chuckers had made sure that information was well-known.

The next day, when Chuckers reported for work, Bowskill asked him if he had indeed told his father about holding the guns.

"Yeah," said Chuckers.

"What did he say?" asked Bowskill.

"He said, 'Next time, give them a roll of duct tape,'" said Chuckers, implying that his father meant the gangsters could conceal the guns themselves in the bathroom, taping them behind a toilet or under a sink.

Curiously, Marsland did not caution his son about the dangers of associating with gun-toting gangsters. He did not insist he quit the nightclub. He did not, apparently, worry about his boy's safety. Indeed,

Marsland later boasted of the "devastating consequences" suffered by the few nightclub patrons who resisted Chuckers and how his son did not suffer a single scratch or bruise.

For some time Chuckers lived between two worlds: the law-enforcement community and the law-breaking community. He often bragged about knowing cops and criminals alike, whether his father and their family friend Honolulu police chief Francis Keala or underworld figures like Naone and Ching. Such a role suited the attention-seeking teenager perfectly.

"Chuck, he wanted to be perceived as someone that was important . . . to be known as someone, or as someone who had information. Or as someone who was, you know, who was worth getting to know," said Mark Keala, the chief's son.

If Marsland wasn't alarmed at Chuckers's interactions with gangsters, it might have been attributable to the fact that Oahu was a small island, and it was inevitable that one would occasionally brush up against less-savory characters, especially at night in Waikiki.

"It was easy to run into the wrong people during that time period," said Mark Keala. "It wasn't surprising that Chuck could find the wrong people, and especially as a bouncer. It seemed to be the type of job you would have if you were looking for trouble or trouble would find you."

Chuckers's girlfriend, Clisby, said that given the frequency with which nightclub employees encountered members of the underworld, it was only natural to become friendly with some of these people.

"You really didn't think anything of it because it just seemed like it was a normal thing. This was what was going on in the world," said Clisby. "You knew who they were. You saw a lot of, um, you know, prostitutes or johns who were your friends. You weren't involved with them, [but] we all would party together because being in the bar business you knew everybody, and everybody knew you."

It was so normal, in fact, that Clisby was not even particularly awe-struck when Chuckers told her that Ching and Naone killed people for a living, though neither man had been convicted of such a crime. Better to befriend alleged killers, one supposes, than make enemies of them. Besides, who else could stop by the police chief's office in the afternoon and then rendezvous with underworld hit men at night. Aside from a few vice cops, no one but Chuckers.

"He sort of felt that he was pretty much invincible," said Bowskill.

"Like a Greek god. Invincible," said Chuckers's roommate, Pedi. "He thought he was above everything."

Chuckers felt so invincible, in fact, that he did the unthinkable one evening. Declaring Ronnie Ching to be too "rowdy," he ejected him from the Infinity. Other club employees went out of their way to avoid such a confrontation with the gangster. Bowskill said that when Ching was in the club, he usually appeared high. He was also cold, beady-eyed, and unfriendly. Everyone knew his reputation as an underworld hit man.

"He looked like a guy you didn't want to mess with," said Bowskill. "You were always cautious when he was in there. It was like a time bomb, and you got the feeling he could go off at any time."

When Chuckers told Ching to leave, the gangster did not explode in a rage. He was, however, visibly angry. As Ching left, he snarled he was going to "get" Chuckers.

In the weeks before he died, Chuckers Marsland was noticeably nervous. At home in his second-story Waikiki apartment, he'd peek out the window while talking to Clisby, checking to see if someone was lurking outside, worried that he was being followed. He told Clisby he was thinking about sleeping at his father's house for a few nights, until he felt safer. He obviously felt in danger but disclosed no reasons for his paranoia. In hindsight, Clisby thinks he might have been protecting her, sparing her from knowing too much.

That, apparently, was Chuckers's problem: He knew too much. And he had a big mouth. In the underworld such a combination can get you killed very, very quickly.

There are a couple of theories about why Chuckers ended up on the side of an isolated stretch of road outside Honolulu with bullets in his head. Each of them involved him tiptoeing too close to Hawaii's underworld. His father believed Chuckers was an innocent victim, targeted by gangsters because he had overheard, or witnessed, something incriminating. Calling the murder "completely senseless," Marsland hypothesized that gangsters feared Chuckers might relay whatever he had witnessed to the police.

"A lot of the underworld people who went in there knew his relationship with the police chief," said Marsland, adding that every clubgoer knew Chuckers was his son too.

It is perhaps predictable that a parent would absolve his child of wrongdoing, finding it hard to imagine any offense that would justify his son being shot to death in the darkness. Despite the occasional fight and Chuckers moving out of the house shortly before his death, Marsland and his son were extremely close. The two men talked constantly.

"[Chuckers] would get up every morning, lay on the couch, make himself a cup of coffee, and stay on the phone for a good hour," said Pedi. "I found out later it was his father he was talking to. Every morning."

Chuckers also visited his father at his office three or four times a week and attended some of his trials. On weekends they scuba dived and had dinner together, sometimes inviting Marsland's mother, Sadie, a former teacher on Oahu who had an outsize reputation on the island as a schoolmarm.

"Everybody interacted really well. It seemed like a very, very loving family," said Clisby, who often tagged along, witnessing firsthand the strength of her boyfriend's relationship with his father.

"We spent a lot of time out at his house with his dad," said Clisby. "[They were] just regular everyday guys enjoying life. . . . They got along famously. They were very, very close."

But beyond Chuckers's loved ones, others were not as willing to pardon the young man's sins. Not only did these people disagree with Marsland's statements that Chuckers was "a likeable kid" who "got along with everybody," but some seemed to believe Chuckers got what he deserved.

If there was indeed fear that Chuckers was talking to the authorities about crime in Waikiki, this concern was well-founded. In one instance Chuckers had told his father and Chief Keala about an illegal gambling game operating on one of the top floors of his apartment building. This game was so well attended that Pedi, Chuckers's roommate, had trouble finding a parking space on the street when the gambling was in session.

Shortly after Chuckers mentioned the gambling game to his father and Chief Keala, the police raided the game. It's unknown if anyone in the police department compromised the confidentiality extended to Chuckers and exposed him to gangsters as the police's source.

Others believed Chuckers was killed over a cocaine debt, though there is dispute over whether Chuckers sold drugs let alone used them. Some high school acquaintances remember him as a dealer at Punahou School, though their recollections lack specifics. Chuckers's close friends from high school don't recall him peddling anything. But a coworker at the Infinity, Joseph Kama Jr., said he once saw Chuckers and Ching snort a footlong line of cocaine in the office of the nightclub. Ching sold cocaine to Chuckers in the men's bathroom too, said Kama, and Chuckers would sometimes duck into the restroom to get high.

"That's when he popped it out and did his trick," said Kama, a security guard. "When he would come out, he would be blowing his nose."

Eventually, said Kama, Chuckers ran up a debt with Ching that he was unable to pay. Ching, on the other hand, said that Chuckers bought cocaine from Naone. According to Ching, Chuckers became panicky in the weeks before his death because he had begun buying yet more cocaine from a rival gangster. Chuckers was afraid Naone might find out.

Such allegations don't square with others' impressions of Chuckers. Bowskill doesn't recall Chuckers sneaking into the bathroom regularly at the Infinity, nor does he remember him ever displaying any other sign of cocaine use. Clisby says she never saw Chuckers use cocaine. In fact, she said he only used marijuana once or twice. And Pedi, their roommate, said he never saw Chuckers use or deal cocaine from their apartment. Yet Pedi was always impressed with the amount of cash Chuckers kept in his wallet.

"If he was, I didn't know about it. No one was knocking on our door. He never brought it home," said Pedi. "If he did, he was doing it out of the club."

Lastly, some wonder if the explanation for the murder was much more straightforward: Chuckers angered someone and paid a heavy price for his misstep. Naone told the police that his Samoan nemesis could have possibly attacked Chuckers out of retaliation for their previous dispute and Naone's flying karate kick. Others wonder if a patron turned away from the club door had sought revenge. Chuckers routinely denied people admission because they were intoxicated or underage. Then there was Ching, who had vowed to "get" Chuckers for ejecting him from the Infinity. On the same day that Chuckers's body was discovered in rural Waimānalo, Ching visited the Infinity and suspiciously told Kama, the security guard, "You don't know nothing."

In any case, it seemed to all boil down to loose lips and poor associations.

"The rumors were that he was talking too much. Saying too many things. Talking to his dad," said James Koshiba, a prominent Honolulu attorney whose criminal defense clientele made him familiar with the Chuckers Marsland murder case and other intrigue in the Hawaiian underworld.

Ching and Naone were fearsome thugs, that much was clear. Yet for all the notorious reputations, rumors, and theories surrounding Chuckers's death, evidence of their involvement was hard to come by. As time went on, and despite Chief Keala's direct involvement in the Honolulu Police Department's investigation, no arrests were made for the murder of the young man. In the days after Marsland's murder, the police interviewed his coworkers as well as Naone and Ching, who had both visited Chuckers just before the Infinity closed. Neither was formally a suspect, and both denied having any knowledge of who killed Marsland. But as noted in a police report, Chuckers's girlfriend told investigators "she wouldn't be surprised if Eric [Naone] or one of Eric's friends was responsible," given their reputations as gun-toting underworld killers.

The same day of the murder, Naone met with police to clear his name. He told a detective he had been with Ching most of the evening and early morning in Waikiki and how they had encountered their friend Chuckers. After they said good-bye to Chuckers, they drove with another friend, Gregory Nee, to Kaneohe, on the other side of the island, so Naone could obtain a change of clothes from his mother's house. Around daybreak, Naone said, they returned to Waikiki.

As the detective wrote of the interview, Naone "knows that Ching is considered a police character but mentioned that he is still a personal friend. He has never seen him do anything wrong and whatever Ching does is Ching's business as long as he isn't implicated one way or another. He knows that Ching and [Chuckers] Marsland always got along and wouldn't encounter the thought of Ronald Ching having anything to do with the demise of Marsland."

Hours later Ching was interviewed by the police. He said little of value. The detective wrote,

> *Although being very cordial and sincere, Ching would not give this writer an oral statement. He only agreed to what Eric Naone stated. He also refused to take a polygraph test. This writer refused to let him know what Naone's statement actually was.*
>
> *He went on to say he doesn't appreciate the police hasseling [sic] him on the streets because that's where he makes his living and it appears the police coupled with their exploits seem to deter his normal life and movement. He does not want to get on the bad side of the police and is willing to come in and talk, requested the police have more tact on their approach to him.*

Five days after Chuckers's death, on April 22, 1975, the young man's funeral was held at Central Union Church in Honolulu. Known by its congregation as the "church in the garden," the tall, grand New England–style stone church was built in 1924 at the corner of Beretania and Punahou Streets. No matter the intensive development of Honolulu in the twentieth century, the church's campus has remained a lush and grassy tropical garden.

Friends and family packed the church to remember Chuckers's life and mourn his death. There were more than two hundred visitors—so many that the funeral service had to be moved from a chapel to the main church. Some of those who attended recall Chuckers lying in an open casket.

Among the large crowd of mourners were Ching and Naone. They had been picked up and driven to the funeral by their mutual friend Nee. The twenty-year-old, who had driven Ching and Naone across the island the same morning Chuckers had been killed, worked as a doorman at the

Polynesian Palace. Nee, who was only an acquaintance of Chuckers's, had not planned on attending the funeral. His friends, however, needed a ride and persuaded him to attend.

"If it had been strictly up to me," Nee said, "I wouldn't have gone."

When the three men entered the church, Nee said, people were crying. He, Ching, and Naone did not stick around for long.

"We went up to the casket and paid our respects and we left," he said.

———

Marsland grew increasingly frustrated by his son's murder investigation, causing his friendship with Chief Keala to fray. The tension between the men reflected an extreme change in Marsland's perception of the Honolulu police. Shortly after Chuckers's death, Marsland had deemed the local department "one of the finest in the nation" and praised the detective division for its nonstop investigation of his son's murder. Furthermore, Marsland lauded Keala as an honorable friend.

"It was the measure of the man that he came to tell me personally [of Chuckers's death]," wrote Marsland. "Not only is he one of my closest friends, but he loved, thought of, and treated Chuckie as his own son."

But friendship counted for little in the absence of arrests. When Marsland eventually began his own personal investigation into Chuckers's death, the tension between the old friends was exacerbated. Keala resented Marsland's efforts and deemed them detrimental to the official investigation. At a meeting in Keala's office, the men traded sharp words. Marsland was unsympathetic to the absence of witnesses and lack of hard evidence associated with the murder. He wanted justice for his son, plain and simple, and he was willing to go to nearly any length to obtain it. At this point, for the distraught Marsland, justice was synonymous with revenge.

Tucking a pistol beneath his coat, he ventured out late at night onto the streets of Waikiki, intent on questioning anyone he thought might know details about Chuckers's death. The well-dressed fifty-two-year-old was out of place in Waikiki, especially at night, when the discos raged, prostitutes crowded the sidewalks, and members of the underworld caroused about town. Nonetheless, Marsland persevered, slowly gathering clues and gossip concerning Chuckers's murder.

Among those he interviewed was Pedi. Marsland invited him to his office, and despite having previously met his roommate's father, Pedi was nervous about the impending conversation. When the men talked, Marsland was tight-lipped about the information he had already collected, mentioning only that he thought a woman might have helped lure Chuckers into the car that took him to his death. Otherwise he grilled Pedi, looking to learn any facts that might have escaped his attention.

"His father was obsessed, totally obsessed," Pedi said of the interview. "He was focused on one thing and one thing only, to find out who killed his son."

During this investigation too, Marsland claimed to have met with a man who told him the names of a handful of people allegedly involved in the murder. If Marsland would pay $20,000, this man said, he would "take care" of these people. As proof of a job well done, the man offered to place a finger from each victim in Marsland's mailbox. Marsland declined the offer.

Marsland also sought answers about his son's murder in the spiritual realm. He consulted a number of psychics, including a sister of his longtime girlfriend. Like Pedi, this sister characterized Marsland as nothing less than "obsessed" with finding his son's killers. In 1975, she conducted a message for Marsland, writing it down in secretarial notebooks. This message urged Marsland not to seek vengeance but instead to think of and remember his son in positive terms and to foster his own healing through the embrace of love and light. The message read, in part, "Prolonged grief is guilt and [Marsland] must cleanse himself of this. . . . The only way he can help his son is by releasing all of the negative hate concerning the death. Thinking of his son only in the light, the death is not an end but the beginning of a new life on a different plane. . . . The moment he releases Chucky in love and continues to think of him in the light of love, both of them will receive the benefits of the divine."

These kinds of divine benefits were of no interest to Marsland. He wanted names. He wanted to know upon whom he must exact revenge. But the psychic message was clear about the folly of that approach:

If you, Charles Marsland, continue on the course you have been on, you will be a victim too, as surely as your son, not of death but of the forces of evil that these people are on. You must free yourself by your own mind, releasing them to their fate and accepting good for you and for your son.

What happens to them is of no importance to you and can serve no purpose in your life. You are not on earth to live anyone's life but your own. Your son was a joy to you. Let him remain so by holding him in the light rays of love. You must now live as light possible to you, acceptive to love and light and giving the best of yourself to every situation, for you have been through a great trial and suffered much. Be kind and tender to all, for you have much to give, but most of all be sensitive to the cleansing rays of light and love and receive these rays.

Marsland would have none of it. More than a year after Chuckers's death, Marsland's fury was undiminished, his outrage unabated. He dismissed the message and further pursued his own investigation, compiling a short list of men he wanted to confront about their alleged involvement in his son's murder. These men proved elusive, or, perhaps, Marsland believed that anything less than a formal interview with these suspects would be useless to police and prosecutors. Abandoning the idea of vigilante justice, Marsland put away his gun and turned to his lawyer, Frank O'Brien, for help in finding the men. O'Brien obliged his client by devising a creative legal solution.

In September 1976, Charles Marsland filed a wrongful death suit against ten unknown defendants, listed as John Does One to Ten, which sought more than $800,000 in damages for the loss of Marsland's son. Part of the motivation for the lawsuit was an impending deadline, as Hawaii law set forth a two-year statute of limitations for wrongful death civil actions. More important, the filing of the lawsuit allowed for O'Brien to depose individuals with supposed knowledge of the crime. In other words, Marsland could confront the men on his short list.

"We were acting like our own little investigative police force," said O'Brien, who concedes that the legal maneuver was a bold one. "Back in those days, we got away with it. . . . I'm always willing to take a whack at something. There wasn't any downside."

Though the gambit cleared legal hurdles, it ultimately had little value. Among the men Marsland was most interested in having deposed was Chuckers's friend Naone. Another was Ching. The reputed hit man, however, would yield nothing.

The gangster came to the deposition accompanied by his lawyer. Ching refused to answer any questions, repeatedly invoking his Fifth Amendment rights. For the length of the short meeting, Marsland stared hard at the man he had been told killed his son. Ching's countenance was no more pleasant.

"[Ching] looked like a mean, nasty son of a gun," said O'Brien. "He wasn't happy to be there."

Thwarted, Marsland pivoted again, deciding to restart his career in criminal law. In 1976, he sought and obtained a transfer from Honolulu's civil law department to the city prosecutor's office. Given his experience combating organized crime in Boston, Marsland would be counted on to handle a heavy caseload. He only hoped that this caseload might one day include the men who killed his son.

"Somehow, some way, two or three vicious, mad dogs ended his life. It was more than one, because no one could have done it on a one-up confrontation," Marsland wrote to his daughter in Boston less than two months after Chuckers's murder. "There's a lot of answers to be found, and few leads to work with. . . . The case will break—but it's going to take time—and I'll see whomever did it in hell."

FOUR

King of Thieves

J. North Conway

The money was there and untouchable. George Leslie knew how to get it.

George Leslie bowed slightly as if being introduced to royalty while graciously shaking Fisk's hand in a hearty, congratulatory way. As in everything he did, Leslie's gesture was deliberate and rehearsed. It was not done solely for Fisk and his guests. He had practiced his outward behavior as if preparing for a part in a play, and perhaps George Leslie did indeed see himself as the leading man in some lavish production of his own creation. He would spend hours standing before the full-length mirror in his hotel room, practicing his bow, his handshake, and his intriguing smile.

Each bow had its purpose—always to show respect, of course, but also to indicate his level of admiration for the person he was being introduced to. A slight bow, more of a tip of his head than anything else, was reserved for those he was not enamored of. A more pronounced bow, bending slightly at his waist with his shoulders thrust a bit forward, was used for those he was interested in becoming acquainted with but had yet to discover why or how. The last bow in his repertoire, a full-blown flourishing bow at the waist, was strictly reserved for the cream of the crop, and Jubilee Jim Fisk was surely one of New York City's finest.

Leslie also took great pains to practice his handshake by using a pincushion and standing in front the mirror. The faint, barely recognizable handshake, limp in nature, was once again reserved for the general populace. It was a handshake that said, "Yes, I am required to do this, but I have no interest in continuing any relationship with you." The indents in the pincushion would be hardly noticeable. His second handshake, reserved for those he was inclined toward knowing better, was a tighter, firmer handshake—not overly aggressive but sincere and memorable, one that was sure to let the person know that he was indeed pleased to be in his or her company and would like to continue the relationship. The pincushion would show the clear definition of his palm and fingers. Lastly, reserved, once again, for the cream of the crop, like Fisk and others whom he greatly admired or in some way wished to emulate, he had practiced a hearty, lasting, congratulatory, and overly animated handshake that clearly conveyed his great admiration and respect. In this case, the pincushion he practiced on would show the effect of his crushing grip.

For the ladies he was introduced to, he had developed a single sweeping gesture that he had practiced endlessly to perfection. This and only this modus operandi applied to every woman, young or old, rich or poor, beautiful or homely. He would bow with great enthusiasm, as if greeting a long-lost friend, cup the woman's hand gently in his, as if not so much holding her hand as balancing it delicately on his own, and with the slightest brush of his lips, he would kiss her hand and then gently remove his own, leaving the woman's hand floating in space. The kiss was always brief and appropriate but tinged with a certain sense of mystery. Rising up from his bow and from kissing the woman's hand in this gentlemanly way, he would maintain deep and penetrating eye contact with the woman, as if judging her response to his ovation. It usually sent hearts aflutter, exactly the reaction he was looking for.

His smile, too, was practiced to perfection, often many times before going out in public. A slight parting of his lips beneath his dark trimmed mustache was reserved for the general public. A broader, more expansive grin, where he bared his pearly white teeth, was awarded to those he would like to get to know better. And a wide, open-mouthed smile that stretched lines in his cheeks—sometimes referred to as smiling from ear to ear—was saved for royalty like Jubilee Jim. Being introduced to Fisk at Delmonico's, Leslie pulled out all the stops. Smiling ear to ear, he bowed deeply and shook Fisk's hand heartily.

Leslie was introduced as a successful architect from Cincinnati, the son of a wealthy Toledo beer magnate. Even before being introduced to the other two people dining with Fisk, Ned Stokes and Josie Mansfield, Leslie congratulated Fisk on his new theatrical venture, the Grand Opera House. Leslie noted that Pike's Opera House—which had been refurbished by Fisk and renamed the Grand Opera House—had been built by a Cincinnati man, Samuel N. Pike. Leslie lavished praise on Fisk for what he had accomplished, making the opera house the most majestic theatrical venue in the entire city. Fisk was not beyond flattery when it came to the theater, and he beamed with pride upon hearing Leslie's unsolicited assessment of the place. His plump cheeks grew rosy red with delight. Fisk immediately offered Leslie free tickets to his newest production, an extravagant musical performance called *The Twelve Temptations*.

Fisk took an immediate liking to the gentlemanly George Leslie after their brief encounter at Delmonico's. Fisk subsequently sent Leslie an invitation to join him at a private party to be held at 79 Clinton Street, the home of Marm Mandelbaum. The invitation intrigued Leslie. He had heard of Fredericka Mandelbaum from friends and was well aware that she was known as the biggest fence in the city. Whatever Jim Fisk was doing associating with the likes of her was beyond him, but Leslie was more than happy to attend. Perhaps Mandelbaum could open a few of the doors that Leslie was hoping to step through. Since he had abandoned all thought of plying his trade as an architect, and since he didn't really know what he wanted to do with the rest of his newfound life New York City, he thought meeting Marm Mandelbaum might be a step in the right direction since he had come to New York City intent on beginning a new career—a life of crime.

—

It wasn't losing the money that bothered Leslie, although the $200 that had been in his wallet was a lot of money by anyone's standards. And it wasn't losing his personal papers that were also in the wallet; he could always replace them. It was the little round metal plate—the prototype of his invention—that was irreplaceable. He had been working on it for three years and had yet to test it out. Somewhere in one of his many notebooks he had sketches of it. But these notebooks, along with the rest of his possessions, were still in transit, coming by train from Cincinnati to New York. Losing this small mechanical device would be a major setback for him. Among his many other talents, George Leslie had an uncanny mechanical ability. His invention, a little tin wheel that he had sarcastically dubbed "the little joker," might take a year or more to duplicate. It had been stolen when someone picked his pocket at the train station.

Leslie had left Delmonico's restaurant feeling on top of the world. He had met the infamous Jubilee Jim Fisk, he'd received free tickets to the Grand Opera House performance of the sold-out show *The Twelve Temptations*, and he'd also received a personal invitation by Fisk to attend the next dinner party at Marm Mandelbaum's.

Fredericka "Marm" Mandelbaum, acknowledged by almost everyone as the "Queen of the Underworld," was also known for throwing some of the most lavish parties in the city, where she entertained many of New York's wealthiest socialites, including businessmen, lawyers, judges, and politicians. Word was that you really hadn't made it in New York City if you hadn't been to one of Marm's exclusive soirees. She was definitely someone Leslie wanted to meet.

Along with being a time of great industrialization in the country, 1869 was also a time of great inventions, both large and small. Thomas Edison created his first invention, the electric vote counter, which could instantly record votes. It was intended to be used in congressional elections, but members of the United States House of Representatives rejected it. He also invented the stock ticker that year, an electrical mechanism that would keep investors updated on their stock-market dealings.

Ives McGaffey invented the first vacuum cleaner, a "sweeping machine" that cleaned rugs. Inventor Sylvester H. Roper built the first steam-powered motorcycle. The first typewriter was invented and patented by Christopher Sholes, Samuel Soule, and Carlos Glidden. In George Leslie's home state of Ohio, W. F. Semple invented chewing gum.

All these inventions in some way revolutionized life in America. Not to be outdone by any of these extraordinary devices, George Leslie also tried his capable hand at inventing. His invention would also revolutionize a certain aspect of American life, specifically banking—more specifically, bank robbing. If he was correct, Leslie was certain that his "little joker" would turn bank robbing into a modern science, no longer requiring holdups, guns, dynamite, or any other previously used, time-consuming apparatus.

In 1862, Linus Yale Jr. invented the modern combination lock. Almost everyone believed that the new combination locks were burglarproof. What they hadn't counted on was something as inventive as George Leslie's little joker. It was a simple device: a small tin wheel with a wire attached to it that would fit inside the combination knob of any bank safe. All anyone had to do was take off the dial knob of a bank lock and place the little joker on the inside of the dial. Then, after carefully replacing the knob, it could be left there undetected. When bank officials opened the vault the next day during regular business hours, Leslie's little joker, still concealed under the safe's knob, would record where the tumblers stopped by making a series of deep cuts in the tin wheel. The deepest cuts in the wheel would show the actual numbers of the combination. Although it wouldn't record the exact order of the numbers in the combination, it would only be a matter of trying several different combinations before the safe would open. Leslie was sure of it.

A bank robber could then sneak back into the bank, remove the knob, and examine the marks in the tin plate. All the robber had to do was figure out the exact order in which the stops were used. Using the device *did* require a robber to break into a bank twice—once to place the contraption inside the dial of the vault and a second time to retrieve it—and not many robbers had the aptitude or patience to perform such a tricky endeavor. It would take a very special kind of person to accomplish the undertaking, someone with brains, patience, and nerves of steel. George Leslie saw himself as that person.

The little joker eliminated the need to use dynamite to blow open a vault. Robbers often blew up more than just the vault door when pulling off a bank heist. Hundreds of times robbers used too much dynamite and ended up blowing up all the cash, securities, and other valuables inside— or worse, injuring themselves. And, of course, the blast from using dynamite drew attention and caused panic, leading to many failed robbery attempts.

The little joker also eliminated the need for long and laborious safecracking techniques used by many robbers—turning the dial this way and that, listening with a stethoscope to determine the right sequence of combination clicks. Safecracking took hours, and it wasn't foolproof. Leslie was sure that his device was the safest, most effective way of robbing a bank. No bank vault would be safe from it.

The most popular method of safecracking was to simply steal the entire safe and move it to a place where it could be taken apart in a leisurely fashion. However, banks and other financial institutions were now investing in huge, complex steel vaults, so moving a safe was no longer an option. Most robbers were forced to use one of four techniques: lock manipulation to determine the combination, screwing the vault, drilling it, or blowing up the vault using either gunpowder or dynamite. None of these methods was expedient.

Lock manipulation required skill and time. The robber would try a series of possible combinations, listening to the tumblers through a stethoscope to determine the exact location where the tumblers stopped. The process could take an inordinate amount of time, and, depending on the number of tumbler stops, it would require the robber to try hundreds, if not thousands, of possible combinations.

Screwing the vault required the robber to drill a hole into the door plate and then tap a thread through it where a heavy machine bolt would be inserted and used to slowly unscrew the door bolts. This was also time-consuming, depending on the thickness of the door. It also required the robber to use dozens of drill bits that would be chewed up in the process.

Drilling required the robber to have access to engineering drawings of the vault's bolt mechanism and then to locate a point on the safe door to drill through. A screwdriver was then shoved through the opening and maneuvered to free the bolts. This process bypassed the vault's combination lock completely. It was also a lengthy process, and without the vault's engineering schematic showing the exact workings of the lock, there was no way of telling where the correct spot was to begin drilling.

Finally, bank robbers could resort to using either gunpowder or dynamite to blow up the safe. Although faster than any of the other three methods, it was fraught with danger. Too little gunpowder and the lock would not be blown. Too much dynamite and not only would the vault door be blown off its hinges but the contents of the safe could also be blown to smithereens. In the worst-case scenario, the robbers could blow themselves up as well. The explosion caused by using either gunpowder or dynamite always attracted attention.

But these methods were all a bank robber had to work with, except for the mythical device that some robbers had unsuccessfully tried to create. It would let the robber know exactly what the vault combination was so that the vault could be opened quickly, safely, and without drawing attention to the crime. Many criminals had tried to perfect such a device, but none had succeeded—that is, not until George Leslie put his mind to it.

The Mandelbaums may have lived in meager surroundings on the upper floor of the Clinton Street address, but Marm's guests experienced only luxury in the lavishly furnished back portion of the building, where she did all her entertaining. As she had accumulated wealth and stature in the criminal community, she gained a certain notoriety in the legitimate world. She became adept at living in both worlds, learning how to deftly balance between the legitimate world and the underbelly of the criminal one.

Although Mandelbaum was the leading criminal fence in New York City, she was, by her own account, still a lady. She had exquisite taste and manners and was an avid admirer of intelligence and sophistication. She wouldn't tolerate foul language around her, especially at her dinner parties. She expected everyone, especially the rough trade she surrounded herself with, to be on their best behavior when they were in her company. Those that couldn't abide by these rules were seldom allowed to do business with her. She was constantly trying to improve the lagging social graces of her criminal friends, imploring them to read and aspire to proper etiquette and good manners.

Her parties were considered the highlight of the city's social season, where thieves and thugs would mix freely with businessmen and politicians. Many of these legitimate guests, ironically, had homes and businesses that had probably been robbed by the very crook sitting next to them at the lavish banquet table Mandelbaum always set. Still, no one who was anyone in New York City could resist an invitation to one of her parties. George Leslie was no exception.

Leslie arrived at his first dinner party at Marm's wearing his best attire: a Highland frock coat, an elegant Wyatt striped shirt with a string tie, wool tailcoat pants, and a Farrington vest, with its high-cut, notched collar—the kind so many businessmen in New York City were wearing at the time. He wore a black Victorian top hat and white formal gloves and carried a cane, a hardwood staff topped with a shiny brass three-knob crown.

Leslie had the carriage drop him off at the front door of Mandelbaum's store on Clinton Street. He held a package under his arm. The store was dark. He strode to the door and knocked loudly, but there was no answer. He was sure he had the right date and the right address. He knocked again and finally heard someone coming.

Mandelbaum's teenage son Julius, fair-haired and slim, opened the door and let him in. Behind Julius stood Herman Stroude, Mandelbaum's part-time clerk and full-time bodyguard. Muscular and tall, he towered over Leslie, who was himself at least six feet tall. Stroude was bald, wore a gold earring in his ear, and had a bushy black mustache. Julius reluctantly made eye contact with Leslie as he explained that he'd been invited to the party by Jim Fisk. He gave Julius one of his cards. Stroude took the card and went upstairs to verify Leslie's story with Jubilee Jim, who was already enjoying the gala event with Josie Mansfield. When Stroude returned a few minutes later, he whispered something to Julius.

Julius led the dandified Leslie through the darkened store to a long corridor, up several flights of stairs, and into a huge, brilliantly lit dining room filled with a bustling, noisy crowd. Guests were laughing, chatting, and eating while a piano player off in the corner played a rousing version of "Little Brown Jug." It was one of the most popular songs in 1869, played in respectable saloons and dance halls throughout the city as well as being a musical staple in the city's so-called free and easies, the more disreputable drinking establishments that provided music as well as prostitutes. These large riotous taverns proliferated throughout the New York City slums. "Little Brown Jug" was written by Joseph Eastburn Winner, the brother of another popular composer during the same period, Septimus Winner. Septimus's songs "Listen to the Mockingbird" and "Oh, Where Has My Little Dog Gone" were both popular dance hall and tavern favorites.

Mandelbaum's dining room was spacious, elegant, and comfortable, with plush carpets of red and gold and an assortment of formal dining tables and chairs as well as upholstered couches and high-back leather chairs. The room featured a coffered ceiling and hand-carved woodwork, including an ornate fireplace and bookcases. Huge pocket doors separated the two parlor sections. The windows were covered with luminously embroidered silk drapes along with carved wooden shutters that concealed guests from prying eyes. The ceilings rose nearly twelve feet high, whereas the cut-glass chandeliers hung at a lower level, in keeping with the practice during the Gilded Age, when lighting needed to be closer to arm's reach for quick replacement.

More than sixty guests dined at the many tastefully set, Chippendale-style mahogany tables with matching chairs, each of which had a shaped crest with acanthus carving on it. Mandelbaum, who was too huge to fit comfortably into one of the chairs, was seated on an embroidered, cushioned bench. All the tables were covered with ornate linen tablecloths and decorated with gold candelabras. The walls were covered with paintings, some framed, some not. The elaborate decor of the dining room was abundant with Victorian elegance and whimsy, all of it stolen from some of the best homes and offices throughout the city and country. Mandelbaum had exquisite taste in stolen property.

Guests dined on lamb and sliced ham that was provided at the party by "Piano" Charlie Bullard. Bullard was a former butcher who now focused on his talent for safecracking. However, when called on, he still provided the best cuts of meat for Marm's parties. Bullard was also a trained pianist, able to perform the most intricate piano concertos. He was known throughout the underworld for having the most sensitive fingers in the safecracking business. No bank safe tumbler was safe from Bullard's nimble fingertips. Bullard often entertained Marm's dinner guests, playing anything from Beethoven to the most popular songs of the day on the white baby grand piano that adorned Marm's lavish dining room. It was Bullard who was playing the rollicking version of "Little Brown Jug" as Leslie entered the room.

As Leslie stepped out of the dark hallway into the crowded, gaily lit, and festive dining room, George Leslie knew he had arrived—in more ways than one.

That evening at Marm's party, Leslie paid his respects to Fisk, thanking him profusely for inviting him. Fisk told Leslie that Marm was anxious to meet him, advising him to introduce himself to her posthaste. He did what Fisk suggested and made his way over to Marm's table straightaway. Mandelbaum was busy holding court in a far corner of the busy dining room. When Leslie introduced himself, Mandelbaum's otherwise downward-curved mouth turned into a smile. Marm asked Shang Draper to move down so that Leslie could sit next to her, a place of honor by anyone's account. The request annoyed Draper, who had become, or so he imagined, second in command to Mandelbaum. He didn't like the idea of having anyone take his place next to Marm, either physically or figuratively. Nonetheless, Draper grudgingly moved over, and Leslie sat down next to Mandelbaum.

Leslie immediately thanked Mandelbaum for the invitation to the dinner party and especially for helping to retrieve his stolen wallet. Leslie had learned from Sheriff O'Brien, to whom Leslie had paid a handsome reward, that he owed his gratitude to Marm. It was only through her efforts that the wallet had been returned, almost intact—sans the $200, of course. Leslie had only been concerned with the return of his little joker, which was now sitting safely in the Fifth Avenue Hotel's safe along with many of his other precious possessions.

Mandelbaum took an immediate liking to George Leslie. Perhaps it was his good looks or his manners. Perhaps it was because Marm always prided herself on being a good judge of character, and she sensed that the handsome, well-mannered gentleman from Cincinnati had a larcenous heart. In fact, being a good judge of character, she knew he did.

Once Leslie was seated comfortably next to Marm, she clapped her hands and a young boy maneuvered through the noisy crowd, carrying a tray of wineglasses. Leslie recognized the boy immediately. It was the young pickpocket from the train station. Along with his many other attributes, Leslie was also gifted with a near-photographic memory. He could look at something or someone for the briefest time and recall the person or place in the minutest detail.

The pickpocket—who was called Johnny Irving—had a shock of blond hair and wide blue eyes. He wasn't dressed in the rags he'd been wearing earlier at the train station; instead, he now sported a white shirt, black vest, and bow tie. Leslie politely took a glass of wine and handed it graciously to Marm. He then took one for himself, all the while keeping his eyes fixed on Irving, who grew more uncomfortable by the minute. Leslie asked after the boy's younger sister. Irving pretended not to understand. Marm intervened, asking if Leslie knew the boy. Leslie explained how he had run into the boy and his sister at the train station. Marm told him that she made every attempt to care for the poor orphaned street children by finding them work. She boasted of running a small school for them on Grand Street. Leslie had heard all about the "school" she ran.

Leslie was bright enough to realize that it was Irving who had stolen his wallet that day at the train station and that he worked for Marm as one of her many criminals in training. It was the only way he could have gotten his wallet back nearly intact. Irving had stolen it and dutifully returned it to his teacher and benefactor, Marm Mandelbaum. It made perfect sense. Still, Leslie had to wonder, of all the possibly hundreds of wallets stolen by Mandelbaum's cadre of young pickpockets, why had his been so readily returned to him? Sheriff O'Brien had only been the go-between. It was Marm who'd had the wallet and Marm who returned it to him. It was a puzzle to Leslie.

With Irving still standing in front of them, Leslie quickly brought up the issue of the stolen wallet. He again thanked Mandelbaum for returning it to him. Marm took no credit for finding the wallet, explaining that it had been all Sheriff O'Brien's doing. She explained that the wallet had simply and miraculously come into her possession when someone, she could not remember who, had brought it into her store, claiming that they had found it. It was pure coincidence as far as she was concerned. God, she told him, worked in mysterious ways. So did Marm Mandelbaum, Leslie suspected.

It was just too bad that he'd lost his $100, Marm said. Leslie winked at Irving, who looked as though he was about to drop his tray and bolt at any second. Both Leslie and little Johnny Irving knew that his wallet had contained *$200*. For one brief moment, the knowledge of that fact struck a tenuous bond between Leslie and Irving.

Marm waved Irving off. Before he could make his getaway, Leslie reached into his pocket and handed him a silver dollar, commending the boy for his fine service. Irving looked at Marm before taking Leslie's tip. She nodded approvingly, and Johnny Irving snatched the silver dollar and tucked it safely away, no doubt relieved that Leslie hadn't revealed his deception to Mandelbaum.

Irving's secret was safe with Leslie. Based on what the police officer had told him, Leslie knew that Mandelbaum's little pickpockets only received a small percentage of what they stole for her. There was, of course, no honor among thieves. Irving must have returned only half of what was in Leslie's wallet. The rest he must have kept for himself and his sister. *Enterprising boy*, Leslie thought.

After Irving left, Leslie explained that he didn't care so much about the money; it was the contents of the wallet that mattered most to him. Some of it was irreplaceable, he said. Marm understood completely. Of all the people in the world who might have appreciated what it was George Leslie was trying to perfect—the Holy Grail for bank robbers—Marm Mandelbaum was at the top of the list. Leslie wasn't the first to try to create a device that could be used to surreptitiously uncover the combination to any bank safe. And now that Marm knew he had a safecracking instrument tucked away in his wallet, she was anxious to find out why. This handsome young man from Cincinnati didn't look or act like any of her other employees. For the first part of the evening, Mandelbaum would not let Leslie leave her side, much to the chagrin of her other criminal guests, always eager to bask in her ample limelight and good favor.

Red Leary tapped Leslie on the shoulder. He pointed to Marm, who was standing on the other side of the room, waiting for him. Leslie bid Tilden and Fisk good-bye. Stokes now sat sullenly beside Mansfield. Leslie saw no reason to engage him further. He headed across the room to where Marm was waiting to take him downstairs to the storefront, the only place they could talk privately. Leslie graciously took the arm of his hostess as she led him out of the brightly lit room, into the dark corridor, and down the stairs.

Although Marm was taken by the gentlemanly Leslie, she was nobody's fool. She needed to test him to be sure he wasn't an agent for the police or the Pinkerton detectives. Mandelbaum had enough money to bribe police and politicians in order to stay one step ahead of the law, but the uncompromising Pinkerton detectives were different. They were incorruptible, which made them dangerous to Mandelbaum and her criminal empire.

The Pinkerton Detective Agency was started in 1852 by Allan Pinkerton, a deputy sheriff in Chicago. It quickly grew to become the vanguard of criminal detection, known for its high moral standards and relentless pursuit of criminals. It was reportedly the prototype for the Federal Bureau of Investigation. During the Civil War, Allan Pinkerton was the head of the Union secret service, responsible for spying on the Confederacy. The agency was also given the job of guarding President Abraham Lincoln. Their slogan was "We Never Sleep," and the sign that hung over their offices in Chicago depicted a huge black-and-white wide-open eye. This logo led to the term "private eye."

In later years, the Pinkerton Detective Agency became known as an instrument of big business, acknowledged more for squashing union riots and strikes than for pursuing criminals. Notably, in 1875, the Pinkertons infiltrated and crushed the Molly Maguires, a secret coal miners' organization in Schuylkill County, Pennsylvania. They also broke up the strike of the iron and steel workers' union at Andrew Carnegie's Homestead plant in Pittsburgh. But before their image was forever tarnished by their link to big business and efforts to suppress the burgeoning labor movement in America, the Pinkerton Detective Agency, under the leadership of Allan Pinkerton and, later, his two sons, Robert and William, was engaged in the pursuit of known criminal gangs and, most conspicuously, Marm Mandelbaum. They were a dangerous force to be reckoned with, and Mandelbaum was not about to take any chances. She had to be sure that George Leslie was not a Pinkerton agent sent to infiltrate her operation.

Alone downstairs in the dingy storefront, far from the gaiety upstairs and from prying eyes, Mandelbaum confronted Leslie. She wanted to know what he was doing with something like the little joker in his wallet.

Although she didn't know Leslie's name for his invention, she certainly knew what the contraption was supposed to be used for. She had seen similar devices before, dozens of times, and she had seen them all fail to produce the desired result—miraculously opening up a bank safe. She laid her cards on the table: she knew what he had in his wallet; what she wanted to know now was why someone of Leslie's upbringing, education, and social standing would have such a device.

Leslie gave it to her straight. He wanted to rob banks, and his little joker would help him do it. He explained to her how it worked and how it would revolutionize bank robbing. Mandelbaum had heard it all before. Leslie explained he'd tested it on his own safe, and it worked like a charm. Mandelbaum still wasn't convinced. There was a big difference between using the device on a safe he had in his room, with all the time in the world to fiddle with it, and actually using it in a real bank robbery where you potentially had someone breathing down your neck. Leslie agreed. He told her that was why he wanted her to give him a chance to prove it to her.

Mandelbaum feigned surprise. Whatever made him think she knew anything about robbing banks? She stared at him suspiciously, complaining that the rich food and wine had upset her stomach. Leslie played along, boasting that if she was looking for somebody to rob a bank, he was the man to do it. He provided a litany of his qualifications, explaining that he had been gifted with a photographic memory. That, along with his understanding of architectural design, allowed him to practically memorize the layout of any building after seeing it only briefly.

She agreed that this was an amazing ability, to be able to size up any room or building so quickly, a gift that must be helpful in his career as an architect. Helpful in perhaps other careers as well, Leslie told her—including robbing banks.

Mandelbaum wanted to know why he wanted to rob a bank. It was dangerous, and if he was caught he could spend years in prison. Leslie assured her that he would never get caught and that his device would take all the danger out of robbing a bank. There would be no need for laborious safecracking, no need for dynamite or any other explosives, and no need for guns or weapons of any kind. He said he had it down to a science.

He still hadn't answered her question about his motive for robbing a bank. He already appeared to be fairly wealthy. He didn't need the money, did he? It was easy enough to answer. People like Jubilee Jim Fisk robbed everyone—banks, trains, other Wall Street brokers, even the government. And Boss Tweed and his political machine—well, they robbed the city blind. The Carnegies, Belmonts, and Vanderbilts, they all robbed from each other and called it good business. And they all put their money in banks for safekeeping. He just wanted to eliminate the middleman, Leslie explained. If all the robber barons put their money in banks, he would just rob the bank. It made perfect sense to him.

It was beginning to make perfect sense to Mandelbaum as well. Still, no matter how taken she was with this handsome young gentleman, she was a shrewd businesswoman and an even shrewder criminal. No matter how much she liked him, his loyalty had to be tested—and it would be, soon enough.

Leslie spent much of the remainder of the evening seated in the chair of honor next to Mandelbaum, an act that prompted some speculation and a great deal of envy, especially from Marm's criminal cohorts at the party. Across from Leslie was Max Shinburn, a German-born criminal whose expertise was burglary and safecracking. He was also one of Mandelbaum's favorites because of his gentlemanly demeanor. Shinburn liked to be referred to as "the Baron." He had spent some of his ill-gotten gains buying a title of royalty in Monaco. He and Leslie hit it off famously.

During dinner the guests drank an array of fine sparkling wines from Victorian etched wineglasses, but after the meal they were treated to a variety of mixed drinks prepared by New York City's most famous mixologist, Jerry Thomas. Thomas was the principal bartender at the Metropolitan Hotel, on the corner of Broadway and Prince Street. He was known as the city's premiere bartender, popular among all the best "club men" and widely known for his famous mixed drink inventions, including the "Martinez," a drink wrongly described as the original martini. Thomas's Martinez was made with sweetened gin, red vermouth, maraschino liqueur, and bitters.

Seeing the attention Marm paid to the stranger infuriated Shang Draper, who didn't take lightly to some tinhorn from Cincinnati cutting in on his turf. Draper worked closely with Mandelbaum, using her as both a fence for stolen property as well as a financial resource for bank robberies. He didn't know who Leslie was or what role he might play in the ongoing business of New York City crime, especially as far as his association with Marm was concerned, but he wasn't about to let anyone come between him and his dealings with Marm, especially not the handsome, sophisticated George Leslie. Draper, who had grown up in the horrific Five Points, had a suspicious mind, and worse, an abiding hatred of the upper class.

Another underworld thug who was not pleased with Leslie's encroachment of Mandelbaum was Johnny "the Mick" Walsh, the leader of the notorious Walsh Gang in the Bowery section of the city. Walsh's violent gangland tactics, including shakedowns of businesspeople and immigrants for protection money, dominated the Bowery. Walsh was no friend of Shang Draper's; he was looking to expand his criminal operations throughout the city, and Draper stood firmly in his way. The two gang leaders had been engaged in a long-running feud, and their gangs had fought turf wars in a series of bloody knife fights and gun battles, with neither gang besting the other. A successful albeit shaky peace had been brokered by Mandelbaum, who saw the feud as bad for business. The truce between Draper and Walsh would be shattered many years later during a bloody shootout at Shang Draper's saloon in 1883, with Draper finally getting the best of "the Mick."

Leslie left the dinner party with private invitations extended to him from three people: Mandelbaum, who wanted to discuss his little joker in more detail; Josie Mansfield, who gave him the dates that Fisk would be in Washington; and exotic beauty Black Lena Kleinschmidt, who, despite Mandelbaum's orders, had found a way to arrange a secret rendezvous with Leslie.

All in all, it had been a very productive evening for George Leslie.

— ◆ —

Mandelbaum organized a gang for the bank job and put Leslie in charge. She felt he could now concentrate his full attention on what was most important: the robbery of the Ocean National Bank.

The old adage "one man's floor is another man's ceiling" wasn't lost on George Leslie as he prepared to undertake his first bank heist. It was more important for Leslie to know whose ceiling was another's floor as he planned his intricate robbery of the Ocean National Bank. The robbery was one part planning and another part hocus-pocus, but it was all sheer criminal genius.

George Leslie pulled off his first bank heist in June 1869, a few short months after his introduction to Marm Mandelbaum. Mandelbaum supplied Leslie with a handpicked gang of her best and most trusted associates, including Johnny Dobbs, Billy Porter, Jimmy Hope, Gilbert Yost, Red Leary, and Shang Draper. Leslie's gang robbed the Ocean National Bank located at the corner of Greenwich and Fulton Streets, getting away with close to $800,000, an unprecedented amount of cash. The take in the Ocean Bank robbery would have been even higher if Leslie hadn't decided that they would only take what they could carry, and only those items—cash, checks, and jewelry—that were untraceable. He saw no point in stealing bank certificates that could only be cashed at the bank itself or gold that would weigh them down. Leslie was particular about what he wanted to steal and how he wanted to steal it, which branded him among other criminals he was working with as a prima donna. Prima donna or not, this was his first heist, but it would by no means be his last.

It was the largest take of any bank job in the city's history up until then, and it was pulled off without firing a shot or blowing open the bank safe. Leslie's little joker did all the work. Although Mandelbaum financed the operation at a cost of $3,000, it was Leslie who masterminded the caper. Leslie had clearly demonstrated his amazing knack for planning and pulling off successful, not to mention highly rewarding, bank robberies. It was the beginning of a great career in crime for George Leslie and an opportunity afforded him solely by Marm Mandelbaum, a fact that Leslie never forgot. Throughout his reign as "the King of Bank Robbers," the title that was later given to him by friends in the criminal world as well as New York City police officials and newspaper reporters, Leslie paid tribute to Mandelbaum either through a direct percentage from every bank job he pulled or by laundering stolen securities and other valuables through her, whether she'd financed the caper or not. This relationship would last throughout his short life.

Shang Draper had not been so keen on Leslie, seeing him as a challenger to his own lofty position within the crime world and especially with Marm. He would later come to see Leslie as a threat to someone even more important to him—his wife, Babe Irving.

Planning for the Ocean National Bank heist took three months, much to the chagrin of Draper and the others, who wanted to simply break into the bank vault and blow up the safe. This wasn't what Leslie had in mind, and, over almost everyone's objections, Marm put the novice bank robber Leslie in charge of the whole operation. Leslie promised her the biggest payday in criminal history, and he wasn't far off the mark. It would take another nine years before Leslie tried to make good on his promise by pulling off the greatest heist in American history, the robbery of nearly $3 million from the Manhattan Savings Institution on October 27, 1878.

Leslie put Mandelbaum's financial backing to good use, providing his gang with the best burglary tools available, bribing several officials, drawing up a full set of plans for the bank's layout, and actually constructing a room identical to the one inside the Ocean National Bank in one of the many empty warehouses Mandelbaum owned. In the end he needed to borrow another $1,000 in cash from Mandelbaum to rent office space. Although it sounded strange to her, Mandelbaum complied. She had complete trust in Leslie, even though he was a novice in the criminal world. She knew true criminal talent when she saw it, and George Leslie had the quickest criminal mind she had ever witnessed. Besides, she knew that Leslie was good for any amount of money she put up to finance the bank job.

No one had ever gone to the extent Leslie did in planning a bank robbery. At the vacant warehouse, Leslie rehearsed with the gang how the entire operation would work—like clockwork, with each member of the gang performing a specific function at a specific time. He had all the gang study the blueprints and drilled into them the step-by-step process they would take during the robbery. Leslie timed each of the steps so that everything would be done within split seconds. Timing was everything as far as Leslie was concerned. Leslie also reenacted the bank heist over and over, throwing in various possibilities and forecasting alternative measures. He even had the gang reenact the robbery in the dark in case something happened to the lighting inside the bank.

Draper and the others weren't accustomed to Leslie's style of lengthy, meticulous planning. They were more adept at blowing things up and taking what they could grab. Leslie wanted a more sophisticated operation, one that he could export to other gangs in the city and across the country—for an adviser's fee, of course. The Ocean National Bank job would be not only his trial run but also his initiation into the New York City crime world. Leslie passed his test with flying colors, not to mention the nearly $800,000 payday in stolen cash, securities, and precious jewelry.

To pull off the bank job, Leslie deposited a large sum of his own money into the Ocean National Bank. This gave him ample opportunity in the months leading up to the heist to visit the institution in the guise of a new depositor. He withdrew his money prior to the robbery. Leslie's many visits to the bank yielded invaluable information, not to mention an in with the bank president. The grounds of the bank were scrutinized until every square inch of the building was known to Leslie. He memorized and then committed to paper the entire layout of the bank, which was located on the first floor of a five-story brownstone. With his knowledge of architecture and his photographic memory, Leslie was able to draw up blueprints of the bank's interior and the outside surroundings that would have put even the most knowledgeable architect to shame. The plans were used to build the replica of the bank where he and the gang rehearsed.

Dining with the bank president and others associated with the bank and its operations, Leslie, who was readily accepted into upper-crust society, was able to learn the name of the company that had built the bank's safe. Leslie did this under the pretense of verifying that the safe where he was depositing his money was indeed one of the best around. He said that, as an architect, he would know a good safe from a bad one, and he wanted to see for himself what kind of product the safe maker was known for. He was able to ingratiate himself with the Yale locksmith responsible for the bank's safe. The locksmith boasted that the lock was impenetrable. It had been tested time and time again, and no one had been able to pick the lock. The safe had even been exhibited in Paris, where a bevy of international locksmiths had all tried their hand at picking the lock but had failed.

Leslie wasn't about to leave anything to chance. With the information he had obtained from the locksmith, Leslie was able to make the necessary adjustments to the little joker—specifically, to accommodate the size and shape of the dial on the Ocean National Bank safe. Yale lock or not, nothing was safe from the little joker.

Once inserted inside the safe's dial, the joker would duplicate where the tumblers stopped after it was opened and secured several times. Of course, there was the matter of breaking into the bank so that he could remove the dial on the safe, place the joker inside, and then replace the dial so no one was the wiser. That meant he and the gang had to break into the bank twice: once to insert the joker and once again to remove it, determine the safe combination, and then actually open the safe. With the safe combination known, it would just be a matter of having a skilled safecracker like Johnny Dobbs, one of the best in the business, try any of the various combinations that showed up on the joker to open the safe. This all seemed too elaborate for most of the gang, but that didn't matter; Mandelbaum had designated Leslie as the boss of the operation, and they all fell into line—most of them, anyway.

Draper remained skeptical of Leslie's plan and his motives. He had already secretly ordered Red Leary, the strongman and muscle behind the gang, to be ready to "take care of" Leslie if he did anything stupid. Draper was sure that the dandified Leslie, with no known experience in robbing banks, would fail miserably. If indeed Leslie was a spy, sent by the Pinkertons to infiltrate Mandelbaum's operation, then Draper, with Red Leary's help, would make sure Leslie never lived to tell about it.

Leary told Draper he was ready to take care of Leslie if and when the bank job went south on them. In fact, Leary had no such intentions. Leary knew which side his bread was buttered on, and it was Marm Mandelbaum who was doing the spreading. If she said Leslie was in charge, then Leslie was in charge. Leary was working for Marm, not Draper, and took orders only from her. And her orders were to do whatever George Leslie wanted him to do—even if he told him to kill Draper. Leary was a company man, and the company was Marm Mandelbaum as far as he was concerned.

The most difficult part of the whole operation was trying to introduce one of the gang into the confidence of the bank. The problem was twofold: First, it had to be someone that the bank trusted to hire in some humble capacity. Leslie needed someone on the inside who could let them into the bank after hours to place the joker inside the dial of the safe and then let him in again to retrieve it. The inside man had to be someone Leslie trusted implicitly, because that person would hold Leslie's career—if not his life—in his hands. It also had to be someone the bank would never suspect. Breaking into the bank once was hard enough. Doing it two times was, in most people's estimation, impossible.

But Leslie knew just the man for the job—a boy, actually: Johnny Irving, the young pickpocket. Leslie knew that he had established an unspoken bond with Irving ever since he chose not to reveal to Mandelbaum that Irving had stolen from her. Using his newfound connections at the bank, Leslie was able to persuade the bank president to hire Johnny Irving, who with his blond hair and sad blue eyes looked his angelic best, to sweep up the bank after hours. It was perfect. Leslie now had his trustworthy inside man.

Besides having an inside man in Johnny Irving, Leslie also needed a backup plan and a way to get his burglary tools inside the bank without anyone noticing. A trip down to the Hartz Magic Repository on Broadway took care of one part of the problem. The second part would be far trickier.

Disguising Jimmy Hope with a fake mustache and curly black wig, he had Hope rent office space in the basement of the bank. The bank only occupied the first floor of the building. The entire basement was rented by William Kell. Posing as an insurance agent, Hope was able to rent a small office that opened out onto Fulton Street. Using forged documents, Hope showed Kell his credentials signed by the New York Insurance Department. Claiming to be Lewis Cole, president of the fictitious insurance company, Hope was able to rent the small office for $1,000, paid in advance. (Leslie chose the name Cole because of his admiration for outlaw Cole Younger, who rode with his hero, Jesse James.) Shortly afterward he had a desk, chair, and a huge cabinet moved into the office.

Having carefully surveyed the structure of the bank, Leslie knew that the small office in the basement that Jimmy Hope had successfully secured sat directly below the bank vault. *One man's ceiling, another man's floor.*

When the time came to enter the bank the second time around, during the weekend, Johnny Irving wouldn't be working at the bank, so he wouldn't be able to let them sneak inside. Leslie decided he would simply drill a hole in the ceiling of the rented office, which would give them direct access to the bank vault and the safe. Of course, there was the question of all the saws and tools they would need, but Leslie had already thought of that. Everything they needed was stored in the huge cabinet that Hope had delivered to the rented office—pure genius on Leslie's part.

Over the course of a weekend in June 1869, George Leslie, Johnny Dobbs, and Red Leary were able to slip into the Ocean National Bank—twice. Billy Porter, the wheelman for the heist, was parked up the street in a getaway carriage. Gilbert Yost, Jimmy Hope, and Shang Draper all served as lookouts. Leslie made all of them wear theatrical disguises procured from the Opera House, different disguises each time. On the night of the second break-in of the bank, Leslie asked Draper to dress as a woman and keep watch in front of the bank. No one would ever suspect that a well-dressed woman, sporting a parasol and a hat, would be a lookout for a bank robbery. Draper balked at the idea, so Leslie went to Mandelbaum. Of all the members of the gang, Draper had the slightest build. He had small, round shoulders and small, delicate hands, and he was clean-shaven. It would not take very much to disguise him as a woman, Leslie thought. He knew Red Leary wouldn't do, not with his brawny build and flaming red beard.

The night of the robbery, Shang Draper, dressed in a powder-blue gown and wearing a long blonde wig and carrying a parasol, stood watch in front of the Ocean National Bank while Leslie, Dobbs, and Leary broke in. The humiliation of it only fueled Draper's animosity toward Leslie.

On the night of the first break-in, Johnny Irving, working late sweeping up around the bank, let the three men in the back door. Using his renowned dexterity and nimble fingers, Johnny Dobbs removed the dial from the safe, following the instructions Leslie had given him. After becoming friends with the safe maker, Leslie had bought a smaller version of the same safe and had it delivered to the warehouse where he had built the replica of the bank. Using what he had learned, Leslie and Dobbs both had ample time to practice removing the safe dial without harming it. The three long months of planning that Leslie had put into the bank heist were paying off.

Dobbs removed the dial on the safe and inserted the little joker inside. Then he replaced the dial so that it appeared as though nothing was out of the ordinary. When bank officials opened the bank vault the next day, Leslie's joker would take care of the rest, recording the combination stops on the lock whenever someone opened the safe during normal business hours.

Leslie knew that there would be more money kept in the bank over the weekend than during the week, so they waited two days until Saturday night. Then they broke in again. This time they drilled a hole in the ceiling of the Lewis Cole & Co. office in the basement of the bank and gained access to the vault through the hole that came up directly opposite the vault. Leslie, Dobbs, and Leary climbed up through the hole to enter the bank for the second time.

Dobbs once again expertly took off the safe dial, removed the joker, and placed the dial back on the safe. Using the series of notches etched into the flat tin plate that had been inserted into the bank dial, Dobbs was able to record the tumbler stops. There were only so many different combinations, and Dobbs began the meticulous process of trying them out. It was only a matter of time before Dobbs established the right combination, and the door to the safe opened easily.

They were in.

———

Johnny Dobbs was one of the most successful safecrackers in New York City. Although there were plenty of deserving candidates to choose from, he was the best. His real name was Michael Kerrigan, and he had earned his reputation as one of New York City's finest criminals by working his way up the criminal ladder, starting as a fence for stolen merchandise and later graduating to bank robbery, safecracking, and ultimately murder. He was in on George Leslie's 1878 world-record bank robbery of the Manhattan Savings Institution, handpicked by Leslie. After the Manhattan bank robbery, Dobbs bought a small saloon, where he tried his hand at going straight. Ironically, it was located almost across the street from the New York police headquarters on Mulberry Street. It was reported that when asked why he'd chosen a saloon so close to police headquarters, he replied, "The nearer to church, the closer to God." His attempt at leading a legitimate life didn't last long, and soon he was back plying his trade in the underworld. Johnny Dobbs enjoyed a near twenty-year criminal career. In 1898, Dobbs was found lying in a gutter, beaten to death. His body was taken to Bellevue Hospital. He died penniless. He was just fifty years old.

Leslie and his gang made off with close to $800,000 in cash, securities, and jewelry in the Ocean National Bank robbery, the largest bank heist in the city's history. They took only what they could carry and only what Leslie told them to steal—no secured certificates and no bags of heavy gold. Not a shot had been fired. Not a single person injured. Not a stick of dynamite used. Not one bit of property wrecked.

Nothing like it had ever been pulled off in the annals of New York City crime. Even the city newspapers gave credit to the culprits: "A masterful bank job pulled off by one very special bank robber," the *New York Herald* proclaimed after authorities were notified of the robbery the following Monday morning. Boss Tweed was reported to have commented, "I couldn't have done better myself."

Leslie had thought of everything, including the fact that if the bank job was performed on the weekend, then bank officials and authorities would not discover it until the following Monday morning, giving Leslie and his gang plenty of time to unload the stolen cash with Marm and make their individual getaways.

Newly appointed police detective Captain Thomas Byrnes was put in charge of the robbery investigation. Despite his expert criminal detection skills, Byrnes's investigation went nowhere fast. Neither Byrnes nor any of the other detectives assigned to the case were able to uncover a single lead in the case. The only puzzlement about the robbery was why the robbers had left behind close to $2 million in cash and securities lying on the vault floor.

Although Byrnes, a top-notch investigator who would go on to become the chief inspector for the city and an incorruptible force in law enforcement, had no leads in the Ocean National Bank robbery, his instincts told him that he was dealing with a whole new breed of bank robber—someone whose intellect was far superior than the usual run-of-the-mill criminal. The only incident noted by Byrnes during his short-lived investigation was the complete withdrawal of funds from the Ocean National Bank by one George L. Leslie. Byrnes was concerned with even the tiniest detail. Through his various sources, Byrnes learned that Leslie was an architect by vocation and a well-to-do gentleman of solid upbringing and education. He wasn't, in Byrnes's estimation, the criminal type. When he learned that Leslie was a frequent guest of Marm Mandelbaum's many dinner parties, Byrnes reportedly remarked, "This can't lead to anything good." How very right he was.

FIVE

The Rock Island Express

Cleveland Moffett

A brutal train robbery on a storied rail line left few clues.

THE THROUGH EXPRESS ON THE ROCK ISLAND ROAD LEFT CHICAGO AT 10:45 p.m. on March 12, 1886, with $22,000 in fifty- and hundred-dollar bills in the keeping of Kellogg Nichols, an old-time messenger of the United States Express Company. This sum had been sent by a Chicago bank to be delivered at the principal bank in Davenport, Iowa. In addition to the usual passenger coaches, the train drew two express cars: the first, for express only, just behind the engine; and, following this, one for express and baggage. These cars had end doors, which offer the best opportunity to train robbers. Messenger Nichols was in the first car and was duly at his work when the train stopped at Joliet, a town about forty miles west of Chicago. But at the next stop, which was made at Morris, Harry Schwartz, a brakeman, came running from Nichols's car, crying, "The messenger is dead!"

The messenger's lifeless body was found lying on the floor of the car. The head had been crushed by some heavy weapon, and there was a pistol wound in the right shoulder. Apparently he had been overcome only after a hard fight. His face was set with fierce determination. His fists were clenched and the hands and fingers cut and scratched in a curious way, while under the nails were found what proved to be bits of human flesh. The pistol wound was from a weapon of .32 caliber, but it was not the cause of the man's death. This, unmistakably, was the blow, or blows, on the head, probably after the shot was fired. All who knew messenger Nichols were surprised at the desperate resistance he seemed to have made, for he was a small, light man, not more than five feet five in height nor weighing over 130 pounds and of no great credit among his fellows for pluck and courage.

The express car was immediately detached from the train and left at Morris, guarded by all the train crew except Schwartz, who was sent on with the train to Davenport. After the first cursory inspection, no one was allowed to enter the car where Nichols lay, and nothing was known precisely as to the extent of the robbery. The safe door had been found open and the floor of the car littered with the contents of the safe.

An urgent telegram was at once sent to Chicago, and a force of detectives arrived at Morris on a special train a few hours later. Search parties were at once sent out in all directions along the country roads and up and down the tracks. Hundreds of people joined in the search, for the news of the murder spread rapidly through the whole region, and not a square yard of territory for miles between Morris and Minooka station was left unexplored. It happened that the ground was covered with snow, but the keenest scrutiny failed to reveal any significant footprints, and the search parties returned after many hours, having made only a single discovery. This was a mask found in a cattle guard near Minooka—a mask made of black cloth with white strings fastened at either side, one of which had been torn out of the cloth as if in a struggle.

Meantime Mr. Pinkerton himself entered the car and made a careful investigation. His first discovery was a heavy poker, bearing stains of blood and bits of matted hair. It was hanging in its usual place, behind the stove. The significance of this last fact was great, in Mr. Pinkerton's opinion; from it he concluded that the crime had been committed by a railroad man, his reasoning being that the poker could have been restored to its usual place after such a use only mechanically and from force of habit and that an assailant who was not a railroad man would have left it on the floor or thrown it away.

Coming to the safe, Mr. Pinkerton found that the $22,000 was missing and that other papers had been hastily searched over but left behind as valueless.

Among these was a bundle of canceled drafts that had been roughly torn open and then thrown aside. Mr. Pinkerton scarcely noticed at the moment, but had occasion to remember subsequently, that a small piece of one of these drafts was missing, as if a corner had been torn off.

All the train hands were immediately questioned, but none of their stories was in any way significant, except that of Newton Watt, the man in charge of the second car. He said that while busy counting over his waybills and receipts, he had been startled by the crash of broken glass in the ventilator overhead and that at the same moment a heavily built man, wearing a black mask, had entered the car and said, "If you move, the man up there will bore you." Looking up, Watt said further, he saw a hand thrust through the broken glass and holding a revolver. Thus intimidated, he made no attempt to give an alarm, and the masked man presently left him under guard of the pistol overhead, which covered him until shortly before the train reached Morris, when it was withdrawn. He was able to locate the place where the crime must have been committed, as he remembered that the engine was whistling for Minooka when the stranger entered the car. This left about thirty minutes for the murder, robbery, and escape.

Returning to Chicago, Mr. Pinkerton investigated the character of the man Watt and found that he had a clean record, was regarded as a trusty and efficient man, and had three brothers who had been railroad men for years and had always given perfect satisfaction. Watt's good reputation and straightforward manner were strong points in his favor, and yet there was something questionable in his story of the mysterious hand. For one thing, no footprints were found in the snow on the top of the car.

Brakeman Schwartz, the only man on the train who had not yet been questioned, "deadheaded" his way, in railway parlance, back from Davenport the following night on conductor Danforth's train and reported to Mr. Pinkerton the next morning. He was a tall, fine-looking young fellow, about twenty-seven, with thin lips and a face that showed determination. He was rather dapper in dress and kept on his gloves during the conversation. Mr. Pinkerton received him pleasantly, and, after they had been smoking and chatting for an hour or so, he suggested to Schwartz that he would be more comfortable with his gloves off. Schwartz accordingly removed them and revealed red marks on the backs of his hands, such as might have been made by fingernails digging into them.

"How did you hurt your hands, Schwartz?" asked Mr. Pinkerton.

"Oh, I did that handling baggage night before last," explained Schwartz, and then he related incidentally that as he was on his way back to Chicago, the conductor of the train, conductor Danforth, had discovered a valise left by somebody in one of the toilet rooms. Later in the day, Mr. Pinkerton summoned the conductor, who said that the valise was an old one, of no value, and, having no contents, he had thrown it out on an ash pile. The only thing he had found in the valise was a piece of paper that attracted his attention because it was marked with red lines.

Examining this piece of paper carefully, Mr. Pinkerton saw that it had been torn from a money draft and at once thought of the package in the express messenger's safe. Now, it is a remarkable fact that no human power can tear two pieces of paper in exactly the same way; the ragged fibers will only fit perfectly when the two original parts are brought together. There remained no doubt, when this test was made in the present case, that the piece of paper found on conductor Danforth's eastbound train had been torn from the draft in the express car robbed the night before on the westbound train. The edges fit, the red lines corresponded, and unquestionably someone had carried that piece of paper from the one train to the other. In other words, someone connected with the crime of the previous night had ridden back to Chicago twenty-four hours later with conductor Danforth.

Mr. Pinkerton at once ordered a search made for the missing valise and also an inquiry regarding the passengers who had ridden on conductor Danforth's train between Davenport and Chicago on the night following the murder. The valise was found on the ash heap where the conductor had thrown it, and in the course of the next few days the detectives had located or accounted for all passengers on conductor Danforth's train, with the exception of one man who had ridden on a free pass. The conductor could only recall this man's features vaguely, and, while some of the passengers remembered him well enough, there was no clue to his name or identity. As it appeared that no other of the passengers could have been connected with the crime, efforts were redoubled to discover the holder of this pass.

So great was the public interest in the crime and the mystery surrounding it that three separate, well-organized investigations of it were undertaken. The Rock Island Railroad officials, with their detectives, conducted one; a Chicago newspaper, the *Daily News*, with its detectives, another; and the Pinkertons, in the interest of the United States Express Company, a third.

Mr. Pinkerton, as we have seen, concluded that the crime had been committed by railway men. The railway officials were naturally disinclined to believe ill of their employees, and an incident occurred about this time that turned the investigation in an entirely new direction and made them all the more disposed to discredit Mr. Pinkerton's theory. This was the receipt of a letter from a convict in the Michigan City penitentiary, named Plunkett, who wrote the Rock Island Railroad officials, saying that he could furnish them with important information.

Mr. St. John, the general manager of the road, went in person to the penitentiary to take Plunkett's statement, which was in effect that he knew the men who had committed the robbery and killed Nichols, and he was willing to sell this information in exchange for a full pardon, which the railroad people could secure by using their influence. This they promised to do if his story proved true, and Plunkett then told them of a plot that had been worked out a year or so before, when he had been "grafting" with a "mob" of pickpockets at county fairs. There were with him at that time "Butch" McCoy, James Connors (known as "Yellowhammer"), and a man named "Jeff," whose surname he did not know. These three men, Plunkett said, had planned an express robbery on the Rock Island Road, to be executed in precisely the same way and at precisely the same point on the road as in the case in question.

The story was plausible and won Mr. St. John's belief. It won the belief, also, of Mr. Melville E. Stone of the *Daily News*, and forthwith the railway detectives, working with the newspaper detectives, were instructed to go ahead on new lines, regardless of trouble or expense. Their first endeavor was to capture "Butch" McCoy, the leader of the gang. "Butch" was a pickpocket, burglar, and all-around thief whose operations kept him traveling all over the United States.

The police in various cities having been communicated with to no purpose, Mr. Stone finally decided to do a thing the likes of which no newspaper proprietor, perhaps, ever undertook before—that is, start on a personal search for McCoy and his associates. With Frank Murray, one of the best detectives in Chicago, and other detectives, he went to Galesburg, where the gang was said to have a sort of headquarters. The party found there none of the men they were after, but they learned that "Thatch" Grady, a notorious criminal with whom "Butch" McCoy was known to be in relations, was in Omaha. So they hurried to Omaha, only to find that

Grady had gone to St. Louis. Then to St. Louis went Mr. Stone and his detectives, hot on the scent, and spent several days in that city searching high and low.

The method of locating a criminal in a great city is as interesting as it is little understood. The first step is to secure from the local police information as to the favorite haunts of criminals of the class under pursuit, paying special regard in the preliminary inquiries to the possibility of love affairs, for thieves, even more than honest men, are swayed in their lives by the tender passion and are often brought to justice through the agency of women. With so much of such information in their possession as they could gather, Mr. Stone and his detectives spent their time in likely resorts, picking up acquaintance with frequenters and, whenever possible, turning the talk adroitly to the man they were looking for. It is a mistake to suppose that in work like this detectives disguise themselves. False beards and mustaches, goggles and lightning changes of clothing are never heard of except in the pages of badly informed story writers. In his experience of over twenty-five years, Mr. Murray never wore such a disguise nor knew of any reputable detective who did. In this expedition the detectives simply assumed the characters and general style of the persons they were thrown with, passing for men of sporting tastes from the East, and, having satisfied the people they met that they meant no harm, they had no difficulty in obtaining such news of McCoy and the others as there was. Unfortunately, this was not much.

After going from one city to another on various clues, hearing of one member of the gang here and another there, and in each instance losing their man, the detectives finally brought up in New Orleans. They had spent five or six weeks of time and a large amount of money only to find themselves absolutely without a clue as to the whereabouts of the men they were pursuing. They were much discouraged when a telegram from Mr. Pinkerton told them that "Butch" McCoy was back in Galesburg, where they had first sought him. Proceeding thither with all dispatch, they traced McCoy into a saloon, and there three of them—John Smith, representing the Rock Island Railroad; John McGinn, for the Pinkerton Agency; and Frank Murray, working for Mr. Stone—with drawn revolvers, captured him in spite of a desperate dash he made to escape.

McCoy's capture was the occasion of much felicitation among the people interested in the matter. Mr. St. John and Mr. Stone were confident that now the whole mystery of the express robbery could be solved and the murderer convicted. But McCoy showed on trial that he had left New Orleans to come north only the night before the murder and had spent the whole of that night on the Illinois Central Railroad. It also appeared that McCoy's associate, Connors, was in jail at the time of the robbery and that the man "Jeff" was dead. Thus the whole Plunkett story was exploded.

Sometime before this the man who had ridden on the free pass, and given the detectives so much trouble, had been accidentally found by Jack Mullins, a brakeman on conductor Danforth's train. He proved to be an advertising solicitor, employed by none other than Mr. Melville E. Stone, who would have given $1,000 to know what his agent knew, for the advertising man had seen the conductor bring out the valise containing the all-important fragment of the draft. But he had not realized the value of the news in his possession, and Mr. Pinkerton took good care to keep him from that knowledge. One hint of the truth to the *Daily News* people, and the whole story would have been blazoned forth in its columns, and the murderer would have taken warning. Not until he had seen the man safely on a train out from Chicago did Mr. Pinkerton breathe easily, and it was not until months later that Mr. Stone learned how near he came to getting a splendid "scoop" on the whole city and country.

The identification of the pass holder removed the last possibility that the valise had been taken into the train by any of conductor Danforth's passengers. And yet the valise was there! How came it there? In the course of their examination, two of the passengers had testified to having seen Schwartz enter the toilet room during the run. Brakeman Jack Mullins stated that he had been in the same room twice that night, that the second time he had noticed the valise, but that it was not there when he went in first. Other witnesses in the car were positive that the person who entered the room last before the time when Mullins saw the valise was Schwartz. Thus the chain of proof was tightening, and Mr. Pinkerton sent for Schwartz.

After talking with the brakeman in a semiconfidential way for some time, the detective began to question him about Watt, his fellow trainman. Schwartz said he was a good fellow and, in general, spoke highly of him. Mr. Pinkerton seemed to hesitate a little and then said, "Can I trust you, Schwartz?"

"Yes, sir."

"Well, the fact is, I am a little suspicious of Watt. You see, his story about that hand overhead does not exactly hang together. I don't want to do him any wrong, but he must be looked after. Now, my idea is to have you go about with him as much as you can, see if he meets any strangers or spends much money, and let me know whatever happens. Will you do it?"

Schwartz readily consented on the assurance that the railroad people would give him leave of absence. The next day he reported that Watt had met a man who wore a slouch hat, had unkempt red hair, and in general looked like a border ruffian. He had overheard the two talking together in a saloon on Cottage Grove Avenue, where the stranger had discussed the murder of Nichols in great detail, showing a remarkable familiarity with the whole affair. Schwartz had a sort of Jesse James theory (which he seemed anxious to have accepted) that the crime had been committed by a gang of western desperados and that this fellow was connected with them.

Mr. Pinkerton listened with interest to all this but was less edified than Schwartz imagined, since two of his most trusted "shadows," who had been following Schwartz, had given him reports of the latter's movements, making it plain that the red-haired desperado was a myth and that no such meeting as Schwartz described had taken place. Nevertheless, professing to be well pleased with Schwartz's efforts, Mr. Pinkerton sent him out to track the fabulous desperado. Schwartz continued to render false reports. Finally, without a word to arouse his suspicion, he was allowed to resume his work on the railroad.

The shadows put upon Schwartz after this reported a suspicious intimacy between him and Watt, and a detective of great tact, Frank Jones, was detailed to get into their confidence if possible. He was given a "run" as brakeman between Des Moines and Davenport, and it was arranged that he should come in from the west and lay over at

Davenport on the same days when Schwartz and Watt laid over there, coming in from the east. Jones played his part cleverly and was soon on intimate terms with Schwartz and Watt, taking his meals at their boarding house and sleeping in a room adjoining theirs. They finally came to like him so well that they suggested his trying to get a transfer to their run, between Davenport and Chicago. This was successfully arranged and then the three men were together constantly, Jones even going to board at Schwartz's house in Chicago. About this time Schwartz began to talk of giving up railroad work and going to live in Kansas or the far west. It was arranged that Jones should join him and Mrs. Schwartz on a western trip. Meantime Schwartz applied to the company for leave of absence on the plea that he wished to arrange some family matters in Philadelphia.

Mr. Pinkerton, being informed by Jones of Schwartz's application, used his influence to have it granted. When the young man started east, he did not travel alone. His every movement was watched and reported, nor was he left unguarded for a moment, day or night, during an absence of several weeks, in New York, Philadelphia, and other eastern cities.

To one unfamiliar with the resources and organization of a great detective system, it is incomprehensible how continuous shadowing day after day and week after week, through thousands of miles of journeying, can be accomplished. The matter is made none the simpler when you know that there must be a change of shadows every day. However adroit the detective, his continued presence in a locality would soon arouse suspicion. The daily change of shadows is easy when the man under watch remains in one place, for then it is only necessary to send a new shadow from the central office early each morning to replace the one who "put the man to bed" the night before. But it is very different when the subject is constantly traveling about on boats or railways and perhaps sleeping in a different town each night. Without the network of agencies, including large and small bureaus, that the Pinkertons have gradually established all over the United States, the shadowing of a man in rapid flight would be impossible. As it is, nothing is easier. Schwartz, for instance, spent several days in Buffalo, where his actions were reported hour by hour until he bought his ticket for Philadelphia. As he took the train, a fresh shadow took it too, securing a section in the same sleeping car with him and taking his meals at the same time Schwartz took his, either in the dining car or at stations. No sooner had the train left the station than the Pinkerton representative in Buffalo reported by cipher dispatch to the bureau in Philadelphia whither Schwartz was going. The exact form of the dispatch, which well illustrates a system in constant use in the Pinkerton bureaus, was as follows:

R. J. Linden,
441 Chestnut Street,
Philadelphia, Pa.

Anxious shoes sucker Brown marbles man other dropping eight arrives put grand fifty marbles articles along or derby coat ship very tan seer wearing these have and is ribbon ink dust central Tuesday for dust to rice hat and paper vest yellow ink get must jewelry morning depot on.

In dispatches of this sort, important information regarding criminals is constantly flashing over the wires with no danger of any "leak."

Thus, from one city to another, and through every part of the country, any criminal may be shadowed today as Schwartz was shadowed, one set of detectives relieving another every twenty-four hours, and the man's every word and action can be carefully noted down and reported without his having the faintest suspicion that he is under observation. The task of shadowing a person who is traversing city streets is entrusted to men especially skilled in the art (for art it is) of seeing without being seen. This is, indeed, one of the most difficult tasks a detective is called on to perform, and the few who excel in it are given little else to do. Where a criminal like Schwartz, on whose final capture much depends, is being followed, two, three, or even four shadows are employed simultaneously—one keeping in advance, one in the rear, and two on either side. The advantage of this is that one relieves the other by change of position, thus lessening the chance of discovery, while, of course, it is scarcely possible for several shadows to be thrown off the trail at once. An adroit criminal might outwit one shadow, but he could scarcely outwit four. A shadow, on coming into a new town with a subject, reveals himself to the shadow who is to relieve him by some prearranged signal, like a handkerchief held in the left hand.

The result of the shadowing in Schwartz's case was conclusive. No sooner was the brakeman out of Chicago than he began spending money far in excess of his income. He bought fine furniture, expensive clothing, articles of jewelry, and presents for his wife and laid in an elaborate supply of rifles, shotguns, revolvers, and all sorts of ammunition, including a quantity of cartridges. The shadows found that in almost every case he paid for his purchases with fifty- or hundred-dollar bills. As far as possible, these bills were secured by the detectives from the persons to whom they had been paid immediately after Schwartz's departure. It will be remembered that the money taken in the robbery consisted of fifty- and hundred-dollar bills.

In addition to this, it was found by the investigations of detectives at Philadelphia that Schwartz was the son of a wealthy retired butcher there, a most respectable man, and that he had a wife and child in Philadelphia, whom he had entirely deserted. This gave an opportunity to take him into custody and still conceal from him that he was suspected of committing a higher crime. The Philadelphia wife and child were taken on to Chicago, and Schwartz was placed under arrest, charged with bigamy.

Mr. Pinkerton went to the jail at once, and, wishing to keep Schwartz's confidence as far as possible, assured him that this arrest was not his work at all but that of detectives Smith and Murray, who were, as Schwartz knew, working in the interests of the railroad people and of the Chicago *Daily News*. Mr. Pinkerton told Schwartz that he still believed, as he had done all along, that Watt was the guilty man, and he promised to do whatever he could to befriend Schwartz. The latter did not appear to be very much alarmed and said that a Philadelphia lawyer was coming on to defend him. The lawyer did come a few days later, when a bond for $2,000 was furnished for Schwartz's reappearance, and he was set at liberty. Matters had gone so far, however, that it was not considered safe to leave Schwartz out of jail, and he was immediately rearrested on the charge of murder.

Whether because of long preparation for this ordeal or because he was a man of strong character, Schwartz received this blow without the slightest show of emotion and went back into the jail as coolly as he had come out. He merely requested that he might have an interview with his wife as soon as possible.

Mr. Pinkerton had evidence enough against Schwartz to furnish a strong presumption of guilt, but it was all circumstantial, and, besides, it did not involve Newton Watt, whose complicity was more than suspected. From the first Mr. Pinkerton had been carefully conciliatory of the later Mrs. Schwartz. At just the right moment, and by adroit management, he got her under his direction, and by taking a train with her to Morris, and then on the next morning taking another train back to Chicago, he succeeded in preventing her from getting the advice of her husband's lawyer, who was meantime making the same double journey on pursuing trains with the design of cautioning her against speaking to Mr. Pinkerton. She had come to regard Mr. Pinkerton more as a protector than as an enemy, and he, during the hours they were together, used every device to draw from her some damaging admission. He told her that the evidence against her husband, although serious in its character, was not, in his opinion, sufficient to establish his guilt. He told her of the bills found in Schwartz's possession, of the torn piece of the draft taken from the valise, of the marks on his hands and the lies he had told. All this, he said, proved that Schwartz had some connection with the robbery but not that he had committed the murder or done more than assist Watt, whom Mr. Pinkerton professed to regard as the chief criminal. The only hope of saving her husband now, he impressed on her, was for her to make a plain statement of the truth and trust that he would use this in her husband's interest.

After listening to all that he said, and trying in many ways to evade the main question, Mrs. Schwartz at last admitted to Mr. Pinkerton that her husband had found a package containing $5,000 of the stolen money under one of the seats on conductor Danforth's train on the night of his return to Chicago. He had kept this money and used it for his own purposes but had been guilty of no other offense in the matter. Mrs. Schwartz stuck resolutely to this statement and would admit nothing further.

Believing that he had drawn from her as much as he could, Mr. Pinkerton now accompanied Mrs. Schwartz to the jail, where she was to see her husband. The first words she said, on entering the room where he was, were "Harry, I have told Mr. Pinkerton the whole truth. I thought that was the best way, for he is your friend. I told him about your finding the five thousand dollars under the seat of the car and that that was all you had to do with the business."

For the first time, Schwartz's emotions nearly betrayed him. However, he braced himself and only admitted in a general way that there was some truth in what his wife had said. He refused positively to go into details, seemed very nervous, and almost immediately asked to be left alone with his wife. Mr. Pinkerton had been expecting this and was prepared for it. He realized the shock that would be caused in Schwartz's mind by his wife's unexpected confession, and he counted on this to lead to further admissions. It was, therefore, of the highest importance that credible witnesses should overhear all that transpired in the interview between Schwartz and his wife. With this end in view, the room where the interview was to take place had been arranged so that a number of witnesses could see and hear without their presence being suspected, and the sheriff of the county, a leading merchant, and a leading banker of the town were waiting there in readiness.

As soon as the door had closed and the husband and wife were left alone, Schwartz exclaimed, "You fool! You have put a rope around Watt's and my neck!"

"Why, Harry, I had to tell him something. He knew so much. You can trust him."

"You ought to know better than to trust anybody."

The man walked back and forth, a prey to the most violent emotions, his wife trying vainly to quiet him. At each affectionate touch, he would brush her off roughly with a curse and go on pacing fiercely back and forth. Suddenly he burst out, "What did you do with that coat—the one you cut the mask out of?"

"Oh, that's all right; it's in the woodshed, under the whole woodpile."

They continued to talk for over an hour, referring to the murder and robbery repeatedly and furnishing evidence enough to establish beyond any question the guilt of both Schwartz and Watt.

Meantime Watt had been arrested in Chicago, also charged with murder, and in several examinations had shown signs of breaking down and confessing, but in each instance he had recovered himself and said nothing. The evidence of Schwartz himself, however, in the interview at the jail, taken with the mass of other evidence that had accumulated, was sufficient to secure the conviction of both men, who were condemned at the trial to life imprisonment in the Joliet penitentiary. They would undoubtedly have been hanged but for the conscientious scruples of one juryman, who did not believe in capital punishment. Watt has since died, but Schwartz, at last accounts, was still in prison.

About a year after the trial, Schwartz's Chicago wife died of consumption. On her deathbed she made a full confession. She said that her husband's mind had been inflamed by the constant reading of sensational literature of the dime-novel order and that under this evil influence he had planned the robbery, believing that it would be easy to intimidate a weak little man like Nichols and escape with the money without harming him. Nichols, however, had fought like a tiger up and down the car and had finally forced them to kill him. In the fight he had torn off the mask that Mrs. Schwartz had made out of one of her husband's old coats. It was Watt who fired the pistol, while Schwartz used the poker. Schwartz had given Watt $5,000 of the stolen money and had kept the rest himself. He had carried the money away in an old satchel bought for the purpose. A most unusual place of concealment had been chosen, and one where the money had escaped discovery, although on several occasions, in searching the house, the detectives had literally held it in their hands. Schwartz had taken a quantity of the cartridges he bought for his shotgun and, emptying them, had put in each shell one of the fifty- or hundred-dollar bills, upon which he had then loaded in the powder and the shot in the usual way so that the shells presented the ordinary appearance as they lay in the drawer. The detectives had even picked out some of the shot and powder in two or three of the shells, but, finding them so like other cartridges, had never thought of probing clear to the bottom of the shell for a crumpled-up bill.

Thus about $13,000 lay for weeks in these ordinary-looking cartridges and were finally removed in the following way: While Schwartz was in jail, a well-known lawyer of Philadelphia came to Mrs. Schwartz one day with an order from her husband to deliver the money over to him. She understood this was to defray the expenses of the trial and to pay the other lawyers. Superintendent Robertson remembers well the dying woman's emotion as she made this solemn declaration, one calculated to compromise seriously a man of some standing and belonging to an honored profession. Her body was wasted with disease, and she knew that her end was near. There was a flush on her face, and her eyes were bright with hatred as she declared that not one dollar of that money was ever returned to her or ever used in paying the costs of her husband's trial. Nor was one dollar of it ever returned to the railroad company, or to the bank officials, who were the real owners.

SIX

The Mad Trapper of Rat River

Dick North

Arctic trails have their secrets.

On July 7, 1931, Indian brothers William and Edward Snow-shoes of Fort McPherson, Northwest Territories, were paddling up the Peel River in their canoe when they came across the camp of a white man. He was sitting under a mosquito bar. One of the Indians nudged the other and said, "He must be Paul Nieman's brother. Paul said he come here soon. His name is Albert Johnson."

One of the Snowshoes brothers then hailed the camp, calling out the name "Albert Johnson." The shadowy figure stirred under the mosquito net before answering. "What do you want?" he asked.

"Are you Albert Johnson?" Edward asked matter-of-factly.

The stranger said he was and then asked the brothers if he was on the Porcupine River. They said no, that he was on the Peel River, adding that the Porcupine River was a hundred miles to the west. The newcomer shook his head in disgust and sat back under his shelter. William and Edward realized the man was finished talking. They shrugged their shoulders and shoved their boat out into the current. The two men continued upriver to where they tended their gill nets and later returned to Fort McPherson. They reported the stranger's presence and in so doing apparently used the name Albert Johnson.

On July 9, 1931, Albert Johnson walked in to purchase supplies from Northern Traders Ltd. in Fort McPherson. W. W. Douglas sold the visitor a sixteen-gauge Iver Johnson single-barrel shotgun and twenty-five shells. Douglas noted that the new man was an ideal customer. Said Douglas, "He knew what he wanted, bought it with no hesitation, and appeared to have plenty of cash." Douglas described the stranger as being about five feet nine inches tall with light brown hair and "cold blue eyes." He also noted that the man was a very taciturn individual.

The quiet man returned upstream and set up his tent across the river from Abe Francis's fishing camp. Aware that there were witnesses, he methodically paced off an impressive target distance by the river's bank and set up two three-foot sticks in the sand. Then, with a pistol in each hand, he shot the top off each stick. He crossed hands and shot again with the same results. According to an Indian who saw this, he whittled about one inch off the top of the sticks with each phenomenal fusillade. Word of his mastery with shooting irons spread like wildfire over the surprisingly efficient "moccasin telegraph" and in a short time became part and parcel of the legend of Albert Johnson. Indeed, this was probably the stranger's intent. If one wanted to ensure isolation, there would be no better way to do so than by demonstrating his infallible accuracy with firearms. The reason for this was probably to discourage prying eyes from seeing he had approximately $3,400 in cash in his possession. Johnson remained there almost three weeks.

On July 21, Constable Edgar Millen met Johnson at Fort McPherson when the trapper was purchasing more supplies. Millen, as a matter of course, asked Johnson where he had come from. This was not done out of idle curiosity. The Depression was in full swing. Many men who were obviously unqualified for such a strenuous occupation were heading north into the bush to trap and hunt. When they got into trouble, it caused considerable difficulty for the Royal Canadian Mounted Police and others to get them out of it. Thus, the Mounties strove to make sure newcomers were properly equipped and knew what they were doing before they went into an area. Casual surveillance and questioning were usually all that was needed to satisfy the Mountie as to an individual's capabilities.

Johnson told Millen he had spent the previous year on the prairies and had come into the Arctic by the Mackenzie River system. Millen was aware the trapper had come down the Peel River and doubted Johnson's story. However, he did not press the matter. There were many men in the backcountry who were reticent about elaborating on their itinerary. This particularly applied to prospectors and trappers because it was in their own self-interest not to tell others where they had been. They were also quite aware in those days that Mounties often prospected and ran trap lines in their spare time.

Constable Millen advised Johnson if he did elect to remain and trap in the area, he would have to purchase a trapper's license from the police and that he might save himself a trip to the nearest police post at Arctic Red River if he purchased one now.

A week later Johnson bought a small twelve-foot canoe from Abe Francis. That same day he walked into W. W. Douglas's trading post and purchased some more supplies. John Robert was clerking and asked Johnson if he would like to purchase a small outboard motor for his boat. "No," Johnson said and flexed his arms, "these are good enough for me. I'm not crazy yet." He then walked down to the river and launched his canoe, which he paddled downstream.

Albert Johnson chose a point approximately eight miles upstream from the site of Destruction City to build his cabin. He placed the structure on a promontory that afforded him a good view on three sides. His cabin was located south of the winter trail that ran through a series of lakes cutting off a bend of the Rat River. This location also happened to be in the vicinity of the trap lines of three men—William Vittrekwa, Jacob Drymeat, and William Nerysoo.

The rest of the summer and the fall Johnson spent building and preparing his eight-by-ten-foot cabin for the winter trapping season and hunting meat for his food stock.

Little was heard about Albert Johnson until December 25, when William Nerysoo walked into the Arctic Red River post for Christmas and complained to Constable Millen that Johnson had been springing his traps and hanging them on trees in the vicinity of Rat River.

The day after Christmas, Millen ordered Constable Alfred "Buns" King and Special Constable Joe Bernard to mush to Johnson's cabin and question the man about the traps being sprung.

King and Bernard mushed to the junction of the Longstick and Rat Rivers. Here they traveled south for eight miles following the course of the river where it tumbles down out of the Richardson Mountains. They arrived at Albert Johnson's cabin at noon, December 28. The shack was about eight by ten feet and made out of spruce logs. King's experienced eyes noticed snowshoes in front of the small dwelling and smoke coming out of the stovepipe. In the time-accustomed manner of the north, he shouted a greeting. Receiving no acknowledgment, he snowshoed up to the four-foot-high door and knocked. "Mr. Johnson, my name is

Constable King," said the Mountie. "I have received a complaint about you interfering with a nearby trap line and would like to ask you a few questions." He received no answer. Puzzled, King looked toward the twelve-inch-square window that was immediately to the right of the door and observed Johnson staring at him from behind a burlap sack. As soon as Johnson saw that King was looking at him, he flipped the sack back over the window.

King, with his experience in dealing with men in the bush, sensed trouble. It was unnatural for an individual to ignore a knock on the door or a greeting when he lived in such a degree of isolation. Under normal circumstances the traveler on the trail could expect to be asked in to have tea and to spend the night if time allowed. The constable thought possibly the man might be wary of him because he represented the law, so he again patiently explained his mission and spent almost an hour waiting for the trapper to make an appearance. However, not only would the trapper not come out, he ventured not a word during the entire time King and Bernard were there.

King realized that he could do nothing more until he acquired a search warrant. He decided the best thing he could do was to go eighty miles down the Husky River to Aklavik and report the incident to Inspector Eames, commander of the Mounties' Arctic subdivision. King figured he would need reinforcements, and there would be men available at Aklavik, whereas none were to spare at Arctic Red River.

The two men went half the distance to Aklavik that day and then completed their trip on December 29. Eames agreed that it would be a good idea to reinforce King and Bernard. He issued a warrant and assigned Constable R. G. McDowell and Special Constable Lazarus Sittichinli to make the trip back to the cabin with King and Bernard. They left early on the morning of December 30 and traveled fast, one of the reasons being they hoped to take care of the Johnson call and then mush on to Fort McPherson in time to celebrate New Year's Eve at Firth's. When they broke camp on December 31, they did not bother to eat breakfast because they felt it would take too much time.

They reached Johnson's cabin at about noon. King left McDowell and the other two men by the riverbank and walked to within hailing distance of the cabin. He shouted, "Are you there, Mr. Johnson?" There was no answer. King had noted smoke coming out of the cabin's stovepipe. He knew Johnson was at home. King shouted again and said he had a warrant and would have to force in the door if Johnson did not open it. Johnson remained silent.

Expecting trouble, King approached the door from the side away from the window. He turned partially sideways, extended his left arm, and knocked on the door with the back of his left hand. Immediately a shot rang out, which in the frigid cold sounded as if a bomb had exploded. A puff of wood and dust indicated the shot had come through the door. It hit King and knocked him into the snow, but he managed to recover enough to crawl to the riverbank. McDowell and the two special constables fired a series of shots into the cabin to keep Johnson down and pulled the wounded man over the riverbank. At the same time, the trapper returned fire, the slugs narrowly missing McDowell. McDowell, Bernard, and Sittichinli lashed King to one of the sleds and started their historic dash to save King's life. They had eighty miles to go. Their dogs were tired, having already run for half a day. The temperature was forty below zero, and twenty-knot winds had blown up. Wind is the bane of mushers because drifting snow fills up their back trail. This means they have to perform the excruciating task of breaking trail all over again. The musher curses the wind with the vehemence of a drill sergeant addressing a stumbling recruit.

Wind also creates another unpleasant situation for the musher, and especially for a passenger. This is the danger of frostbite. A twenty-knot wind at forty below zero will plunge the skin-freezing chill factor to ninety below. Such a gale will slash the face of a man, turning his features into a white mantle of frost with each labored breath. Even with a parka, fluid from a running nose freezes in a man's nostrils, and an ice film will collect on his eyelids. His cheeks will freeze and eyes close if he does not constantly warm them with his hands. Consequently, King's comrades had to stop and rub his face to prevent frostbite, but at the same time they could not spare precious minutes to rest. In only a few hours darkness had enveloped the trail as they plunged northward toward Aklavik.

Mile after mile, men and dogs bent their heads into the biting wind while they pushed their way toward Aklavik. It took them twenty hours to reach Aklavik, which was good time considering the difficulties. Once there, King was rushed to the settlement's small hospital. Resident doctor J. A. Urquhart found that the bullet had passed through the left side of King's chest and had come out the right side. The slug had missed any vital organs. King, who was in excellent physical condition, recovered quickly and was up and around in three weeks.

Inspector Eames had a total of eleven men under his command in the Aklavik subdivision. Eames chose a force of nine men and forty-two dogs to go after Johnson. The party left Aklavik on January 4, 1932.

Two days later, the police posse stopped briefly at Blake's post and found Constable Edgar Millen and an Indian guide, Charley Rat, waiting for them. Millen was presumably the only member of the party who had ever seen Johnson face-to-face. Blake had seen him, but he was not to join the search until later. At Blake's, Eames purchased twenty pounds of dynamite.

The next day, the police and deputies journeyed to the junction of the Longstick and Rat Rivers and made camp. At this point, Johnson's cabin was roughly eight miles away. That night they decided that the best course to take was to circle Johnson's cabin and approach it from the upstream side.

At dawn they set out to follow an Indian trapline trail that would take them off the Rat, as they were afraid there were too many places Johnson could ambush them in the tangle of willows and brush along the river.

The posse tramped all day. When it came time to make camp, Charley Rat assured them they were only a few miles above Johnson's cabin. However, the next day they found they were seven or eight miles above Johnson's camp. By the time the posse had reoriented itself near their Longstick River starting point, they had mushed twenty-eight miles in two days and had used up most of their supplies.

In the meantime, two men had been detached to make a quick scout of Johnson's location by going directly downriver. While circling his cabin, they noticed that smoke still poured from the chimney, and they figured the trapper was still there.

The two men reported back to Eames, and the inspector set up camp close to Johnson's cabin. The next morning the posse advanced up the river. The temperature hovered at forty-five below zero, a point where supplies take on overwhelming importance for sustaining a party of men and dogs in the bush. As the men approached the lonely refuge of Albert Johnson, they wondered if he would still be there. Surprisingly enough, Johnson had not moved. It was shortly before noon, January 9, 1932.

Eames and his men moved up to the riverbank, which extended in a half circle around the trapper's cabin. He shouted for Johnson to come out, explaining that King was still alive. At least Johnson would not be up for a murder charge. Only ominous silence greeted Eames's confrontation. In fact, during the entire length of his defiance of the police, Johnson was never heard to say a word.

All manner of ruses and diversions were used to gain access to the cabin, but the men came under such heavy fire it was impossible to persist in the attack long enough to batter down the small four-foot door of the structure. Johnson appeared to have punched loopholes on all sides of his cabin, but somewhat confusing was the level of fire coming from them. Muzzle blasts showed Johnson was either lying prone on the dirt floor of the cabin or was standing or kneeling in a pit.

During one sortie a man slammed the butt of his rifle against the door, jarring it open. Johnson was shooting from a pit, firing "two hand-guns." These later proved to be a sawed-off shotgun and a .22 rifle with the stock sawed off.

As the hours went by, the cold began to register a telling effect on the posse. At forty-five below zero, a man has to keep moving to stay warm, but in order for the men to keep watch on the trapper's cabin, they had to remain posted along the sides of the riverbank. The longer a man stays outside at such low temperatures, the more food he needs to replace the body heat. Consequently, his system works overtime to keep his body at a ninety-eight-degree temperature.

Inspector Eames was well aware that the two days he lost circling the cabin had taken a significant toll, as he had only two days' supply of dog food left, and supplies for his men were running low. He knew that he would have to break through Johnson's defenses soon or retreat for more supplies.

Fires were ordered built for the men to take turns getting warm. Here the men of the posse congregated briefly and discussed the incongruities of the desperate individual they faced. They asked each other why he had shot King and why he did not try to escape after the shooting. And who was he? None of these questions were satisfactorily answered at that time.

Darkness in January comes early at this location above the Arctic Circle (67°40' north latitude). The siege had begun near noon, and now it was nine o'clock and quite dark. Eames ordered flares to be lit, figuring the glare of the flares might blind Johnson. He also ordered the dynamite thawed out. Thawing out dynamite is a tricky process, as once the explosive is frozen, it must be handled delicately because of crystallization. Finally, this tedious task was accomplished successfully, and Eames commenced throwing the dynamite sticks at the cabin in hopes of dislodging some of the logs, the door, or the roof of this seemingly impenetrable structure. The dynamite sticks were ineffective.

The men continued their raids, but hour after hour the stubborn Johnson held out against the determined efforts of the nine-man posse. The temperature dipped even lower. Something drastic would have to be done as the men of the posse could be outwaited by the man in the cabin. Johnson was fighting off the police party from the relative comfort of a heated cabin. The posse, on the other hand, was exposed to the cold.

Midnight came. The flares had long since gone out. Knut Lang volunteered to propel his lanky six-foot-four-inch frame over the bank and to throw dynamite onto the roof of the cabin. Under cover of enfilading fire, he carried this off successfully. The resulting explosion blew a hole in the roof and knocked off the smokestack. Lang launched himself through the cabin door and found he was looking at Johnson, but for some unexplained reason he froze and failed to shoot him. Johnson recovered quickly, and when the smoke cleared, he continued firing undeterred by the blast. Lang retreated back to the riverbank.

It was near to three in the morning on January 10, 1932, when Inspector Eames decided on one last effort to dislodge Johnson from his redoubt. Eames bound up the remaining sticks of dynamite—four pounds in all—and heaved the deadly bundle across the twenty-yard clearing. The resulting blast ripped the roof off the cabin and partially caved in its sides. In hopes of gaining access to the cabin if Johnson was dazed by the blast, Karl Gardlund and Inspector Eames charged across the clearing. Gardlund carried a flashlight with him that he hoped to use to temporarily blind Johnson. When he reached the cabin, he held the light at arm's length and shone it through the wrecked door of the cabin. However, to the surprise of Gardlund and Eames, the besieged woodsman was not only alert but shot out the flashlight in Gardlund's hand. This attack failing, Eames and Gardlund retreated to the safety of the riverbank.

Although some members of the posse suggested burning out the trapper, Eames wanted to take him alive. He then decided to go back to Aklavik. At 4:00 a.m. the force of nine men left the scene of one of the most unusual battles fought in the history of the North American frontier. One tough man had defied nine others for fifteen hours and was still at large.

On January 14, 1932, Constable Millen and Karl Gardlund were sent back to Rat River to keep an eye on Johnson. They found that Johnson had abandoned his cabin and escaped.

Gardlund and Millen went through the wreckage of the "Mad Trapper's" cabin and found it hard to believe their adversary had survived the last dynamite blast. They scoured the area in an effort to find a clue to Johnson's identity but found nothing other than a carefully concealed stage cache suspended among some trees with no articles that could be identifying. They also found the canoe that he had purchased during the summer.

They looked for his trail, but a heavy snow that had begun during the night of the siege and continued all the next day had obliterated Johnson's tracks. At that time of the year, there was only a brief period of daylight, meaning a limited period of visibility. Since they had no idea of the direction Johnson had taken, many men would have to spread out and search a one-hundred-square-mile area from the Richardson Mountains on the Yukon border to the Mackenzie River on the east.

It was obvious that Albert Johnson was no man to be taken lightly. Eames wrote in his official report, "I note in press reports that Johnson is referred to as the 'demented trapper.' On the contrary, he showed himself to be an extremely shrewd and resolute man, capable of quick thought and action, a tough and desperate character."

By January 21 a second, smaller party led by Edgar Millen were faced with the dilemma of choosing a direction in which to search for the trapper. The Rat River valley and its tributaries were nothing short of a jungle of cottonwood, willow, poplar, and spruce. Windfalls caused by summer squalls and winter storms served to make the tangle even worse. It was difficult enough trying to find men who became lost unintentionally without having to find a man who was avoiding them by design.

All that Millen and his men could do was to surmise what they might have done had they been in Johnson's position. They decided to continue up the Rat River. Though they had dogs, it was a slow process. The difficulties of low temperatures, drifting snow, and short days made the task of finding Johnson's trail incredibly tough. The man had the entire vast wilderness to run in, and there was always the possibility that one day he might not run, choosing rather to ambush his trackers.

The four-man party patiently worked its way up the Rat River. They combed the timber from one side of the valley to the other. From dawn to dark they scanned the snow for any telltale sign that would enable them to pick up the trail of the fugitive trapper. During this time they discovered two caches. One was loaded with half a ton of food, which they left for bait, hoping the trapper would come to it. They lay for hours in the piercing cold watching the cache through field glasses, but like a sly old wolverine, Albert Johnson did not fall for the inducement and avoided the trap.

January 28 the temperature hit forty-seven below zero. The trackers had put in another frustrating day searching in vain for Johnson's trail. Each one of the men could run thirty miles a day behind a dog sled without getting tired. They were trail-hardened men used to long hours cutting wood, breaking trail, stabilizing heavy supply-laden toboggans, chopping ice for water, breaking up dog fights, and performing other tasks in temperatures at which every movement was an effort. But now even they were beginning to show signs of exhaustion. Their supplies were down to a little tea, hardtack, and bacon, and they were almost out of dog food. They traveled long and far that day, and frost collected on the insides of their parkas and froze. They stopped on the way back to an outcamp they had established. They built a fire and boiled tea to warm up.

Friday, January 29, as the temperature dipped even lower, they managed to trail Johnson through several old camps but finally lost him completely. However, they were getting to know his habits. Johnson never crossed a creek except on glare ice. Like a wolf, whenever possible, he traveled the ridges where the snow was packed and a trail was hard to find. They noted he often made a long zig-zag pattern where he might watch the men pursuing him from one side of the "z" as they proceeded up the other side. They noted that Johnson's stamina seemed to be almost superhuman. The trapper was snowshoeing two miles to every one stepped off by his pursuers, and he was toting a heavy pack. To avoid detection in the extreme cold, he could only build fires under cover of a snowbank. He had to take time out to snare squirrels and rabbits for food as rifle shots for bigger game would give away his position. He spent long, arduous hours climbing cliffs, trotting on his snowshoes through spruce forests, and crawling among seemingly impenetrable clusters of willows and buck brush. He expertly ran such a pattern of trails that at one point two of the trackers met head on.

The searchers now found themselves far up the Rat River. They were conferring on which way to turn when an Indian came mushing upriver to tell them he had heard a shot from the vicinity of the Bear River, the point where Millen and his men had first picked up Johnson's trail. There was a distinct possibility that Johnson might have taken a chance on shooting a caribou to replenish his food supply, figuring that his trackers had lost the trail and the shot could not be heard. Millen was quite aware that anyone could have fired the shot, but though it was a slim lead, he decided to follow it up anyway. The men retraced their trail to the Bear River. Here, by continued circling, they picked up the trapper's tracks again. They followed him out of the Bear, down the Rat River, and five miles up a small creek that empties into the Rat River about a mile northwest of the confluence of the Rat and the Barrier Rivers. In trailing him, they found odd quarters of caribou, confirming the Indian's report. They climbed a ridge running parallel to the creek but shortly thereafter lost Johnson's trail again. Then one of the men looked down into a steep canyon below them and spotted a wisp of smoke. It marked Johnson's camp.

The searchers followed the ridge until they were almost above his camp. They could see the edge of a tarp and a fire, but they could not see Johnson, though they could hear him puttering and whistling among the trees. The trackers waited for two hours in the cold for a chance to get the drop on the fugitive trapper, but they never did actually see him. Waiting so long in the chill of minus-fifty degrees took its toll. Frost again collected inside the men's fur clothing, and at dusk they headed back to their outcamp.

The temperature was thirty-six below and a blizzard was raging when the four trackers set out directly across the hills to apprehend Johnson. They arrived at the canyon unnoticed by the trapper. Two men descended into the canyon and managed to take up positions only fifteen yards from Johnson without his seeing them. Consequently, Johnson was hemmed in against a steep cliff. Millen and a second man then started down the ridge to the creek bed. However, one of them slipped, making enough noise for Johnson to come alert and rack a shell into the breech of his rifle. He spotted Millen moving, and his 30–30 Savage barked in the Arctic air. Millen dropped to the ground and returned fire. Johnson evidently saw a better place to settle, jumped across his campfire, and flung himself behind an overturned tree. Karl Gardlund, a veteran of the Swedish army, was ready for him and shot at him as he leaped across the fire. He thought he hit the fugitive because Johnson seemed to collapse in a heap behind the overturned tree.

Millen yelled for Johnson to give up but failed to get an answer. The four men did not dare approach the spot where Johnson had fallen. They waited to see if there was any sign that the trapper was disabled.

Minutes went by and there was no sign that the "Mad Trapper" might be still alive. An hour went by. No sound came from Johnson's direction. Silence descended on the dramatic scene being played out near the top of the world. The four trackers realized there was no room for mistakes with a man as dangerous as Johnson. All the men were as tough as the country in which they chose to live, yet they were now aware that they had run into a man who was tougher than they. Not only was he a man capable of great feats of endurance, but he was also crafty almost beyond belief. In fact, his senses were so acute and his ability to defend himself so apparent—even in the face of blasts of dynamite—the men were led to believe that Johnson might have had special training and experience, possibly police and military, at some point in his life. And since his age was estimated to be between thirty-five and forty, he might well have seen service in the First World War.

Thus, the men waited, but if they thought they could outwait a man of Johnson's capability and woodsmanship, they were sadly disillusioned.

After two hours had gone by, "Spike" Millen decided to break the stalemate. Darkness was approaching, and if someone did not go in and rout Johnson out of his place of refuge, he more than likely would make good another getaway, if he was still alive. Millen elected to go in after the trapper.

Millen and another man had walked about five paces when a shot rang out. Millen spotted the movement of the fugitive trapper's rifle barrel, dropped to one knee, and snapped off a shot. The noise of his high-powered rifle echoed loudly through the canyon in the depressing cold. Johnson replied in kind with his Savage. Both men missed. Millen fired again with the trapper returning two shots so quickly that the rifle blasts seemed to come as one quick burst. Millen suddenly rose up, whirled, and fell face down into the snow, his rifle falling beside him. He did not move. Karl Gardlund crawled to the fallen man and, under covering fire from his companions, tied the man's legs together with laces from his mukluks and dragged him out of Johnson's line of fire. A quick examination showed that Millen had been killed by a shot through the heart.

The three remaining trackers built a stage cache to keep Millen's body out of reach of predators and then retired to a campsite they had established a mile away. Sergeant Earl Hersey was waiting for them with the supplies. The next morning Hersey retrieved Millen's body. At the same time, the men found that Johnson had made good his escape by climbing the vertical cliff located behind him. To do this, he had chopped handholds in the snow and ice with his ax and upon reaching the top of the cliff had cascaded snow over his escape route in an effort to hide his trail. The men seemed to be fighting a demon rather than a human being, and the demon had won again.

— ❦ —

The longer Johnson avoided capture, the greater was the feeling for him on the part of the public, hoping the underdog might win out and escape altogether. Throughout North America people remained by their radio sets waiting for news about the great chase across the "roof" of the world. Each follower had his own opinion of the case. Whether he was a cab driver in New York or a newsman in Vancouver, the mere mention of the "Mad Trapper" was enough to bring forth an extended conversation as to how the chase would turn out.

Inspector Eames knew the toughness of the man he pursued. Anyone who could travel on foot the distances Johnson had and still remain out of reach of trackers using dog teams was a person to be reckoned with. To Eames's credit, he requested that a plane be dispatched to the north country for use in bringing in Johnson. Many people scoffed at the idea, for a plane had never before been used by the Royal Canadian Mounted Police in tracking a man down. The necessary landings and takeoffs would be perilous under the adverse conditions of such a manhunt. Eames, however, saw the not-so-obvious value of the plane: it could help alleviate his constant supply problem of feeding the dogs of the many teams involved in the search.

February 2, 1932, two days after going on the radio to request a plane and volunteers, Eames set off down the well-worn trail to Rat River. February 5, the party found that Johnson, after climbing the cliff to escape Millen's men, had disappeared in the jumbled array of creek beds and canyons that made up the watershed of the Rat and Barrier Rivers. Johnson took to the hardpacked snow between the upper reaches of the creeks, enabling him to make fast time.

Wop May piloted the Bellanca monoplane into Aklavik via the Mackenzie River valley on February 5 and actively joined the search on February 7. He landed near Eames's party and began ferrying supplies to the searchers near the Barrier River.

May was already a living legend in Canada. During the First World War, he became a double ace, shooting down thirteen German planes. This included having played a part in decoying the German ace Baron Von Richthofen (nicknamed "The Red Baron") when fellow Canadian pilot Roy Brown shot him down.

Johnson had been living off the land for thirty days when Wop May joined the search with his Bellanca. He had escaped during a blizzard, and several more blizzards had swept the area since that time. The temperature rested between thirty and forty-five degrees below zero during much of the time Johnson was pursued, yet he was still at large.

February 9 had seen a blizzard rip through the Rat and Barrier River watersheds. The blizzard swept the entire Mackenzie Delta, grounding the plane and grinding patrols to a standstill. Yet during this snowstorm, the "Mad Trapper" chose to bolt across the high ridges of the Richardson Mountains in his bid for freedom.

Outside of the few passes in the area, the Richardson Mountains represent a formidable obstacle for man or beast. They are an extension of the Rockies and at that far northern latitude consist of barren, windswept crags and precipices. Storms continually rake the mountains, and wind-chill factors reaching the hundred-below-zero mark are common.

Local Indians said that the trapper would never try to go straight across the mountains in winter. The white trappers and veterans of the north country agreed with them. No man could cross those mountains after being chased for thirty days. The men watched the passes but did not see Johnson. On February 12, Peter Alexie brought the message that Johnson was on the other side of the Richardson peaks and still going strong.

After Johnson went over the mountains, he followed a small creek to the Bell River, cutting southwest to avoid La Pierre House. In doing this he shortcut a bend in the Bell and started heading southward along the Eagle River, which flows into the Bell.

February 13, one search party flew to La Pierre House from Aklavik. At the same time, a second party started across the mountains through Rat Pass.

The airborne party landed at La Pierre House about noon. May set out immediately in the Bellanca to look for Johnson's trail, and in a short time he found it leading up the Eagle River from the Bell. Here Johnson's tracks disappeared among the many trails of a herd of caribou. Johnson, always wily, had obviously decided the best chance to hide his trail was by following the caribou as long as they were headed away from his pursuers.

On Sunday, February 14, flying conditions were poor, and Wop May was able to get in only an hour's flying time. However, it was enough to pick up Johnson's trail twenty miles up the Eagle River from its confluence with the Bell.

By February 15, the party that had undertaken the trip through the pass arrived at La Pierre House. That same day fog closed in, forcing the plane to stay on the ground. However, the dogsled party from across the mountains, after a short break, set out to find searchers who had left on foot to follow Johnson earlier in the day. Within a few hours, the two parties were united and proceeded together up the Eagle River.

The Eagle River winds like a snake through a country of low-rolling hills and little timber. The trackers cut across numerous bends to save time. In order to show Wop May where they were when visibility became good enough for him to fly, the men cut spruce trees and formed arrows in the snow pointing out their way.

February 16 the fog was still bad. The Bellanca was grounded as the searchers continued up the Eagle River. News of the progress of the manhunt radiated down the Porcupine River valley to Old Crow. Neil McDonald recalled that the men of Old Crow were busy forming another posse to stop Johnson if he went down the Porcupine. But an elderly woman shaman of the Old Crow band told them, "You no go look. One sleep and he die."

The sky was gradually clearing when the posse started out on the morning of February 17. As it turned out, they were on one of the many hairpin turns in the river, the trackers having camped on one side of the "pin" and Albert Johnson on the other. The posse made considerably more noise than usual because the snow was all cut up by caribou tracks.

Johnson probably heard this from his side of the "pin" and thought the trackers were coming downriver rather than going up. In addition, he had gone upriver and run into ski tracks of Bill Anderson and Phil Branstrom, partners who trapped the headwaters and middle section of the Eagle River. Fearing the ski tracks represented advance scouts of the posse (Gardlund had been using skis), Johnson had turned around and was backtracking.

Shortly before noon the posse ran head-on into Johnson. Sergeant Hersey, with his strong team of seven Mackenzie River huskies, was in the lead. "Johnson was backtracking, stepping in his old tracks, and obviously thought we were behind him. He was startled when he saw me. He put on his homemade snowshoes, which I recognized, and started for the bank of the river," he reported.

Hersey grabbed his rifle and started to fire. Johnson ran a few steps and then whirled and snapped off a shot at Hersey. The slug of the 30–30 Savage hit Hersey, who was in a kneeling position firing his rifle. The impact of the deadly missile lifted Hersey right off the ground, and he cartwheeled into the snow. The bullet had smashed through his left elbow, plowed through his left knee, and then ripped through his chest. Constable Sid May and Joe Verville now arrived.

May, who thought Hersey had been killed by the trapper, signaled for the party to break into two segments, and they moved up both sides of the river toward the trapper, who had by now run forty yards and thrown himself into the snow. He rolled over onto his back and eased his arms out of the pack and then used it as a bulwark. Karl Gardlund, Frank Jackson, John Moses, and Constant Ethier darted to the east bank of the river and ran north, firing as they went. Lazarus Sittichinli, Constable William Carter, Peter Alexie, and Sergeant Riddell swept up the west bank of the river, also concentrating their fire on Johnson. Inspector Eames joined Constable May in the center of the river and shouted twice for Johnson to surrender.

In the space of a few minutes, Gardlund, Jackson, Moses, and Ethier had outflanked Johnson and were located on the high bank of the river with Johnson below and between the two groups. The sniping from above shortly began to take effect. One shot hit ammunition in Johnson's pocket, and he jinked violently when it exploded and took a chunk of flesh out of his thigh. Another bullet slammed into his shoulder and still another into his side, but the trapper kept on firing.

Inspector Eames, for the third time, called on Johnson to surrender, but there was no answer other than the bark of the 30–30 Savage and a wave of his arm. The posse poured fusillades of lead into the trapper's shallow sanctuary.

Wop May had been shooting pictures of the battle from the air. It was so cold they could even hear the rifle shots above the roar of the engine. Said May, "We came roaring down the river and once again I peered down at Johnson in his snow trench. Then, as I circled over the posse, I saw a figure lying on a bedroll and realized that one of our party had been hit. I circled back upriver, passing over the posse and Johnson. As I flew over the fugitive's lair, it seemed as though he was lying in an unnatural position. Swinging back, I nosed the Bellanca down till our skis were tickling the snow. Johnson, I could plainly see as I flashed past, was lying facedown in the snow, his right arm outflung grasping his rifle. I knew as I looked that he was dead."

May rocked the wings of his plane to indicate that Johnson was dead. At about the same time, Sid May walked forward, rifle in hand, ready for anything. He hooked the rifle barrel under Johnson's body and turned him over. The "Mad Trapper" was dead; a bullet through the spine was the shot that ended his life.

Wop May landed the Bellanca and walked over to look at Johnson. "As I stooped over and saw him," said May, "I got the worst shock I've ever had. For Johnson's lips were curled back from his teeth in the most terrible sneer I've ever seen on a man's face. . . . It was the most awful grimace of hate I'd ever seen—the hard-boiled, bitter hate of a man who knows he's trapped at last and has determined to take as many enemies as he can with him down the trail he knows he's going to hit."

Johnson's body was taken to La Pierre House by dogsled and the next day was flown to Aklavik, where pictures were taken of him and Dr.

Urquhart conducted a complete physical examination of his body. Later, he was buried in an unmarked grave.

A coroner's jury found, "Albert Johnson came to his death from concentrated rifle fire from a party composed of members of the Royal Canadian Mounted Police and others on February 17, 1932."

SEVEN

The Ax Murders of Saxtown

Nicholas J. C. Pistor

They were certain they had found the killer. Were they wrong?

THE CLEAR SKY WAS STREAKED WITH ORANGE AND BLACK. A SOUTHERN wind collided with the cool air blowing in from the northern high plains. It was winter's last murderous struggle, but spring was winning out. The weather mirrored the range of human emotion that would be traversed that day, from calmness and serenity to madness and horror. Something terrible had happened.

It was Friday, March 20, 1874. The temperature was unusually high, begging to be knocked out by a thunderstorm. It was the kind of day that drove mutts to run in circles. The wind was still, but the old folks could feel something coming. They always did.

The rivers of the Mississippi valley were swollen, nourished by melting snow and heavy rains. The stagnant water brought all kinds of bugs and flies and rats. Most of the area surrounding the Mississippi looked like a swamp—and felt like one. Humidity wreaked havoc on the bone joints of young and old.

Ben Schneider's legs must've felt the pain. But he ran. Hard and fast with no hesitation. It was instinctive. He *had* to run.

Ben wasn't running *to* somewhere. He was running *from* somewhere.

His heavy leather boots, breaking apart with age, clogged deep into the mud and left footprints that would later be questioned by dozens of wannabe sleuths.

It was about five o'clock in the afternoon, most newspapers would later agree. That's when his screams were first heard, or at least when someone took note of them.

His panic had caused him to revert to his native German tongue. He couldn't think straight enough to even stutter in English.

Ben screamed deeply from his stomach with a windblown holler that some within earshot could have mistaken for a Confederate war cry, that war still hanging in the background. The local boys, who had worn Union blue a decade before, heard the sound only in their nightmares. Until now. It was the kind of shout that happened naturally and couldn't be re-created without a shock of horror or a cattle prong.

Horror was in Ben Schneider's wake.

Five minutes before, ten at most, Ben had gone to the nearby Stelz-riede farm to pick up potato seed he had bought from Fritz Stelzriede the day before. Germans were funny about potatoes. The vegetable triggered bad memories. The Irish had their potato famine—and so did the Dutch. In 1840, the German population had grown large; it relied on the potato to sustain it. When a disease struck potato crops across the land, rural Germans swelled into a panic that still played with their minds. Several agrarian crises ensued. Many people fled the country.

Potato planting must be done with care and attention. Ben knew that. Superstition scared everyone into planting potatoes before St. Patrick's Day. But the wet weather had left Ben at the mercy of the gods. It was already three days past, so he reckoned he'd pick up the seed on Friday afternoon.

Ben later wished he'd never gone.

Barrel-chested. Average height. Strong. Hunched back. No educa-tion. He was not a patrician farmer who milled about the land drinking bourbon. Nor was he a famed "Latin farmer" who debated the merits of agricultural theory. Ben worked the land himself like a slave. His body, at just twenty-eight years old, was assaulted by life on the farm. He had lost most of his teeth, and his hands were so badly calloused they looked like the belly of a snake. Today, he intended to carry the sacks of potato seed a mile home on foot by balancing them on his shoulders.

The Stelzriede family—Fritz, his wife and two children, and Carl, the family patriarch—were Ben's neighbors.

Ben marched to the Stelzriedes' farm like a caveman. The Germans here didn't take their time.

He paused as he approached the small Stelzriede house.

The animals on the farm were in a panic. Chickens pounced at his tattered homespun trousers. The cows hunched in distress. They hadn't been milked. Crows and buzzards circled up in the sky. No smoke was coming from the house's chimney.

Something was wrong. There was a strange stillness.

Monk, the Stelzriedes' Newfoundland dog, howled in the unseen background. The big dog sounded like he was penned behind the house.

"Fritz!" Ben yelled from the road.

He listened. No answer.

Everything seemed strangely quiet at the house. Ben wondered why.

Ben approached the house with caution and stepped across an old, creaky wood-planked porch. He rapped at the front door with his left hand.

Silence still.

He checked the door to see if it was locked. It tipped open; he peeked inside like an intruder. Darkness. He swung the door open and allowed the fading sun to flood the house's front room, where the Stelzriede family slept. It was a sight that made his blood run cold.

Observers would later say the place looked like a domestic slaughterhouse, with its inhabitants struck down and butchered like hogs.

Three severed fingers were scattered on the floor like spent gun shells. A head, nearly severed from its body, lay three steps from the doorway. A few feet away, a woman lay dead with her two children, whose heads were pounded so hard they looked like raspberry jelly.

Blood was everywhere. Brains were spattered on the white walls. And the house had been ransacked.

Ben ran out.

Soon, his screams summoned the world to Saxtown. And soon, Ben's left hand would make him a suspect in the biggest crime to happen in America since the murder of Abraham Lincoln.

Murder had happened here before, but nothing like this. A vagabond on the loose killing a passerby? Sure. A crazy man killing for quick sex? Yes. Just a month earlier, a German farmer riding in the fields had been shot and killed in broad daylight. Days later, another farmer was beaten and assaulted in his wagon. But those crimes were standard fare, representative of the Reconstruction era, not blood feuds or love triangles. "These brutal affairs," the *St. Louis Dispatch* reported, "were attributed to a gang of negroes." Arrests were made.

But now men would come from far away. From places named Belleville, Waterloo, and Maeystown. From St. Louis and its gritty neighbor,

East St. Louis. And from even farther. Men boarded trains in the smoky dins of Chicago and Kansas City and bolted to tiny Saxtown, a place unknown to them just days before. Sleuths and police and newspapermen couldn't stay away. The simple details of the terror commanded attention—and attracted the brave and curious and downtrodden by the wagonload.

Saxtown was easier to find than when the Stelzriedes had first arrived all those years ago. Railroads now crisscrossed southern Illinois, a symbol of progress and the present economic malaise. But travelers still lacked one convenience. A technological marvel, a bridge longer than any in existence using steel, was rising over the Mississippi at St. Louis. The Eads Bridge was a stunning symbol of the coming industrial age, a beautiful hulk of limestone arches crossing the river and connecting the western and eastern railroads in St. Louis. But those wanting to use the structure to get to Saxtown would have to wait. The bridge wouldn't open to traffic until July 4—almost three months away.

Still, against the violent, nasty black of the sky, the men came at once. They had heard what happened. Now they just needed to know who did it and why. Rumors wafted that the German family had been butchered over a secret fortune—some in their sleep, others in a death struggle.

Dead. Dead. Dead. Dead. Dead. All of them.

As the sun dropped in the evening sky, Ben Schneider stood in the barren fields and told neighbors of what awaited behind the wooden facade of the Stelzriede home. In his breathless German, Ben painted a gruesome picture of blood-spattered walls and dead children.

George Schneider, his brother, was the first to hear the news. He immediately became shaken. He knew the Stelzriedes. They were German immigrants just like himself who struggled daily to make a better life in Saxtown, a shared experience among neighbors. George, who lived about three-quarters of a mile from the Stelzriede home, had seen the family often and knew their daily habits. He had spent most of the winter with some friends chipping at a coal bank near their property. He could recount when young Fritz Stelzriede fed his animals and when the old man left the house for one of his rambling walks into the wilderness that surrounded them.

A few days before, Fritz had bought a dog named Monk from George Fritzinger, one of George Schneider's mining buddies. The Stelzriedes were looking for extra protection. A dog known for its giant size and strength helped. The massive Newfoundland was found at the crime scene penned into an interior room of the Stelzriede house.

George Schneider's grief was questionable. Coal miners didn't bear the cleanest character, locals noted, and Schneider boarded a number of them on his property. They were hard-drinking men unfazed by bloodshed. The newspaper columns of 1874 showcased violent tales of labor riots and worker uprisings.

The poor men who boarded with George Schneider weren't that extreme—or industrious. They were said to take out just enough coal "to pay for their winter's whiskey." For sure, they were capable of killing one another. But would they slaughter innocent children for plunder?

George was skilled with a knife. When he wasn't mining, he was a butcher. He killed pigs and cleaved cattle. For years his steady hands had turned livestock into food for supper. But now they trembled when his brother repeated the news of a human slaughter.

The police were needed. Fast. A fiendish killer was on the loose and likely watching the events unfold, pretending to be unaware of the crime. Help was needed to unmask the killer and prevent the horror from happening again.

The first clue was the sodden ground beneath their feet. The roads to and from Saxtown consisted of a heavy mud that would have required a massive drawbridge for a quick exit. Saxtown might as well have been a moated castle. The ground served as leg irons. The murderer had to be among them.

"The roads are in almost impassible condition, and as the news spread like wildfire, it seems almost impossible for the murderers to get away with any rapidity," affirmed one written account.

Everyone agreed on that. The dirt pathways were soaked by an abnormally wet season that swelled the rivers and threatened the idea of easy transportation. Countless headlines had told Saxtown residents the tale of punishing river levels that swallowed whole villages like a muddy monster. Anxiety increased daily in the downstream river towns of Memphis and New Orleans as the Mississippi would rise with suddenness and rapidity, like a night stalker.

The Schneider brothers notified others nearby, mainly farmers and laborers who were finishing up their daily work. Locals learned in rapid-fire succession that one of Saxtown's original families had been wiped out. Fred Eckert Sr., a farmer who was one of Saxtown's largest landowners and who lived a quarter mile north of the Stelzriedes, was told. As were George and Charles Killian, two of the miners who boarded at George Schneider's house. All greeted the news with disbelief.

The news spread as fast as a man could run or a horse could gallop. Distraught voices interrupted the cool dusk. Men quit work in the fields to understand the fuss. Women abandoned their preparations for supper. Children, ignorant of the mayhem, played and laughed after school until the adults struggled to explain what had happened. Then the fear began to sink in.

People ran about in different directions, as if they were taking shelter from a sudden summer storm but still wanting to keep an eye on the sky. The St. Clair County sheriff was headquartered in Belleville. It would take hours to get the news to him and still more hours before law enforcement could arrive. For the time being, Saxtonites were on their own. The investigation was up to them. And so was their safety.

A group of men—including Eckert, George Schneider, and the Killian brothers—agreed to go to the murder scene and keep vigil. They went together, likely traveling across the same muddy path the unknown assailant had walked earlier. Certainly they thought about that. And certainly they thought about each other's circumstantial peculiarities. The young Killians had bad reputations. Eckert was the murdered family's closest neighbor and would become an administrator of old man Stelzriede's will. And, of course, there was the trembling George Schneider.

As they marched along the soft dirt path to the Stelzriede home, George Schneider grew nervous and excitable. His whole body convulsed, which drew sharp glances from the group. His miner friends helped calm him down.

The men pressed forward. There wasn't time to wait. Soon, the Stelzriede farmstead appeared in the dark distance. Its large gray barn resembled a giant tomb.

The Stelzriede house was set up close to the road that sliced through Saxtown and stood square in the ghostly shadow of the three-story barn. It looked like the house of a practical German farm family. It was small and spartan and much less prominent than the nearby barn. The house was simple and rustic—like the frontier birthplace of Abraham Lincoln.

The group stopped and stared at the house, but no one would enter it. Not one man would step over the limestone slabs that led to the front door and cross the threshold to verify Ben's account. Questions rushed through their minds. Would the killer strike again? Was the murderer walking among them? Was some evil force at work?

The fear prevailed until the area's well-respected schoolteacher approached. Isaiah "Esquire" Thomas was considered the most educated man in Saxtown. He was thirty-one years old but had the visage of a man much older and wiser. He spent his days in a small schoolhouse teaching the young farm boys about the outside world, from history to horticulture. Thomas had an air of sophistication. He was tall and known to carry a thick and shiny silver-headed walking stick, which he often used as a prop to punctuate his speech. On special occasions he was known to wear a long coat and top hat. Intellect wasn't the only thing that set him apart from the others. He had been born in Ohio, not Germany or St. Clair County. He had bought a small plot of forty acres in Saxtown in 1869.

Thomas was passionate, independent—and a natural leader. Just the kind of man needed to take control of this extraordinary situation. He was also a local justice of the peace.

Ben had told Thomas of his discovery. At first Thomas didn't believe it. The men gathered outside swore that Ben was telling the truth, and after some back-and-forth, he took their word. Thomas agreed to enter the house and make sure the Stelzriedes were all dead. Several other men followed, just so long as they weren't leading the way.

But not George Schneider. He remained outside, struggling to keep his composure. With the house in his view, he staggered up against a wood fence and fainted. The Killian brothers rushed to help. They took him off to the side and splashed water on his face to revive him. He regained consciousness but remained on the ground.

Isaiah Thomas was undeterred by the commotion. He walked over the Stelzriedes' front porch and into the crime scene. Several others peeked from behind. He was on a mission.

Dead bodies were scary enough to view in full daylight, but a lantern's firelight provided something more haunting and sinister. The flicker played tricks with its ever-changing shadows. Points of light unequally distributed—just as the horror before him. Thomas counted the bodies. Five of them. Three in the bed and two on the floor. No survivors.

Stillness reigned. The air was heavy with the smell of dead flesh. A playful young boy, a sick baby girl, a devoted mother, an ambitious father, and a tired old man had all been rendered lifeless. Three decades of their laughs, their cries, and their screams were now nothing more than faint whispers soaked into the bare, blood-drenched floorboards.

The men could barely look at the bodies. They covered them with bed sheets as a sign of respect for the dead. The act disturbed the crime scene. It was now tainted.

George Killian stood outside the house and watched his friend George Schneider gather himself. Killian was a man small in stature and red in the face. He wasn't known to care for others; his eyes often displayed an uninviting expression. Killian decided to leave Schneider there. His friend was too distraught.

Killian walked into the Stelzriede house at dusk. It was so dark inside that he could barely see his way. The faces of the dead were covered. Killian motioned to the other men to remove the cover over Anna, witnesses remembered. He remarked, "Let me see how bad her head is hammered out of shape and if that eye is sticking out yet."

The comment drew curious glances from the other men and reinforced what they already knew: suspects were everywhere.

◆

The men looked like outlaws checking the exits before holding up a bank. But they were eyeing one another, then looking away in attempts to mask their thoughts.

They stood on the front lawn of a brutal crime scene as night fell. Isaiah Thomas had ordered everyone out of the house to preserve the crime scene until the sheriff arrived. He wanted everything watched and nothing disturbed. They had stayed in the house only a matter of minutes. Few would have wanted to stay longer. The place smelled awful.

Ben Schneider had gone to Millstadt to notify the constable and summon law enforcement help.

Suspicion built like a symphony. Slow and steady to a loud crescendo. Minds raced. Thoughts flashed here and there and back again. Who did it? Why? How?

As time passed they began to spin theories. The first one—and the only one that gave them brief comfort that the killer wasn't among them—was that the Stelzriedes were killed by an unknown passerby.

"The theory of the murder," the *St. Louis Democrat* reported, "is that some traveler had been given lodging in the house that night ... and had cruelly abused the kindness shown him by killing and robbing his benefactors."

As the men waited for the sheriff and struggled with what to do next, they heard footsteps in the distance. A man's silhouette appeared to the soundtrack of boot heels padding the young grass.

The man who came into view was John Afken, someone they all knew. He was a fellow German who had worked in the area for years as a farmhand, passed from farmer to farmer like a bottle of strong whiskey.

Afken stood tall and firm with the hulking form of a steam engine. He was a powerful 180 pounds with a long, muscular frame. The newspapers said he seemed as "strong as a giant." He had bright blue eyes that looked at the men "fierce and straight." He had light hair and skin so pale that it appeared unaffected by the sight splayed before him.

Make no mistake: Afken was an ugly customer. His face was so scary a newspaper reported that "on first sight [it] would condemn him as a criminal."

Afken was thirty years old. He was born in the Lower Saxony town of Oldenburg, Germany, a land that didn't treat him well. It was a feudal society that didn't have much to offer someone with little intelligence and a bad family tree. He eventually packed up his things and left. He showed up in St. Clair County in the 1860s and earned his bread working odd jobs on farms. His hands were his asset, not his brain. For a time he lived in Belleville before ambling to the farms of Saxtown.

Afken wore on his face the staid expression of a Methodist. He was calm and quiet. He looked at the Stelzriede house and listened to everything the men said. His ear turned to one conversation and then to another as the men gossiped about who might have killed their neighbors.

Afken said nothing . . . for the whole night, in fact. But his body did the talking.

He didn't flinch when hearing the descriptions of the hacked body of Fritz Stelzriede. Not once. The others noted his lack of a reaction. Mainly because Afken knew the family well. He had once lived with and worked for them.

Then his body language turned "taciturn and scowling." It appeared he suffered from an "unrest of mind."

Soon, everyone's eyes drifted from analysis of his mannerisms to subtle glances at his muscular frame. Afken's body was the product of his work. He spent long hours plowing soil in broiling summers and biting winters. Sometimes his muscled arms would spend days plucking apples from the trees. Sometimes his knees would be bent all afternoon as he pulled wild strawberries from a patch.

Afken lived a few miles away on a farm owned by Henry Boeker, a longtime resident of Saxtown. Boeker employed Afken and boarded him at his house.

Afken was a grubber in the weeks and months before the murders. His main tool was an ax.

Illinois farmers didn't have heavy machinery in 1874. On the untamed frontier, they often needed help with the grubbing (or removal) of tree stumps, a common chore on tree-heavy German farms. Grubbers like Afken could swing an ax from any direction.

They could work fast to destroy brush, tree roots—or people.

The grounds of the Stelzriede farm glowed with the orange light of oil lamps and handheld torches. A few hours had passed since the Stelzriede bodies had been discovered. The tough Saxtown farmers arrived one by one, then in groups. Some on horseback, others on foot. Many showed up on the property with their families. They were too afraid to leave them home alone.

Isaiah Thomas worked to calm the frenzy. First the lawn was filled with dozens of people. Then fifty. Then one hundred. They spilled out from the hinterland the moment they heard the news, like animals running to higher ground from a flood.

Horror. Panic. Fear. Worry.

The tension filled the cool March night air and hung on sad faces. It was compounded by the fact that no one knew what to do. The only thing that seemed right was to keep vigil until the sheriff arrived.

Thomas knew it was only a matter of time before people asked to enter the house. He knew a riot could break out if they did. The horror was too gruesome. Worse than even the darkest imagination.

How long would it take before the sheriff arrived? Before order could be restored?

All they could do was wait.

William G. Bangert, the constable, had heard the news that evening. It was his job to get the sheriff in Belleville, the county seat. In March 1874, Belleville had the most needed man in Saxtown: Sheriff James W. Hughes.

If anyone could find the Saxtown killer and exact justice, it was Hughes. St. Clair County's top cop was a lawman of unquestioned integrity and intellect but one also of incredible stubbornness.

Hughes believed in swift, tough justice. The vengeful farmers of Saxtown wanted that, and they took solace in knowing of Hughes's law-and-order pedigree. Sheriff Hughes knew St. Clair County well—and nearly all of its crooks and crannies.

Some said James Hughes stood as high as six foot three. His broad chest made him look even taller. His face was boyish and intense. His blue eyes had fire behind them. His clothes fit him well, as did the trimmed mustache that sat just above his lips.

That facial hair was a sign that Hughes wasn't an ordinary man. Or an ordinary cowboy sheriff like people were reading about out west. His looks made it clear that he was a politician. A man who commanded respect.

Hughes embodied his office with a theatrical appearance. From top to bottom, he always looked immaculate. He wore a white coat and a white vest, which accentuated the lace of his gold watch. A Stetson sat on his head, a .44 Colt on his hip, and shiny boots on his feet. He cared so much about his footwear that inmates in the county jail were ordered to keep them at a high shine. Always.

The sheriff was at his home on South Charles Street in Belleville when a deputy told him of the Saxtown murders. Under his roof was his wife, Sarah Scott Hughes, and their six children—Julius, Virginia, Loulou, Elizabeth, Whitfield, and Emma. His oldest son, twenty-two-year-old Julius, served as a sheriff's deputy. While it's unknown how the sheriff reacted to the news, it's almost certain that his first action was to dress.

Hughes was said to have marshaled his staff like a "general would call upon his troops." He gathered supplies and a few deputies (including his son), telegraphed the coroner in East St. Louis, and left Belleville at about ten o'clock on a wagon pulled by two horses. The race for justice was on. Belleville residents saw the sheriff's hurried departure into the cool mist and wondered what was amiss. They would find out in the morning. A messenger in town had slipped a telegraph to the *St. Louis Daily Globe* newspaper.

The sheriff and his deputies plodded through the wet pathway to Saxtown and stopped for a brief respite in Millstadt, as did most travelers. The horses needed water, and the lawmen needed to prepare themselves for what they were about to see at the end of their hastened voyage. In Millstadt they found the townspeople in a panic. Hughes had no words to calm them—he himself knew only the basic details. As the sheriff's horses and wagon departed south for Saxtown, a group of folks spilled out of the taverns and houses of Millstadt and followed Hughes.

The landscape supplied natural drama. The gaslit caravan plodded through the wet mud and methodically crossed a creaky wood bridge across Roos Creek, the final barrier to Saxtown. The murder scene appeared as a flashpoint of firelight. Almost no one spoke.

The crowd waiting for the sheriff was made up of neighbors and Stelzriede friends. Smoke from fire and torches hung over the crowd like a canopy of death. They needn't be reminded that the killer could be among them.

The sheriff's arrival calmed Saxtown's nerves like a stiff drink. Finally, help had arrived. Finally, an investigation would begin.

Hughes arrived to a big audience made up of dozens and dozens of scared farmers. Isaiah Thomas greeted Hughes almost immediately and told him the basic particulars of what he knew: five people, all dead, bodies inside the house, very gruesome, no suspects, discovered by Ben Schneider.

Hughes wanted to speak with Ben. The person who finds the crime is often the person who did the crime. It was quite common for murderers to show up at crime scenes while unwitting detectives attempted to solve cases. They liked to assess their bloody work from a close distance. Little is known about what Ben told the sheriff other than that he had found the bodies and they appeared cold.

Ben had already caught the attention of Isaiah Thomas. He had found the bodies, and his brother, George, had been acting strange. Deputy Julius Hughes surveyed the crowd and asked questions, searching for anything that could crack the case or provide motive. When did you last see them alive? Did they have any enemies? Did you see anything unusual in the days before the murders? Do they have any relatives living nearby?

The young Hughes gathered answers as best he could from a crowd still struggling with the shock of what had happened. The torches placed around the farm grounds were said to have created an eerie scene of "flame, smoke, and faces." Those faces included the nervous Schneider brothers, the watchful Isaiah Thomas, the grim-looking George Killian, and the quiet farmhand John Afken.

Hughes entered the dark death house with his deputies. Their oil lamps illuminated the draped windows, so, unbeknownst to them, their movements could be seen by the large crowd outside—a shadow play as the lawmen methodically inspected the scene. They catalogued each body, going from one part of the room to another.

They moved nothing other than the sheets that covered the dead, wanting to keep things as they were for the coroner. The position of the bodies would be an important clue in determining who was the first to die. Anna was still in the bed with her two children, indicating she may have been killed first. The yellow-haired infant daughter's hands were still clasped around her mother's neck, and her split-open head was on Anna's bosom. Anna's skull appeared to have been crushed, as did the children's. The young boy's head had been smashed with such repeated hacks that he no longer had a human form.

Fritz's body was also in terrible condition. His head was nearly detached, his body soaked in a pool of blood. Three of his fingers had been cut off and laid nearby. Carl's body had also taken a beating. His clothes were pocked with marks of blood and "congealed gore." The sheriff took note that the old man, whose body was on the floor, had his coat in his hand.

The interior of the home presented what was called a "sad scene of confusion." The murderer had opened bureaus and closets. Their contents were strewn on the floor, creating a mess of blood and clutter. Everything had been at least partially emptied, from the closets to wooden boxes and suitcases.

Hughes remained focused, although he surely was affected by seeing two young children, one an infant girl, hacked and cleaved to death. After all, he had an infant daughter, Emma, waiting for him back home.

Hughes examined things like the locks and the doors.

At first the evidence matched the early theory of a murderous lodger. It was noted that the rear door was found locked, and the front one appeared to have been unlocked from the inside. The murderer had either lodged with the Stelzriedes or been secretly concealed inside the house.

The wooden doorjamb bore another clue. Deep cuts and indentations were found in the entryway to the old man's room. Possibly misguided swings of an ax. The marks indicated they came in at a particular angle, as if an ax had been swung left to right. Meaning the murderer may have been left-handed.

Police work wasn't scientific. It was largely based on emotion and observation. On what someone saw—or, at least, what someone *thought* he or she saw.

Hughes eventually walked out of the house and back into the crowd. Legend grew that he spent considerable time observing the neighbors of

Saxtown to see who was left-handed—even going as far as to hand them something, like his cigar, to see what hand they would use to retrieve it. That apparently brought his attention to Ben Schneider, the lefty who had discovered the bodies.

But if Hughes did that, he never said so.

Later, as he stood among the frightened folks of Saxtown, he was asked what he had witnessed inside the house. Hughes didn't mince words.

"I think it is the most revolting crime that I have ever seen or heard of," Hughes said.

Someone asked, "What is your belief as regards the manner in which the murders were committed?"

Hughes responded with some early details to satiate the onlookers' curiosity.

"It is my honest belief that the crime was committed by one man and that that one man completed his work inside of ten minutes," Hughes declared. "I think he entered the house, in some way to me unknown, and killed the mother and her children first. One blow was sufficient to kill her, because if it were not she would have moved in bed or changed her position in some way; as she lies now, she laid when she was struck, with the baby pressed closely to her breast. The man used an ax or a heavy hatchet. When he had dispatched the mother and little ones, or before he had got through, I believe that the woman's husband, Fritz, who from all appearances was lying on the lounge there, was aroused from his sleep. He must have fought for his life, for you see he has changed his position on the floor once or twice. The noise awoke the old man in the next room, and as he opened the door he was struck in the forehead and knocked down, then his throat was cut. The whole thing was done so quick that there was no chance for anyone to escape or give an alarm."

Then, with the investigation still fresh, Hughes made a startling revelation.

"The murder was certainly committed by someone who did not care for money, as two pocketbooks containing greenbacks were picked up, and the drawer in which the old gentleman kept his notes and money was opened, but neither the notes nor money were touched. The man who committed this murder did it simply because he wished to clean out the entire family. He wanted none of them, and he has left none of them."

The crowd chattered and gossiped all night. Hours passed. The spectators were tired but too afraid to shut their eyes and sleep. A brutish killer was on the loose. Perhaps the attacker would strike again.

In a daze of excitement and fear, the residents of Saxtown watched the sun rise. They had lived to see another day, but there was much work to do. The bright light would help the investigation. Now all of the grounds could be seen.

A search party fanned out, looking for anything to help solve the case. Everything needed to be looked at: creek beds, wheat fields, haystacks, footprints.

It was now March 21, 1874, the day after Saxtown residents had learned their neighbors had been slaughtered by an unknown assailant. The search soon uncovered a major revelation. Blood and bloodstained tobacco leaves were found on a road about a mile north of the Stelzriede house.

Tobacco was commonly used to stop bleeding and to treat wounds.

The killer may have been injured.

On the following morning, the headlines hit everywhere men could read and women could cry. New York, San Francisco, Chicago. Newspapers hammered readers with the frightening details from Saxtown, Illinois. It was enough to make even iron-stomached farmers sick.

The bodies had decayed fast. Rigor mortis appeared gone. Hour by hour the Stelzriede family had withered in their own death.

It was common for reporters to be allowed inside a murder scene in the nineteenth century. Their presence, of course, provided little good other than to satiate the appetite of interested readers, but perhaps on a good day they could point out some clues for detectives who lacked manpower and science. But they weren't trained investigators and could perhaps complicate the crime scene.

They wanted to paint a picture of the murder scene—but they also wanted to help reveal who was responsible for the carnage. It was the morning after the bodies had been found. The killer was loose, perhaps in the crowd outside watching them or perhaps long gone. Every detail mattered, and reporters could help put together the puzzle.

St. Louis Daily Globe editor Joseph McCullagh's reporters, known for their vivid writing, walked through the wooden front door and found a room full of bodies. There were so many it was hard for their eyes to fix on anyone in particular. Looking down at their own boots was perhaps the easiest. But maybe not. At their feet was a pool of blood. Time had turned it into a congealed mess. Everyone almost stood still as they took in the scene, but if they hadn't watched their step, they would have gotten their feet wet. Less blood would have dried fast, but there was too much of it, which created a big puddle of red muck.

The blood source was Fritz Stelzriede, whose body lay nearby with gaping wounds on his head, face, and neck. Fritz was lying on his left side, they observed. His head dangled on his arm. Head and arm were surrounded by a thick pool of blood. Nearby lay three decaying fingers that had been torn from his hands. They looked like darkened nubs. His white skin no longer had the color of flesh. Fritz's face had turned black. A lot of blood had lodged in his head.

His throat had been cut from ear to ear. This was no accident. Someone wanted to make sure he was dead. Fritz was the strongest, ablest member of the family. The most likely person to fight back to stave off the rage against his family and protect their fortune.

Fritz wore a pair of denim pants and a blue shirt. He didn't bother with real sleeping clothes or fancy pajamas. Fritz was always ready to work, even while asleep.

The *Globe* reporters theorized that "he had evidently been lying on the lounge from which he arose to meet the assassin's instrument of death." Within seconds he was hacked to oblivion.

He fought back, for sure. The missing fingers were a sign of that. His hands were no match for sharpened metal.

The reporters' eyes wandered to the doorway of the adjoining room, which was Carl's bedroom. The door was open. The dead old man lay on the ground. It was said to be "the most terrible sight that ever a human being looked upon."

The man who had run from death his whole life—surviving harsh winters, hot summers, fires, death, and everything else—looked like butchered meat. He did not meet the saving grace of Job. His body had been mutilated even more so than his son's. Many thought that was a clue to motive: the murderer appeared to hold the most animosity for the old man's bones.

Who were his enemies? the investigators wondered.

His throat was cut and chopped a little below the chin, and his head was crushed. Pounded and pounded with the force of something very strong. Still, his old skull held up better than the soft bones of his grandchildren.

"From all appearances he had been first struck with an ax or some heavy weapon and knocked down and then butchered in the awful way in which we saw him," a *Daily Globe* reporter observed. "His bed was still unmade and seemed as if he had just left it. He was dressed in a white shirt and a pair of drawers. Both on the shirt and drawers were clotted drops of blood, and, like the picture in the other room, congealed gore was seen all around him. The old man's hair was jet-black, and, strange to tell, not a sign of blood was noticeable in his locks."

The centerpiece of the murder scene was the large four-post bed. The wooden frame, which normally held the exhales of tired breath, displayed "the most heart-rending scene of all." Anna and her two children lay in it. Their faces of death unforgettable.

"The mother's face was a complete mass of blood and hair and was, in fact, scarcely recognizable," a *Daily Globe* reporter wrote.

In her arms she held a little infant, pretty even in the bed of death, and its little arms were closely clasped around the neck of its mother. It was a little girl, [eight] months old, with light flaxen hair and blue eyes, which were open and seemed to beg for mercy. The mother's bosom was exposed, and close to it she held the babe. Both looked as if they had sunk in sweet sleep and never afterwards awoke. On the inside of the bed lay little [Carl], whose head was also crushed in, and whose features were not to be seen because of the blood and bruises which disfigured his little face. The mother had a deep gash in the throat, but the children were killed by a single blow each. Little Anna, in fact, could not have been struck with an ax or hatchet but rather with a club. There they lay, all huddled up together, as they had gone to rest, and God only knows whether they ever awoke to see the weapon raised above their heads, and, if they did, whether they looked only once and then all was over.

The reporters scribbled notes as fast as they could (mistaking some facts, like the baby's age and boy's name). At first it was hard, because of the terrible scene, but soon they got their wits about them. The first-person details they were getting would please their boss, McCullagh, and their readers.

What was most difficult for the reporters to look at wasn't the bodies but the things. Real people lived in this house, and real people had died in it, the reporters were reminded. Anna's clothes hung on a chair by her bedside. A cough syrup and spoon were on the bedside table—a reminder that the young Stelzriede baby had been sick. It appeared that the baby had thrown a toy on the floor near the foot of the bed. Several trinkets belonging to the children were scattered about the room. Their little boots and stockings were hung neatly.

"The whole scene bore a likeness to a bed chamber where the family group had sought shelter, never thinking it would be their last night on earth," the *Daily Globe* wrote.

The clock on the wall drew a lot of attention. It had stopped at eighteen minutes after six. "A number of those inclined to be superstitious pronounced it the time the murderer was at work."

The identity of the murderer was now on everyone's mind. The sheer harshness of the crime had settled in. Thoughts quickly turned to *who*.

"Who was the murderer, and can he be caught?" the newspapermen wondered. What clues within the dead family could lead to the perpetrator?

The reporters exited the crime scene and began the process of getting their story back to St. Louis for the next day's paper. They would compare notes, and one man would remain behind to catch any new details. An inquest, which would push the investigation along and provide the first public legal proceeding in the case, would begin as soon as the coroner arrived.

As time passed, the gossip flew. Everyone suspected this person or that person. John Afken was on the list. As were the Schneider brothers. And George Killian's mysterious comment the night before was being repeated, and most likely embellished, as Saxtonites performed their own investigation.

Isaiah Thomas escorted the reporters around the front yard and continued his own investigation. Rumors began to swirl of a family feud. One of the Stelzriedes' distant family members must have wanted them dead, some supposed. That would be the only reason to snap off an entire branch of a family tree.

But everyone disagreed about which side of the family was to blame. Curiously, none of the family's relatives had yet come to the house. Not Anna's sister or her brother-in-law, Fred Boeltz. Not Carl's brother, Charles, who had moved away from Saxtown several years before after a feud with the old man and never returned.

But a new clue soon materialized. Investigators, intrigued by the talk of a family feud, put together that the bloody tobacco leaves, found about a mile north of the Stelzriede house, were dropped on a road headed toward the home of Boeltz—the man who had not even bothered to come to the Stelzriede farm when news spread of the murders.

Faint drops of blood appeared to point in the direction of Boeltz's house. Investigators followed the lead at once.

———

"One of the most terrible and revolting murders ever committed in the history of this or any other country has taken place in this county."

The cursive handwriting in the Western Union telegram was the screed of St. Clair County sheriff James W. Hughes. His message was addressed to John L. Beveridge, a former lawman and the current governor of Illinois.

Hughes needed to get Beveridge's attention. At once. The governor was one of the few people in the state who could marshal resources—money or manpower—to help smoke out the unknown killer of the

Stelzriede family. Reward money, Hughes knew, was an easy way to get people to come forward with criminal information or enlist private detectives to help investigate.

St. Clair County had already offered a staggering sum of $1,000. Saxtonites had cobbled together an additional thousand. That was enough money to grab the attention of thrill seekers and wannabe sleuths all over the Midwest. But Hughes wanted more—and he sought it from the state of Illinois.

The problem: Beveridge, an inch over six feet tall with gray hair and gray eyes, was a Civil War veteran and no stranger to blood or death. It would take a lot of both to get his attention, especially because the murders happened hundreds of miles south of Chicago, the governor's political base.

While there is no question the Stelzriede murders were terrible and revolting, many in Illinois, and most in the state's capital city of Springfield, would have placed it second to the murder of Abraham Lincoln—now almost ten years past. Perhaps Hughes was being a little dramatic with the words in his telegram. The steadfast Democratic sheriff, who cared little for Lincoln, might have disagreed.

The telegram arrived on the governor's desk as rain fell on Springfield, a city that looked like it was still mourning Lincoln's death.

Beveridge, at forty-nine years old, lacked gravitas and was leading a state in the middle of a nationwide economic crisis. Times were tough. Money was tight. All that meant difficult choices for the governor and lots of political debts that went unpaid. There wasn't enough cash to be the chief executive that everyone wanted.

On top of that, Beveridge was no friend of the Germans in southern Illinois. In 1874, Beveridge supported the state's Dram Shop Act, which made it harder to sell alcohol.

"Beveridge was, on account of his prohibition views and religious bigotry, very unpopular among the German element," wrote Belleville Republican Gustave Koerner. "Besides, a great many Americans would never have voted for a Chicago man as governor. No one from that city had ever filled the governor's chair, and those who had been candidates for the office had been always defeated."

Also, Beveridge was no friend of Sheriff Hughes. Politics made sure of that. One was a staunch Republican, the other a Democrat. Hughes's telegram to Beveridge was straightforward. The sheriff asked for $5,000—a hefty sum considering budget constraints and the economy.

After the dramatic opening line, the telegram read, "The county offers one thousand dollar reward, the administrators [of the estate] one thousand. The state should offer at least five thousand or more. Telegraph me at once what the state will do so I can get out my bills. Don't delay."

Hughes did have some reason to hope Beveridge would offer a helping hand. The governor was the former sheriff of Cook County. That law enforcement past, Hughes hoped, would help Beveridge understand the severity of the situation. Hughes was bolstered by the *St. Louis Times*. On March 24, the newspaper reported, "Governor Beveridge has also been telegraphed to by the sheriff on the subject of offering a reward, and although no answer has as yet been received, it is thought that [Beveridge] will increase the amount of the award two thousand dollars."

Beveridge's response to Hughes would be just as simple. The *Stern des Westens* reported that Beveridge rejected Hughes's request, saying he couldn't provide the incentive money "because there are no appropriations made for such cases." Beveridge simply offered moral support.

The news was a blow to Hughes, who thought it was a blow to the investigation. A bigger reward could only help. Or so he thought.

Regardless, in Saxtown the existing reward money was already luring sleuths looking to make a buck during tough economic times and contributing to a frenzy of finger pointing and distrust.

Hughes started dealing with the accusations minute by minute. One neighbor gossiped about another. Everyone seemed to suspect each other.

Hughes was in Saxtown on Saturday afternoon in preparation for the inquest. The area burned with excitement, even more so than when he had left. While Hughes awaited the coroner's arrival and the inquest's beginning, he started sifting through the tips.

One from a railroad conductor caught his attention.

Conductor Fleischert, who ran a train on the Cairo Short Line, had read the early news accounts of the murders. Fleischert, whose route traveled from Belleville to St. Louis, reported that a strange man had gotten on his train the morning of the murders.

Fleischert eyed him closely and said the man "had a guilty look upon his face."

The *St. Louis Dispatch* later reported, "Around the roots of the man's fingernails there were blood gatherings, and though his clothing showed no signs of blood, the impression was so deeply made in Fleischert's mind that no sooner had he heard of the awful murder of the Stelzriede family than his thoughts naturally reverted to this unknown passenger."

The tips created a puzzle. And Hughes was struggling to put it all together. Did the railroad conductor come face-to-face with the murderer of the Stelzriede family? Was it a neighbor? A stranger? A friend? A relative?

It was too early to tell. The inquest was soon. All the suspects would be there.

Fleischert gave a vague description of the man but confidently said he could identify him among "ten thousand convicts."

———

Fred Boeltz arrived at the Stelzriede farm against his will and faced a crowd that wanted him to die a brutal death. He was said to look "like the most wretched-looking man that probably ever stepped outside a lunatic asylum."

He had been told early that morning that his wife's relatives—Carl, Fritz, Anna, and the kids—all had been murdered the previous night. Boeltz, who lived in a ramshackle house on a nearby farm with his wife and five children, appeared to have shown little concern—for anyone. Even if he didn't care about the Stelzriedes, neighbors thought he would have at least been concerned that a killer was on the loose. The neighbors had pleaded for Boeltz and his wife, Margaret, to go to the crime scene. They had refused.

Boeltz first said he couldn't go because he could not get on his boots. He said they were too wet from "wading in water the night before." Newspaper reporters called it the "lamest of excuses."

With Boeltz's claim about his boots not passing muster, he pleaded sick. He said under no circumstances could he look on a dead man— much less five of them.

Sheriff James Hughes was startled when he heard of the refusal. Why would a relative not come to the murder scene? Only if he had something to hide, Hughes suspected.

Everything was pointing in Boeltz's direction. His boots were wet. The bloody tobacco leaves had been found along the road in the direction of his house. For a space of about 150 yards, drops of blood appeared as if they had dripped from wounds or a bloody garment. And now Boeltz's uncaring behavior did little to reduce the suspicion.

Tobacco was often used to draw blood from wounds. The sheriff wondered, was Boeltz wounded? He would soon find out.

Hughes, who liked his orders to be obeyed, called on Boeltz by having his deputies tell him "that as he and his wife were the only living members of the family, it was nothing more than their duty to go to the house and attend to matters."

Hughes was wrong. Boeltz and his wife weren't the only living family members. Carl had an estranged brother who lived hours away. But that side of the family seemed to have slipped from the sheriff's mind as he began to narrow his focus on Boeltz. Hughes tended to be very myopic. He overlooked less obvious things in favor of what was most prominent.

When officials arrived on Boeltz's farm, he was found hidden away having a discussion with John Afken, the grubber and former hired hand of the Stelzriedes. The two were said to have been in an intense conversation. That detail commanded attention as detectives wondered why the two were together. Afken was already rumored to have been keenly interested in everyone's conversations at the murder scene and known as one of the best locals at swinging an ax.

At first Boeltz rebuffed Hughes's request, saying he didn't have time to go to the murder scene. Hughes responded by serving him with a subpoena and had his deputies bring him to the Stelzriede house by force. Boeltz, who was agitated, cautioned that he wouldn't look at the dead people.

He could scarcely recognize the Stelzriede farm. People were packed on the grounds like they were attending a cattle auction. Old men and young men walked in all different directions looking for clues and discussing the case's sordid details. By the time Boeltz appeared, the crowd numbered three hundred and growing.

The group resembled a small-town lynch mob. Word had spread through the crowd about the tobacco found near Boeltz's farm, about his wet boots, about his disinterest in coming to tend to his sister-in-law's affairs, and about a feud he had been having with the Stelzriede family.

Many of the local farmers knew that Boeltz had borrowed money from the Stelzriedes—hundreds of dollars over three years—and that it had been a source of arguments between them. The Stelzriedes had placed a chattel mortgage on Boeltz's property until the debt was repaid. (The Stelzriedes had a lien on two of Boeltz's mules and sixteen acres of his wheat.) It was said that Boeltz grew embarrassed by financial woes and became offended when the Stelzriedes asked him to pay his debt. Words were had and tempers flared. Both sides dug in. Carl, who drank too much and increasingly found himself in arguments with everyone, including his own son, Fritz, didn't back down easily.

The situation escalated until Boeltz refused to speak to the Stelzriedes. Then he forbade his wife from visiting them. For several months leading up to the murders, Margaret couldn't murmur a word to her sister, lest she draw the ire of her angry husband. To make matters worse, Carl made no secret of Boeltz's messy business affairs and told anyone he stumbled across about the unpaid loan.

Now the people who knew Boeltz were quick to hang him with unflattering descriptions. Based on their comments, the *St. Louis Daily Globe* reported that Boeltz "does not bear the cleanest character in the world among the Germans in the neighborhood," though they never gave a specific reason as to why.

The crowd watched Boeltz as he arrived.

"His limbs knocked together, and his whole frame seemed to be agitated," the *Globe* reported. "Perspiration was perceptible, and these maneuvers, together with the rumors existing, placed Fred in an unenviable light."

Aside from his wife and children, Boeltz didn't have a single friend among the hundreds of frightened and angry people stamping across the Stelzriede lawn.

The *Daily Globe* continued: "His clothes were scrutinized, his boots were a subject of much comment, his every movement betokened something to the excited crowd, and not one among them believed him to be innocent. There seemed to be a terrible feeling aroused in the hearts of the German friends of the murdered family!"

"Do you think these men would hang the murderer if they were to catch him today?" a *Daily Globe* reporter shouted to one of the men leading Boeltz to the crime scene.

"Sir," the man responded, "he would never be hung!"

"What do you mean?" the reporter asked.

"I mean that hanging would not be sufficient punishment for the brute."

An unnamed law enforcement official jumped into the conversation.

"Well," he said, "my duty is to keep the peace, but if the murderer is ever caught, and these people desire to punish him in their own way, I will be absent on business."

The crowd clattered with that kind of talk. The burning desire for vengeance coursed through everyone's heads—even the people who didn't know the dead family.

"He should be torn to pieces," came a shout from the crowd, which started to gather around Boeltz.

"Tortured," another man yelled.

"There's the man there!" screamed a man with a thick German accent, pointing to Boeltz. "He did it! I'll bet my life on it!"

The crowd's rage began to grow. The men and women had already judged Boeltz based on gossip.

Sheriff Hughes stood before the people and sought to calm them. He discussed his theory of the murders—that they happened fast, by one assailant, not for money—and answered some questions. Everyone wanted to know about the bloody tobacco leaves. Hughes had little additional information to offer about that, but he played to the crowd.

"The murderer was injured in some way, and he took some of the old man's [Stelzriede's] tobacco and tried to stop the bleeding. The tobacco was found bloodstained near the road about one mile from here and in the direction of that man's house," Hughes said.

He pointed his finger straight at Fred Boeltz.

Hughes then questioned him about everything. The bloody tobacco leaves. His whereabouts the night before. The borrowed money. The family feud.

Boeltz appeared so nervous and scared that a "confused and ominous murmur" ran through the crowd. He was stripped of his clothing and searched, but he appeared to have no visible wounds.

Every piece of clothing was inspected for dried blood. But nothing could be found. His damp boots, however, appeared to have red streaks around the toes, as if blood had been scraped off. Still, it was impossible to tell if that's what it really was.

Were Boeltz's boots really wet from wading in water, or had he tried to clean them? The answer was unclear.

Hughes didn't care about the uncertainty. Having already made up his mind, and with Boeltz's answers making little difference, he ordered the man to be held pending results from the coroner's inquest. He expected Boeltz to be arrested after the jury came back with a finding.

Hughes felt the situation was under control. He didn't need to be present for the inquest, so he left to handle business in Belleville.

Schoolteacher and justice of the peace Isaiah Thomas, Constable William Bangert, and the *Daily Globe* reporters left the scene to search Boeltz's property, which was about three miles from the Stelzriede farm. Based on the circumstantial evidence, they expected to find something linking Boeltz to the crime—namely, something with blood on it. Blood-stained clothes. Bloody weapons.

"The locality is neither beautiful nor picturesque, and it is not of that kind that fills the soul with poetic thoughts but rather makes one feel for himself and guard himself when in the vicinity," the reporters remarked.

The search party arrived on the farm with great fanfare. Margaret, Anna's sister, was there. They told her they were given authority from the sheriff to search the premises. She didn't stop them. They searched everything: haystacks, corn cribs, chicken houses, onion beds, featherbeds, trunks, bureau drawers, attics, cellars. Everywhere anything could be hidden. For two hours the party tore apart the farm, dismantling everything, looking for the slightest clue or the smallest drop of blood.

The effort was futile. They found nothing and gave up.

"We left the house as wise as when we entered it," a *Daily Globe* reporter remembered.

If Fred Boeltz murdered his in-laws, he smartly got rid of the evidence, they thought.

One item they did remove from the property was Boeltz's boots. Mud boots with soles studded with broad nails were taken to make footprint impressions. Investigators could compare them to prints left around the Stelzriede property.

They arrived back on the Stelzriede farm, where the crowd had swelled to over five hundred people. Excitement built for the inquest, as if the crowd was anticipating a grand performance. Coroner John Ryan had arrived at about two o'clock from East St. Louis. He was accompanied by East St. Louis police chief John Webster Renshaw and several of his officers, city marshal Michael Walsh, and two physicians. The added police presence stoked the tension.

Coroner Ryan wasn't a pretty sight. He had a "gnome-like" face that appeared to lack eyebrows or eyelashes, which accentuated his buggy eyes. His diminutive body was stiff. He stood in stark contrast to the dashing Sheriff Hughes.

Ryan knew little about medical science. He had investigators for that, men who could measure head wounds, dig out bullets from flesh, cut open dead bodies. That work wasn't for Ryan. He just knew the procedures of holding an inquest, a formal inquiry before a jury to determine how someone died.

The medical examination was performed by Dr. Adolph Schlernitzauer, a physician who practiced in Millstadt.

Ryan got down to business right away and began the task of finding a six-person jury to judge the inquest. Their chief job would be to decide the cause and manner of death of the Stelzriede family. The proceeding could expand on information already obtained during the fledgling investigation.

Ryan, with Dr. Schlernitzauer by his side, examined the bodies inside and then looked over the areas surrounding the Stelzriede house. He and his investigators found blood traces in the yard, as if somebody had dragged a bloody ax across the ground. Footprints on the wet ground also were an important clue. The person suspected of the crime appeared to have worn shoes with nailed soles. The prints "undoubtedly showed nail prints," the investigators deduced.

Dr. Schlernitzauer's physical examination of the bodies led to testimony.

The inquest was done on the Stelzriedes' front lawn, before the large crowd. Fred C. Horn, of the nearby town of Flora, was named the foreman. Five other men were selected to join him.

The jury was sworn in. Silence fell over the crowd. This is what they were waiting for.

Ben Schneider was the first person to be questioned. He testified, according to the St. Louis–based *Anzeiger des Westens*, that "he just happened to stop by the Stelzriede farm in order to get some potato seedlings." He said everything appeared strangely quiet, and when he opened the front door he discovered the bodies. Schneider said he ran away to inform the neighbors and get the justice of the peace, Isaiah Thomas.

Thomas appeared before the jury next and corroborated Schneider's story, saying that Schneider had alerted him of the discovery and that the bodies were found just as he had described. John Afken, the grubber and former employee, also was called as a witness. He testified that he was the first to tell Boeltz of the murders that morning. Of course, they had been found in a spirited conversation that day. Investigators were theorizing that Afken may have been an accomplice to Boeltz. After all, he was much larger and capable of producing a higher body count than Boeltz. But under rigid questioning, and knowing he was a possible suspect, Afken "kept wonderfully cool."

Even if Afken was guilty, he held up like a fine stage actor. Only occasionally did the blood "mantle his face."

The crowd was unbelieving. The *Daily Globe* reported that "taken altogether, he seems to be a man put up for murder or stratagem."

And who would have put him up for that? Ryan then called the witness everyone wanted to see and hear: Fred Boeltz. Although Ryan's investigation consisted of determining the cause of death, he had some limited leeway going beyond those bounds in questioning.

Boeltz was small in stature and appeared "rather weakly built." He certainly didn't display the type of brutish muscle that could kill an entire family. He was thirty-five years old and had lived in the country for about six years.

"He has chin whiskers, but no mustache, and is not a powerful man by any means," a *Daily Globe* reporter wrote. "His features are rather on the delicate order, and he has a meek expression."

Boeltz was religious. The residents of Saxtown knew that. He taught Sunday school.

"It is said that he is a little crazy at times on the subject of religion, and it is argued by some that he might have committed the deed under the influences of religious fanaticism," the *Daily Globe* reported.

Boeltz was sworn in. He was immediately made to look at the bodies, the very thing he said he didn't want to do. Boeltz resisted, but he was eventually pushed through the front door of the Stelzriede house and forced to look at his dead in-laws. The jurors examined his face and body language. They didn't do him any favors.

At once, he turned his back to the bodies, although there were so many it was hard for him to position himself. When asked why he couldn't look at the dead bodies, he responded that when he was a little boy he had seen a friend who had drowned and he could never look at a dead body afterward. Under questioning, however, he admitted that he had seen other dead people but clarified that he meant that he couldn't look at people who had suffered an "unnatural death."

Boeltz appeared agitated during the questioning. At one point it looked as though he would faint. "His voice was tremulous and his answers incoherent," the *Daily Globe* reported. He often answered with rambling sentences that found no end.

But his physical discomfort was somewhat of a red herring. The smell was so bad inside the house that the jury could enter only in the presence of the coroner's physicians for fear that they themselves would faint.

Still, after having been pushed before the bodies, Boeltz wouldn't look at his brother-in-law, Fritz, who lay in a pool of blood. So he was forced.

"He writhed in agony, sank into his chair like a woman, his eyes looked as though they would start from their sockets," the *Daily Globe* reported. "Such a picture has never been seen before in the West. This man had professed to be a Sunday school teacher, and, while nobody had accused him, or even hinted to him of being implicated in the murder, he shrank from the ghastly sight as if from a snake."

The investigators turned over Fritz's body in front of Boeltz. Exposed in front of him was his brother-in-law's crushed skull and thrashed body. The sight sickened the crowd. Men and women alike had a hard time handling the view. Boeltz was said to have taken it in "without a look of pain, a look of anger or a look of sorrow."

"Nothing but a vacant stare," the *Daily Globe* reported.

Boeltz was questioned about the tobacco, for which he had no answer. It was shown that the tobacco found along the roadway near Boeltz's farm came from the Stelzriede house.

While being questioned Boeltz showed "terrible fear." As time passed, however, he appeared to grow more comfortable. He became exceedingly guarded and cautious in his answers and "very artfully avoided incriminating himself."

One of the jurors, assuming the murderer had been injured because of the tobacco leaves, asked for an examination of Boeltz's body. That examination, just as the one the sheriff had conducted, showed no wounds.

The lack of wounds made what once appeared to be an easy arrest much less certain. The jury determined that Boeltz's extreme behavior was understandable and that there was no longer a reason to be suspicious.

Before a hushed crowd, as midnight approached, the jurors made public their findings: The three oldest persons died of hitting, stabbing, and cutting wounds. The two children died of blows to the head. All by unknown hands.

Boeltz was set free. The crowd reacted with shock. Public opinion had already judged him guilty, especially based on his conduct at the inquest. Did a murderer just get set loose? Would he attack another family?

"Many of the influenceable and rich citizens of the area had a meeting with Coroner Ryan, discussing the necessary steps to be taken for finding the murderers," the *Anzeiger des Westens* reported. "They all agreed to hiring secret police to heavily guard the entire area. In Saxtown itself, in [Millstadt], at Centreville Station, in Belleville, private secret police were hired to follow the weak leads that were known. The citizens of St. Clair County are decided to shed light on the terrible deed, and they are prepared to spend any money and use all their endeavor to bring the suspects to justice."

The crowd remained into the night, most afraid to be alone. They drank beer and ate deer meat and prepared for what to do next.

Coroner Ryan got in his carriage, left the rural chaos, and headed back to his home in East St. Louis. When he arrived he gave an interview with reporters from the *Anzeiger des Westens* and the *St. Louis Democrat* that offered stark disagreements with Sheriff Hughes's original investigative work and public assertions.

Ryan first stated that he had "seen many horrible things during his lifetime, but that he had never set his eyes on a crime scene so gruesome and terrible as he witnessed in the house of the Stelzriedes in Saxtown."

Ryan then began poking holes in Hughes's theory that one person committed the crime. Ryan said he was convinced that two people were involved.

The *Anzeiger des Westens* reported his theory thus: "One of the murderers had only a knife and the other one only needed an ax. It is not possible that only one person could change the murder weapons [knife and ax] so quickly, committing five murders in such a short period of time. One person alone would not have had the time to set down the knife and then use the other weapon."

He also noted that Hughes was inaccurate when he said that money wasn't stolen. Witnesses testified that Fritz should have possessed at least one hundred dollars he had received from the mill. And that money was missing from the scene. Not to mention any possible gold fortune. No gold was found at the scene. Just an empty basket that had been seen hanging around Fritz's neck earlier in the week.

Ryan said that just because *some* money was left in the house, it didn't mean that the murders were not committed for plunder. Pocketbooks found in the victims' clothing only had seven dollars in them. Ryan said it would have been too dangerous for the murderers to take them for risk of getting bloody. Ryan cautioned that the "whole affair will take time to be brought to light."

As Saxtonites remained scared and fumbled for protection, the investigation was already in dispute.

EIGHT

The Lufthansa Heist

Henry Hill and Daniel Simone

The inside story of a headline heist that stole the nation's attention.

THE STAGE WAS SET, THE CURTAIN ROSE, AND THE PERFORMERS READIED for act one.

In this predawn hour of Monday, December 11, 1978, a black Ford van with six passengers is entering Kennedy Airport from the northeast end, a zone with a chain of cargo hangars. A silver Pontiac Grand Prix, the chase car, is trailing the van. The two-vehicle motorcade continues to travel southbound on the JFK Expressway, and at the Federal Circle intersection it veers off the ramp and heads east on Nassau Expressway. Within a half mile, the driver of the Ford van, Angelo Sepe, has in his sight the yellow florescent Lufthansa sign atop cargo building 261.

"It's a quarter to three. We're five minutes early," Sepe says.

DeSimone glances at his wristwatch. "You better slow it down, Angelo. We shouldn't get there before ten to three."

Sepe steers into a maze of parking lots until he reaches the targeted hangar, the German airline freight complex. The chase car passes the van, idles to the rear of the three-story Lufthansa building, and parks in front of a loading dock. The Ford van then stops near the main entrance, and everyone inside hardly breathes as they peruse the environment. White lighting splashes out of the third-floor office windows; at this restful hour, though, Kennedy Airport is dormant, and even a watchdog can find peace. The six armed robbers can hear the sound of a truck and the swishing tires of a courier panel van somewhere in the distance. The takeoff and landing of aircrafts is nonexistent, an eerie contrast to the frenetic daytime traffic at the world's busiest airfield. The quietness and stillness is strange to the marauders; they've never roamed the inner roadways of the airport at three in the morning. It spooks and confuses them.

"Shit, I hope we don't run into ghosts," Sepe says. But in the perimeter of the Lufthansa compound, no phantoms are in sight, and the burglars' breathing restarts, their hearts throttling back to a slower beat. Sepe then shifts the van into drive and eases on a hundred yards to the east of the hangar, where the chase car has been waiting. He brakes to a halt twenty feet from a chain-link fence. A padlocked gate encloses the loading ramp.

A square, man-size gaping hole opens widely on the side of the van as the door slides open. Four of the six men—Frenchy McMahon, Joe Manri, Tommy DeSimone, and Louis Cafora—have been in a squatting position on the metal floor. Sepe throws the gearshift into park. "OK, it looks clear. Get out now." He and the gunman seated to his right stay put in the vehicle, and their four compatriots, in a disguise of black ski masks and dark clothing, disembark. Two of them hop out with agility; overweight Manri and Cafora roll out as if they are two giant pillows bouncing off a bed.

In case someone spots them, Sepe waits three or four seconds—poised to scamper away—but the seas are at peace, and he climbs out of the van. The man in the front passenger seat, Paolo Licastri, also bails out. A short Sicilian immigrant without a visa, Licastri is on hand as John Gotti's envoy. Licastri and his bunch clump in front of the van.

McMahon peers at his watch. "OK, guys. Mr. Hychko should be coming soon."

Mike Hychko, a shipping clerk, is due back from collecting air bills from various airlines that, through Lufthansa, forward shipments to Europe. He regularly finishes these errands in time for the 3:00 a.m. meal break.

And here he pulls up with punctuality. Hychko, medium built with a square jaw and refined facial features, parks his pickup truck next to the Ford van, and the half dozen people grouped near it unnerve him. Five of the shadowy figures, he notices, are wearing wool caps. Hychko's eyes blink with alarm. "What're you guys doing here? And . . . and you can't park this van here by the gate."

The sixth interloper, Sepe, head and face uncovered, tackles Hychko. With the butt of his Colt .45 Gold Cup semiautomatic, a marksman competition firearm, Sepe thwacks the Lufthansa clerk on the skull and restrains him in a headlock. Hychko's wound gushes blood, tinting his light, wavy hair, and he roars out a piercing scream. "Rolf, Rolf, c'mon out here. Call Port Authority. I'm getting kidnapped. Call nine—"

Manri rams his shotgun into Hychko's stomach. "Shut the fuck up, or I'll put a couple ounces of lead in your temple." Hychko's hollering is echoing, and he's writhing to break free from Sepe's forearm hold. The gash on his scalp is deep, and his face is sodden with blood. DeSimone pitches in and grapples Hychko from Sepe, who's fumbling to slip on his mask.

Too late. Hychko's memory bank has photographed a snapshot of Sepe.

Sepe puts on his ski cap. He plucks Hychko's wallet and waves it in front of the man's eyes. "OK, Mr. Hychko, I got your wallet, and now we know where you live. Somebody's gonna be parked on your block. If you rat on me, you can kiss your family good-bye. Got it?"

Anguishing over his fate and, more immediately, the life-threatening loss of blood, Hychko doesn't answer but nods in full understanding. DeSimone then handcuffs Hychko and bullies him. "Where's the three-sided key?" He raps the wounded man on his head. "Gimme the key. In which pocket do you have it?" DeSimone grabs the lapels of Hychko's coat and shakes him. "I said, gimme the fuckin' three-sided key."

The three-sided key? They have inside information, Hychko perceives. Panting, he mumbles, "It's . . . it's in my left side pocket."

DeSimone gropes in the pockets of Hychko's trousers and finds the specially shaped key that deactivates the loading ramp motion detectors, a system wired to the Port Authority headquarters at the airport. "Mr. Hychko, where's the switch for this key on the gates?"

Hychko's wincing contorts his face. "It's on the right post of the gate. Right there. You see it?"

DeSimone slides the key into the cylinder and switches the tumbler to the Off position. "You better not have lied, Hychko. 'Cause if the alarm is still on, you're gonna be a bag of broken bones."

Hurriedly, with a bolt cutter, Cafora swiftly shears the thick chain that's padlocked to the gates. He pushes them inward. DeSimone prods the wounded Hychko inside the fenced grounds, manhandling him to the top of the loading platform, the rest of the gunners following with soft steps. Sepe quickens his pace, trots ahead of DeSimone and Hychko, and reaches the small service door to the hangar. He presses the handle downward and steps indoors, everyone else at his heels. Werner had informed Manri that this door, the one used for foot traffic, will be unsecured. So far, Werner's input has been accurate, and the pirates are hoping the upcoming sequences will be faultless.

They storm inside, and a Lufthansa shipping agent, Rolf Rebmann, hears the shuffle of feet and a commotion of energetic movement. Rows of steel shelving stacked to the ceiling grid the ground level of the warehouse, and Rebmann's workstation is at the end of those lanes. He cranes his neck into the open space and, on seeing the charging gunmen, tenses. Rebmann's lips freeze, and he can barely speak. "Hey . . . hey, what's going on? Who are you?"

With the snap of a lisping snake, Licastri leaps at Rebmann's throat, and Sepe binds the man's wrists behind his back.

Rebmann struggles futilely and succumbs, his knees shaking. "Don't hurt me. I'll do whatever you want. I got two kids and a sick wife."

"Join the club," DeSimone replies. "I got a wife who plays sick too. I've never known a married woman who isn't sick. The minute you marry them, they get sick and stop fucking."

Sepe says, "Take it easy, take it easy, Mr. Rebmann. Keep your mouth shut and nothin's gonna happen. And if any of you steps out of line, you'll all get it." To stress the threat, Sepe, in mock, raises the barrel of his semi-automatic to his temple. "See? Get my drift?"

The gunmen were clued in that at the end of the shelf rows, somewhere near the high-value vault, a security guard may be loafing out of sight. Up to now, the lone watchman has not yet detected the intrusion. Manri, whom Burke appointed in charge, directs the assailants and, in a whispery voice, says, "Frenchy, you and Cafora go find the guard. He's an old dog, so go easy on him." Manri indicates the direction where the watchman may be stationed. "He's probably goofing off back there next to that pile of pallets. Go get him; we'll wait here."

McMahon and Cafora, crouching, walk stealthily down the aisles. They turn a corner and see the guard slurping hot soup from a Styrofoam cup and listening to a radio broadcasting the weather. His face is gaunt and gray. His frame, tall and fleshless, is curved forward, and from a side view it forms a *C*. He's a dozen years past his golden days and doesn't belong on the night shift protecting Lufthansa's cargo hangar.

The two commandos rush the watchman. He glimpses them, and in a delayed reaction his body flexes, and the soup spills onto the floor. Cafora, his gun aimed at the wrinkled geriatric, says, "It's OK, Granpa. It's OK. Nothin's gonna happen. Come on with us." McMahon and Cafora each gently clasp one of his arms and walk him through the maze of shelving to reunite with their compatriots.

Petrified out of his wits and vibrating faster than a tuning fork, the brittle guard doesn't know how to react. His job calls for him to arrest trespassers and detain them until the police respond. How can this senior, who's in pain from a slipped disc and rheumatism, enforce security? He can scarcely stand upright, never mind wrangle 250-pound armed robbers.

For his will, though, he deserves an A. "What do you think you're doing? We got cops all over the airport. You don't know it, but the loading dock outside has an alarm, and you probably tripped it. And . . . and Port Authority will be here any minute."

McMahon chuckles. "We know about it, Pop. As we said, it's all gonna be all right. And because you're the oldest here, when we get upstairs, tell everybody there to behave and not to do anything stupid. OK? And nobody will get hurt."

"Or killed," adds Cafora, and the watchman gasps, his freckled hands trembling.

Manri sees that McMahon and Cafora have the guard in their custody. "Good. You found the old man." Under his breath, out of earshot of the captives, he calls out, "Frenchy, Tommy, Roast Beef, and me will take these three with us and go upstairs to round up the rest of the night workers. Angelo, Paolo, you two stay down here. If anybody shows up, tie the fuckers and take them to the lunchroom."

Werner had instructed Manri to locate and account for the night supervisor, seven employees, and one guard. Nine in total. And Werner specified that at 3:00 a.m., the night shift groups in the lunchroom for the meal break. This was the reason for initiating the raid at 2:50 a.m.

Paolo Licastri questions Manri's directive and in his thick Italian accent suggests, "Why I no go with you? If you gotta kill somebody, I can do easy."

"The Gent don't want nobody killed here tonight. And if you do, you'll be the next one to go. Got it?" Manri promised.

"Whatsa matta? Burke no have big *collioni*, eh? Ah, ah, ah."

Manri exhales heavily, bellies up to Licastri's chest, and hovers over him. "You just do what I say, you little prick." Inches from the Sicilian's eyes, Manri rams the air with his finger. "Because if you don't, we'll send you back to your boss, Mr. Gotti, in tomato sauce jars." This silences Licastri—for the moment.

Manri motions with his sawed-off shotgun for McMahon, DeSimone, and Cafora to follow him up the stairway. DeSimone and Cafora are dragging along the two Lufthansa cargo expeditors and the old gent, jabbing the younger two in their spines.

Manri flips off the light switch in the stairwell; he and his co-holdup men, flashlights in hand, nudge along the three captives, and they all file up to the third floor.

They're climbing two flights of stairs. Leading, Cafora stops on the landing and signals with his hand for everyone to halt. "Hold up." He can smell microwaved food, and murmurs are rumbling from one end of this floor.

"They're supposed to be in the lunchroom," McMahon says under his breath.

The melody of a song is seeping from the cafeteria. Faintly audible, the lyrics are escaping into the hallway: "Monday, Monday, can't trust that day . . ."

Handcuffed and standing between the watchman and Hychko, Rebmann informs them, "They're all in the cafeteria. The supervisor, Rudi Eirich, is the only one who doesn't come up here." This submissiveness is Rebmann's way of ingratiating himself in the hope the brutes will spare him harm.

Suddenly, a chirping of rubber soles, then the jolly whistling of a man nearing the stairwell.

"I guess they're not *all* in the lunchroom. Are they, Mr. Rebmann?" DeSimone chides. "Listen, Rebmann. Don't try to be cute, because you're gonna get your ears cut off. You're already a donkey, and you'll look even stupider without ears. So who the fuck could be walkin' around in the hallway?"

Rebmann's intent to cooperate is misconstrued and reeks of deception. He explains, "No . . . no. That . . . that could be the supervisor, Eirich. I . . . I told you he's the . . . the only one who doesn't come to the lunchroom on his meal break."

"Shut the fuck up and don't say another word," Cafora shushes, tightening his jaws.

Manri prods DeSimone to step out into the corridor with him and grab hold of whoever is wandering outside the cafeteria. Guns up high, the two robbers spring into the brightly lit hallway and plant their feet two yards from cargo agent John Murray. Not to draw the attention of those in the cafeteria, DeSimone says quietly but harshly, "Put your hands up. What's your name?" His .38 Magnum pearl-handle Smith & Wesson is aimed at Murray's midsection.

The abrupt appearance of the masked gunmen terrifies Murray. Only because adrenalin is anesthetizing him, he dares to ask, "Who are *you*?"

Manri and DeSimone move in, flanking Murray, the shotgun and the Smith & Wesson scraping his temples.

"We're asking the questions, not *you*." Manri's eyes are spearing Murray's through the eyeholes of the ski mask. He jams the barrels of the shotgun into Murray's forehead. The cargo agent twitches, the veins in his temples now blue and swelling. "If you wanna be a wiseass, a blast from this thing will make a tunnel through your head."

DeSimone has ten pairs of handcuffs in a satchel strapped to his shoulder. He pulls out one set and fetters Murray's hands while Manri holds the shotgun inches from him. "Mr. Murray, where's everybody else?"

Murray points with his chin at the doors of the lunchroom. "Some of them are in there."

"Where's everybody else?"

"The supervisor is downstairs in his office. Rolf Rebmann, Mike Hychko, and the security guard are somewhere in the warehouse," John Murray answers genuinely, unaware three of his coworkers have already been corralled.

Werner had said the night supervisor, Rudi Eirich, often stays in his office on the warehouse level. Manri does some math in his head. "Mr. Murray, how many people should be in the cafeteria?"

"Probably seven." Murray assumes he is the only one captured; otherwise, he would've confirmed only four workers in the lunchroom.

Werner had also spoken about a cleaning service. "Where are the porters, Mr. Murray?"

Murray is shaking like a leaf in the wind. "They're . . . they're gone. They leave early." Judging by the scent of fresh wax and the high luster of the blue vinyl-tiled floor, Manri and DeSimone believe him.

Manri knows of the independently contracted porters, the number of personnel in the building, and their identity. It's clear, Murray thinks, a Lufthansa employee must've spelled out the indispensable facts to the robbers. And though the sight of Manri's shotgun is short-circuiting Murray's brain, he's convinced the ring leader of this holdup is Louis Werner.

Everyone in the building now accounted for, Manri and DeSimone walk Murray to the stairwell, and Manri nods at his companions to take the captives into the cafeteria. He touches his nose as a reminder to maintain silence. "We got everybody who's supposed to be in the building. There should be four more in the lunchroom down the hall."

Single file, the four thugs herd the hostages down the tunnel-like corridor. They stride up to the swinging doors of the lunchroom; DeSimone kicks them open and hurls Murray inside. McMahon gives Hychko and Rebmann each a hard push, and Cafora and Manri lurch in with the watchman.

In this moment, the four in the cafeteria are unflustered by the incursion. "Oh, c'mon, what kind of a joke is this. You guys got nothin' better to do?"

"It's . . . it's no joke," warns Rebmann, his mouth quavering.

"Oh, please. Get the fuck outta here. Who do you think you're fooling?" says one of the workers.

Manri flaunts his weapon. "This ain't no joke, and if you don't believe this shotgun is real, lemme put a shot in your fuckin' head."

The harrowing invasion nearly stops the heartbeats of the Lufthansa night shift, and the leisurely meal break erupts into bedlam.

His shotgun sweeping side to side, Manri shouts, "Get on the floor facedown, and don't look up."

Two of the Lufthansa staffers had been dozing. Having been jarred from sleep, but not quite fully awake, their grogginess sees this head-whirling moment as the absurdity of a dream.

The seven hostages do as they're told and scramble to the floor.

Manri yells out, "Like I said, everybody keep your fuckin' eyes down and don't look around the room."

One of the detainees, Wolfgang Ruppert, can't seem to concentrate on keeping his gaze on the pavement; his eyes rove from Cafora to McMahon to Manri.

Cafora goes up to Rupert and presses his booted foot on the man's neck. "We told you not to look around. If you lift your head again, you better say your last prayer."

Ruppert complies and starts weeping. "I have a family of five. Two of my sons are three and four years old. They need me."

Cafora grins. "Yeah, well, everybody needs their father."

One by one, the captors rifle through the pockets of the prisoners, take their wallets, and hurl them at DeSimone for him to keep in his satchel. The robbers then take turns addressing the Lufthansa staff. This tactic is to lessen the chance for the gunmen to leave traits or clues of their identities. McMahon is in rotation to speak. Mimicking a professional master of ceremonies, he clears his throat. "You all must've heard the story of the unsung hero. The message I'm trying to drive home is this: we're as concerned for your safety as you are yourselves."

Burke had chosen McMahon to give this speech because his manner was the exception within the Robert's Lounge gang; his pronunciation was indistinct, unlike the rest of them, whose New York Brooklynese accent could be singled out even by a foreigner. "We got your wallets, and we know who you are and where you live. So please do what we say. If any of you doesn't obey, *remember*, we can find you. You should also understand that the damage we're going to do tonight to Lufthansa, a corporation with millions and millions of dollars, will be as minute as a mosquito bite on a horse. But if you try to be a hero, well . . . it may cost you your life. Now that's a big loss. So no heroes, please!"

Manri and DeSimone lift Murray to his feet and shove him into the corridor. "Mr. Murray, pay attention," Manri says. "I want you to call your supervisor and have him come up here."

"You mean Rudi Eirich?" Murray asks.

"Yeah, him."

Supervisor Rudi Eirich is responsible for the high-value vault and the alarm keys.

"You want me to get him up here? What do you want me to say to him?"

Cafora is up at bat to do the talking. "How about telling him he's got a call from headquarters in Germany. When Germany phones, he's gotta take the call. Right? So don't play stupid. If you don't get Eirich here, I'm gonna mix your brains in your dinner." Cafora glances at his watch. "Germany is six hours ahead of us. Let's see, it's 3:15 here. There, it's 9:15 in the morning. So it's likely they could be calling. Right?"

Holding Murray by the arms, Manri and Cafora take him to his workstation. Cafora unshackles him so he can dial. The cargo agent picks up the phone on his desk and punches in Eirich's extension.

Manri grasps Murray's wrist and interrupts his dialing. "Before you call Eirich, lemme warn you. Don't get the idea to use tricky words to give your boss a heads-up. Remember what we said in the lunchroom: no heroes, please."

Murray bobs his head and redials. "Rudi, it's John Murray. Listen, I . . . I got a call on hold from Germany. They wanna talk to you. Said it's important."

Manri and Cafora assume Eirich to be saying, "Switch the call to my extension."

"No . . . no, Rudi," Murray stammers. "The call . . . the call came in on the open line." The open line is a dedicated telephone toll cable for overseas communications.

There's a lapse in the phone conversation. Seconds pass, and Murray hangs up the receiver. "Mr. Eirich's coming." He's perspiring but relieved.

Cafora removes his gun from Murray's temple. "Good, good."

Manri, too, bows with appreciation. "Good job, John." By now, they're on a first-name basis.

Towing Murray along, Cafora and Manri go to the far end of the hallway where the steel door to the stairs is. They keep Murray standing against the wall, and the two holdup men position themselves out of sight on the sides of the stairwell.

Manri says to Murray, "Don't make a move." Forty seconds clicked, and Eirich hasn't arrived. Manri frowns at Murray. "I hope you weren't foolish enough to have said something to give Eirich a hint."

Murray's forehead douses to a drench. "Hell, no! He . . . he'll be here. It's a long walk from his office. He'll be here . . . soon."

He isn't lying. In ten seconds, Eirich pushes open the fireproof door and emerges with urgency from the stairway. To his dismay, Eirich runs into the deadly end of a high-caliber pistol and a stubby, double-barreled shotgun. And so sinister are the sizes and shapes of the felons toting the artillery.

"What the hell . . . ," Eirich utters, and his body braces.

Cafora wiggles the tip of his gun on Eirich's cheek. "Relax, relax. You missed the speech in the cafeteria. The bottom line is we don't want you to be a hero. Everything's gonna work out, and nobody will get harmed. *Or killed.*" Cafora nods. "Let's have your wallet. "

Hands trembling, Eirich promptly produces it.

"In the next half hour," Manri forewarns, "a couple of hot-headed guys, who have no respect for a human life, will be parking themselves in front of your house. Know what I mean?" Eirich nods, and Manri says, "I know you do, Mr. Eirich. Now let's go to the cafeteria."

Envisioning a prelude to death, Eirich lowers his head, and the two robbers pull him by the arms for the hike to the lunchroom.

On seeing his staff sprawled on the cafeteria floor with an armed, hooded burglar standing over them—a heart-skipping picture—Eirich wets his underwear. More wrenching, he sees blood dripping from

Hychko's scalp, leaching onto the pavement as though it were a slow-moving red river.

Manri bumps Eirich's back with the shotgun barrels. "These are eight of your people. Is everyone here, or is someone missing? And don't bullshit me."

Eirich counts eight pathetic men, one's hair bloody and tangled. "Yes, they're all here." His fingers unsteady, he indicates Hychko. "Eh, he's losing a lot of blood. He needs an ambulance." The supervisor feels his urine warming the left thigh and frets that the expanding stain on his pants might be noticeable.

"Yeah, yeah. The sooner you get the money room opened and closed, the sooner we get out of here and the sooner you'll be able to get help for Hychko. OK?" Manri waves the shotgun in the direction of the stairs. "Let's go downstairs."

Manri, Cafora, and McMahon take Eirich two floors below to his glass-enclosed office, where the alarm control panels are mounted on a wall. Cafora tugs roughly at Eirich's sweater. "You got the key for the alarm?"

Shivering from fright, Eirich straightens his collar and points to a safe anchored under the control panels. "When I'm in the building, I keep it in there."

Manri nods at the safe. "Get it."

Burke's orders to his field marshal, Joe "Buddha" Manri, are not to injure anybody. But unaware of such considerateness, these hell-bent raiders portend a fatal ending. Hand trembling, Eirich works the combination dial, opens the safe door, and reaches in for the key.

All the while, Licastri and Sepe have been standing by on the loading platform. Earlier, Licastri removed a key from Rebmann's pocket, and with it, he, Licastri, turns on the switch next to the overhead door. It opens, and Sepe backs the Ford van into the cargo bay. The van now indoors, Licastri switches the door shut.

Manri instructs Eirich to disarm the alarm, a delicate procedure. The position of the switch must be precise, a deliberate exactness intended to trip unauthorized tempters. Eirich steadies his thin fingers, huffing and wiping his brow. He sets the knob to the supposedly correct setting. "The alarm is off."

"Hear me out, Eirich. Before we go and unlock the door to the vault, let's get one thing straight. If you're doin' some kind of trick and an alarm goes off at the Port Authority, we'll . . ."

Eirich loses his composure and bangs on the alarm panel. "Oh, stop this shit. I don't want to be no hero, and I don't want any trouble. I got a family to go to. All I want is for you people, whoever you are, to take what you want and get the hell out of here. And leave my workers unhurt. God damn it!"

Eirich's outburst surprises the robbers, and Manri doesn't want to test Eirich's sincerity. "Here's what I'm gonna do. If you got nothin' to worry about, then when we leave here, you won't mind coming with us until we're out of the airport. All right?" Manri squares his shoulders and speculates, "If you did what you weren't supposed to do, and we get a tail of cops on our asses, well, then we can kill you right then and there. How's that?"

Cafora breaks out into a laugh. "That's a good one, Joe."

Eirich doesn't see the humor; his knees as rubbery as overcooked linguini, he feels he's about to faint.

⌒

McMahon and Joe Manri leave Eirich's office, and Cafora stays to guard him. McMahon and Manri huddle in a corner to mull over the supervisor's fate.

"Joe," McMahon says, "I don't think it's a good idea to take Eirich with us."

Manri crimps his lips. "Why not?"

McMahon shakes his head. "Let's say we make it out of the parking lot, and somewhere down the highway we get into a chase with the cops. You know how DeSimone and that nut-job Licastri are. They got balls but no brains and the common sense of a two-day-old spic."

The common sense of a two-day-old spic! McMahon's disparagement incenses Manri, a South American himself, though he can't defend himself against the slur. It must remain secret that he isn't of Italian descent. Inwardly, he's boiling with rage and would love to strangle McMahon.

"If things get hairy," McMahon reasons, "with Eirich *and* those two empty-headed nitwits in the van, anything can go wrong. Then we'd have a murder rap on our hands." Affecting a psychological dominance, he palms his gloved hand on the wall above Manri's left shoulder. McMahon's uniqueness to the Robert's Lounge gang is one of value; though he's a schizophrenic, his cleverness and keenness are attributes Burke needs to keep the rest of the louts in check.

Seething, Manri glares fiercely at McMahon and doesn't answer.

McMahon pauses and lets four or five seconds linger. "Me, I'd rather take my chances with the cops. I mean, Sepe is a hell of a driver." McMahon senses he's mollifying Manri.

Manri studies the cement floor, and McMahon recaps, "I believe Eirich is playing it straight. He doesn't seem the type to risk it all. And for what? So when he retires, Lufthansa will give him a twenty-dollar watch?"

Manri isn't the sharpest knife in the drawer, though his smarts are a notch above the rest of Burke's flock. He mulls it over for a moment or two. "All right, Frenchy, I'll go along with you on this, but if something goes wrong, it's on you. Let's get Eirich to open the vault."

———

The high-value chamber is built as two separate vaults, an outer and an inner. The cartons of money are stored in the inner room. To access the second vault, after deactivating the alarm, one must unlock the door (door 1) to the outer chamber. Once inside there, door 1 must be closed before opening the one to the second vault (door 2), a critical step. If door 1 and door 2 are simultaneously left open, a warning sounds off at the Port Authority.

Settled on trusting Eirich, Manri and McMahon trot back to his office.

"Are we taking him with us?" Cafora asks.

"No, we ain't," Manri answers with an air of finality.

"Why not?"

"Let's just get this done," Manri says.

McMahon looks severely at Eirich. "OK, the moment of reckoning is here."

Manri presses the barrels of his weapon against Eirich's spine, and they fast-step to where the vault is, McMahon following them.

Again, Manri prods Eirich with the shotgun. "Open it. So far you've done good. Don't blow it now, Eirich." The four-inch-thick cast-iron door can only be unlocked by turning three handles to the left and to the right in a preset sequence, and Eirich does so. No alarms or sirens so far.

"Thank God!" Eirich mutters, his inhalations slowing.

The faces of Manri, McMahon, and Cafora are glistening with perspiration, and their pulses have suddenly quickened. They seem to be wondering if a silent alarm is alerting the police. A battalion of cops could be here in two to three minutes and surround the Lufthansa complex.

"Get inside." Manri jostles Eirich through the doorway of the vault. "There's supposed to be an alarm button somewhere on a wall. Where is it?"

Eirich points to a red knob next to the light switch. "It's right there."

"OK, Eirich, sit down in the middle of the floor."

Listening for sirens, a torrent of misgivings rushes through Cafora's mind. He's been keeping watch on Eirich; McMahon snaps him out of his anxieties. "Pay attention, and make sure Eirich don't go near that red button over there."

"How many times do I have to say it? I don't want trouble," Eirich appeals.

"Yeah, yeah, we believe you, but we can't take chances," Manri says. "Now you're the man of the hour, Mr. Eirich. Stand up and shut the outer door airtight before you open the second one."

They know about the distress call knob and how not to set off the alarm when opening the door to the inner vault, strengthening Eirich's belief. Definitely inside information.

Only a handful of Lufthansa managers know that coded succession, and a name booms in Eirich's mind: *Louis Werner*. The robbery isn't yet over, and two employees of the German airliner have already pegged blame on Werner.

Eirich gives the gunmen access to the inner vault. Hundreds of packages in a variety of dimensions and sizes are piled on steel shelving. A clipboard hangs on a shelf post, and a sheaf of invoices and bills of lading are clipped to it. Manri leafs through the paperwork to pinpoint the parcels with the cash. Werner's data has been on point; one night's work, at last, is about to make everyone flush.

But what if there isn't any money? Well, then, Mr. Werner should buy a ticket to the far end of the world because Jimmy Burke will hunt him until the end of time.

In the outer vault, from where he's standing, Eirich can spy Manri sifting through the tissue-thin freight manifests rubber-banded to the clipboard. The tell-tale signs of an insider's role are plain, and Eirich can't contain his curiosity. "One thing I'd like to know."

"Yeah, what's that?" Cafora says, his gun pointed at Eirich.

"I'd love to know who's your inside man." Another spell of panting, and Eirich feels his pulse thumping.

"Maybe we'll send you a postcard with his picture," Cafora jokes. "We *do* have your address, you know."

McMahon snaps the clipboard from Manri and quickly isolates the money packets. "Here, Joe! I think these are what we're looking for."

Teeth gritting, Manri reproves, "Watch yourself! Don't call me by my fuckin' name in front of Eirich."

McMahon covers his mouth, glances slyly around him. "Shit, I'm sorry." Unfazed by the blunder, McMahon speedily unravels one of the bundles, and the content is green. "Yeah! These are the ones," he gloats, his broad grin flashing through the mouth opening of his ski mask.

Sepe has been in the driver's seat of the Ford van, waiting for Manri's cue to back it close to the vault. His heart is racing; he's imagining a SWAT team staking out the loading dock outside, waiting to ambush the robbers. In the interim, Licastri joins Cafora in guarding Eirich. Manri motions for Sepe to start the engine; Sepe glances at him through the sideview mirror and rolls the van so the rear bumper is four to five feet from the vault. He jumps out of the cab and helps his confederates transfer the one-cubic-foot boxes from the inner room, across the outer vault, and into the van. The engine is running, and the exhaust fumes are fouling the cargo bay with carbon monoxide.

"Shut off the motor before we all get gassed," McMahon squawks.

The stickup men need six minutes to load the loot.

Manri and McMahon practically lift Eirich by the armpits. "This is your final act, Mr. Eirich," McMahon jibes. "Now look into my eyes. Without fuckin' around, close the doors of the vaults, *the right way.*"

Eirich first closes door 2 and then opens door 1. Despite Eirich's assurances, McMahon and Cafora fear the unknown, an automatic signal going off at the Port Authority. McMahon prompts, "C'mon, Mr. Eirich, let's make this fast and finish locking door one. We wanna get out of here."

Eirich completes securing the outer vault door, and Licastri and Sepe board the Ford van, now laden with three hundred pounds of treasure. McMahon, Cafora, and Manri haul Eirich upstairs to the lunchroom. DeSimone has the cargo agents sitting quietly on the floor, and he's been hankering for one of them to provoke him.

Cafora and McMahon are prodding Eirich, Manri strutting ahead. They bound into the cafeteria, and DeSimone seems glad to see them. He slides the ski mask over his forehead and wipes his cheeks of perspiration. "Did you find what we came for?"

"Pull down your damn cap, man," shouts Manri. "What're you, a moron?"

McMahon glances at two of the Lufthansa shipping clerks, who are in a direct line of sight to where DeSimone is standing. He stews, realizing a second gunman has revealed himself to the Lufthansa workers.

Rebmann and Murray surely will not forget DeSimone's visage. Hychko also has locked Sepe's face in his mind from the glimpse he caught of it earlier.

McMahon points his gun to the floor and draws an imaginary ring with the left hand. "All right, everybody. Sit on the floor in a circle with your asses inside the circle."

The armed men string together the cargo agents, arms behind their backs, and DeSimone gags everybody's mouth with silver duct tape, a well-thought-out drill.

DeSimone is about to strap the tape on Eirich's mouth, but the supervisor recoils, his face red and filmy. "This is not necessary, goddamn it! Even if we wanted to scream for help, nobody can hear us. We're too far from the other buildings. We've been gentlemen all through this."

DeSimone hurls the tape at Cafora and pats Eirich on the shoulder. "You're right. You have been gentlemen. If you weren't, by now you'd be at the pearly gates talking to St. Peter."

Eirich gazes pitifully at Hychko. Though he can't make out the seriousness of the man's lacerations, he sees a sickening flash of blood and pulp on his cranium. Eirich implores the robbers, "Hychko is in bad shape. He needs medical care. Immediately!"

"He'll get it soon enough. First we gotta finish our job," Cafora says with the callousness of a hangman.

Of the nine hostages, eight are handcuffed. The burglars do not cuff Murray but loosely rope his wrists, enabling him to free his hands and phone for assistance.

Manri scowls at Murray, his jaw clenched. "Wait twenty minutes before you call 911. Even if you get free, *wait* twenty minutes. *Got it?*"

The Port Authority can block the four airport exits within fifteen minutes. Three days ago, during the same early morning hours, Manri and McMahon drove from the Lufthansa cargo hangar and out of the airport in six minutes. Ample time to escape.

To ensure the victims are tied snugly, McMahon checks each one. "Remember, no heroes, please! When you're asked what we sounded like, be smart, say you were too shook up and don't remember a thing. We're going to remind you again. We know where you live."

McMahon and DeSimone are ready to follow Manri and Cafora to the stairway. They quick-step four or five paces, then turn around to face the lunchroom. Unscripted, McMahon bids, "Good night, and have a nice day tomorrow. You're going to be on TV and in newspapers, so dress up in your Sunday clothes."

"Let's get out of here." DeSimone taps McMahon's forearm, and they scurry to the stairway.

They catch up with Manri and dash below to the ground level. Cafora remains on the landing, slams the door, and counts to sixty.

"... Fifty-eight, fifty-nine, sixty." He plows his 360 pounds into the door and forcefully reopens it, bursting into the corridor, an intimidating effect. "Didn't I say not to move for fifteen minutes?" Cafora shouts, his voice lasting in the hallway as he fades down the staircase.

Burke's highwaymen regroup on the loading ramp and pile into the Ford van. McMahon presses the Up button on the wall, and the corrugated roll-up door of the warehouse starts to open. The van exits, and he walks out the side door of the cargo bay. McMahon jogs to where the chase car, the Pontiac Grand Prix, is parked and folds his six-foot-one frame into the bucket seat on the passenger side. He tears off the woolen ski mask, and a gust of wind refreshes his cheeks. The engine is idling, and the heater fan is blowing warm air.

"Turn off the damn heater," McMahon complains. "I'm sweating like a pig."

"How did it go?"

"All right. We got it, Frank." McMahon fans his face with a hand and lays his head on the headrest. He lets out a sigh of relief and shuts his eyes.

Licastri engages the Down switch, and the twenty-four-foot-wide door begins to lower, its rollers screeching loudly, fracturing the complacency of the early dawn. With Sepe at the steering wheel, the van turns left into the driveway of the Lufthansa compound and onto the Nassau Expressway.

"Stay close behind the van, and keep checking for cars that might be following us," McMahon says to his driver, Frank, Burke's oldest son.

Duly respecting the forty-five-mile-per-hour speed limit, Sepe decelerates and shifts his eyes from the solitary road to the rearview mirror. "Oh, shit!" he exclaims.

"What's wrong?" Manri asks.

"Some kind of car with flashing lights is creeping up behind the Pontiac. Could be cops."

Everybody becomes rigid and stares through the rear windows of the van.

"Fuck," Cafora curses, "an alarm must've gone off."

"Hit the gas, Angelo. Floor the goddamn pedal," DeSimone yells.

Panic breaks out inside the van. Manri looks at the closely tailing Pontiac carrying McMahon and Frank Burke and squints to focus three hundred feet farther back on the vehicle with the orange emergency beacons, flashes careening in the darkness.

They scramble for their weapons. "Cool it, cool it," Manri yells. "They're not cops. Those lights are orange. It must be a tow truck or somethin'. Only ambulances, fire trucks, and police cruisers have red emergency lights. Everything else got orange lights."

"Whew!" The desperados exhale heartily, releasing a surge of breath they'd been holding in, and bellow in unruly laughter, palms slapping with one another.

"A close one," cries out Cafora, wheezing and winded.

"You ain't shittin'," Sepe remarks.

A tune comes on the radio, and Paolo Licastri amplifies the volume to the maximum. It's a new hit, "Gonna Fly Now," from the soundtrack of the film *Rocky*. The music incites Burke's scholars to a rocking mood; they're richer than they were an hour ago, and they clap to the beat of the song. Manri quells the excitement. "Whoa, whoa! Cool it. Paolo, turn it down. You can hear it from outside. Let's not attract attention at the last minute."

"It's all under control, man. I got an eye on the rearview mirror. All is quiet, and the seas are calm," Sepe wisecracks. "Just Frank and Frenchy in the Pontiac. We're home free. *We're home free!*"

Sepe veers onto the entrance ramp of the northbound lanes of the Van Wyck Expressway and hums in sync with the radio.

DeSimone is sulking over the ultra-foolish move of removing his ski mask in the Lufthansa cafeteria, but he rises above it, dreaming about tomorrow, the heftiest payday of his felonious career. And to forget the dark thought of that stupider-than-stupid move back there, he jokes, "How can you go through life with a name like that Lufthansa worker, Wolfgang Ruppert?" DeSimone was a bully from the moment he'd sloshed out of his mother's womb, and in his school days, had he come across a boy named Wolfgang, he might've slapped him just for laughs.

"If my old man named me Wolfgang, I'd kill the bastard," Sepe assures.

Rowdy guffaws crackle in the crowded van, and foul odors from perspiring bodies taint the air. And though the temperature is at the freezing mark, the passengers feel as if they're broiling in an oven—it's been a nerve-racking night.

Paolo Licastri, though, has been moping; he can't relate to the humor in DeSimone and Sepe's heckling. His English isn't much better than that of a retarded parrot. Moreover, he's stewing over Manri's orders back at the Lufthansa hangar not to harm anybody, offending him in the company of his equals, a discourtesy he will not ever bury.

In the dawning hours of December 11, 1978, the Lufthansa cargo complex underwent two cleaning services, one by the contracted porters and the second a costly scrubbing by the Jimmy Burke company of convicts. Afterward, as John Murray unshackled his wrists, he bolted to his workstation and sent a mayday call to the Port Authority headquarters a mile to the west of Lufthansa.

Fingers fluttering, Murray dialed the Port Authority. "Eh, this . . . this is cargo building 261 re . . . reporting an armed robbery. I'm, eh . . . shipping agent John Murray. One of us is bleeding badly. Please send an ambulance."

"Emergency response units will be on the way, Mr. Murray."

In the next twenty minutes, as the magnitude of the theft flew over the wires to the regional and federal law enforcement agencies, a fleet of police cars, unmarked vehicles, ambulances, crime scene trucks, and Brinks patrol cars swooped into the Lufthansa parking field.

Nine miles from Lufthansa ground zero, traveling south on the Van Wyck Expressway, exhaustion was weighing on Sepe's eyelids, and the Ford van swerved slightly, riling McMahon, who was watching the zigzagging getaway vehicle from the chase car. "Damn, look at this jerk Sepe driving all over the road. He's gonna get stopped."

Indeed, if the gunmen attracted the interest of a cruising patrolman, a shootout could definitely ensue.

"Ouh!" Cafora yelped. "Angelo, what're you, sleeping at the wheel? Paolo, give 'em a smack before he falls asleep."

Paolo Licastri refrained; nobody could slap Sepe and go on unscathed.

Sepe shook off his doziness. "I'm OK. We only got a few blocks to go."

"You sure?" Manri second-guessed. "'Cause I can drive the rest of the way."

"Nah, nah, I'm all right."

They were headed to Metropolitan Avenue in Maspeth, Queens, where an industrial park with factories and commercial buildings spanned blocks on end.

"Slow down, Angelo. It's the second building on the left," Cafora said.

"Are you sure?" Sepe questioned.

"You're a real mammalook. Wasn't I here just a couple of hours ago to drop off Jimmy?"

Sepe decelerated. "I see it." He nosed the van into the driveway of the warehouse, and Manri bounced out. He banged on the roll-up door, and in seconds it began rising. The warehouse was John Gotti's contribution.

The gangly Black man Stacks was waiting inside, his finger on the button of the electric opener. "All right! All right! C'mon in. You got plenty o' room," he directed, waving on the Ford van. Sepe drove it in, the Pontiac chase car immediately behind.

Outdoors the street resumed its stillness. Inside the warehouse, the lighting was dusky at best, and everyone spilled out of the van. Draped in a black full-length wool coat, its collar and a white cashmere scarf enveloping his neck, Burke came forth from the shadows, seemingly in a slow-motion, soundless stroll, hands deep in his pockets. He smiled at Manri. "How did it go?"

"Smooth, Jimmy. Smooth," Manri informed him, kissing his thumb and index fingers. To feel accepted, he overcompensated in mimicking the Burke gang of Italians.

A flush warmed the Gent's face, and he had the look of a child who couldn't wait to unwrap a gift. "What're you waitin' for? Unload the cash and lemme get it out of here."

This startled the robbers. "Jimmy," Licastri spoke out, "why we no count the money now?"

Everyone else gazed at the floor, and Burke stared at Licastri. "You think we're gonna stand here counting for the next three hours? I wanna be off the streets in case the cops put up roadblocks."

"How I know how much we steal?" Paolo Licastri clucked his tongue, his rotting teeth as pointy as a pitchfork.

"You're gonna have to trust me. And if you don't, tough shit. Now let's get this cash out of the van," Burke said.

In a minute, the warehouse changed into a setting reminiscent of Santa Claus's shop of elves. Everyone lined up, forming a human conveyor belt. They unloaded the cartons of money from the van and reloaded them into a switch car, a second vehicle for ferrying the booty to where it'd be hidden—a precaution if perchance a witness had seen the black Ford van on the Lufthansa property. Burke and his stickup men packed the bundles into the trunk of the switch car, a white Toyota Corona. As a decoy, they added twelve pounds of foul bagged bluefish over the packets of cash. This tactic, Burke's idea, served two objectives; it hid the money, and if an inquisitive cop started searching the trunk, the nostril-gassing odor would fend him off from digging further. Who'd conceive of cash camouflaged under rotting fish?

Sepe pinched the tip of his longish nose, the outline of a ski jump. "Whooh! Sure as shit, nobody's gonna wanna go near this car."

"Pheeew. Jimmy, after this run, you're gonna have to junk it," Manri said. "You'll never get the stink out of this car."

"OK, we're done," Burke said, wired energy in his speech. "Frenchy, let everybody squeeze into the Pontiac and drive them back to Robert's Lounge. Frank and me will go stash the loot." The Gent's son, Frank, a tall, skinny nineteen-year-old, would be inhaling the putrid fish fumes, and Senior . . . well, he'd be basking in the defeat of the Red Baron.

The Toyota loaded, Burke said to Stacks, "Listen carefully." He dropped his hands on the Black man's shoulders. "This van's gotta disappear faster than immediately. Understand? You know where to take it. Change the plates, and go there now."

"I got you, Jimmy," Stacks said.

The gunners changed their clothes. Manri threw the outfits and ski masks into the van. John Gotti had arranged for an auto-wrecking yard in the Flatlands section of Brooklyn to crush-compact the getaway vehicle and all the paraphernalia used in the robbery.

Burke's thieves huddled around him. "All right," he coached. "After we all leave here, I want you to do whatever you've been doin' and don't change your routine. I don't want none o' you to phone each other. If you got something to say, do it in person. *No phone calls.* Got it?" The Gent peered at them one by one. "Five days from today, Joe Buddha's gonna come to see you all and square up with your cut." Burke leered at Licastri. "Paolo, tell John that I myself will be straightening out with him." The whole crew gave signs of understanding, then disbanded. Licastri, though, wore a glare of disdain for Burke.

<hr />

Frank and his father drove to their house in Howard Beach and pulled into the driveway, the black, overcast sky losing its darkness and streaking to a violet hue, shades of the new aurora. The Gent got out of the Toyota, took a remote control out of his coat pocket, and clicked it; the garage door opened. He waved Frank on to roll the car in. In the middle of the garage floor was a four-by-twelve-foot wooden hatch. Beneath it, the Gent had dug a pit two yards deep, originally for a mechanic to work on the undercarriage of an automobile.

Into that hole, an oily and grease-saturated trench, Burke ditched the Lufthansa haul.

<hr />

Minutes after Burke and Frank had driven out of the warehouse, Stacks snuffed out the lights and backed the Ford van out onto the sidewalk; the electric overhead door closed automatically. He was headed east on Metropolitan Avenue and tuned the radio to an FM jazz station. He hummed, floating into a reverie while listening to the fast-skipping blues notes of the sax musician, Sonny Stitt. Stacks glanced at the digital clock on the dashboard: 5:54 a.m. "I gotta get this van to the junkyard before it gets light out," he muttered to himself. A distraction titillated his thoughts: Shelly, a "fine sistah" with whom he curled up from time to time. She sported a claret-dyed afro, a cushiony fluff in style with the one Angela

Davis trended in the late sixties. Shelly had had four children with four different men, or possibly five. She herself had lost count.

Stacks was cruising at forty-five miles per hour, careful not to speed; the license tags on the van, number 508HWM, were stolen. Sonny Stitt's saxophone was lulling Stacks into the mood, and he suddenly longed to stop by Shelly's; he'd stay with her for a couple of lines of cocaine and a romp in the sack, then scram to the Flatlands area of Brooklyn to dump the van.

At the auto-wrecking yard, the operator had been waiting to crush the Ford van into a bale of scrap metal. Stacks, instead, boarded the west-bound lanes of the Belt Parkway at the Cross Bay Boulevard intersection. He traveled on the Belt for seven minutes and exited on Rockaway Parkway. He then swung north for two miles toward Canarsie until reaching East Ninety-Fifth Street. Shelly lived in a garden apartment, a drug exchange center, crack the leading neighborhood commodity. The tenants were five-dollar prostitutes, drug runners, social assistance scammers, and addicts. A balanced blend of citizens. On the grounds outdoors, weeds were littered with trash and newspaper debris, empty bottles of Gypsy Rose wine strewn here and there.

Clunkers with rotted fenders lined both sides of the block. The late-model Ford van, clean and shiny, was bluntly out of place on this ghetto street. Stacks absentmindedly parked it near a fire hydrant; he locked the door and traipsed to Shelly's doorway.

Nailed to the door was a piece of cardboard with a handwritten message, "Bell No Work." Stacks knocked. No answer. He knocked again, and after thirty seconds in the frosty climate he heard the jangling of a safety chain and the clanking of the doorknob.

"Who is it?"

"It's Stacks, baby. Open up. "

The door opened, and Shelly appeared, yawning and sleepy, a brown infant crying in her arms. "Stacks, it's five o'clock in da mornin', honey. Whatchu doin' here so late?"

He hugged "his lady" and kissed her, the baby howling louder. "I wanted a snort o' coke, baby. And I know you got a little stash," he said, plugging his nostril with a thumb, a hint of his craving.

"C'mon in," Shelly mumbled with reluctance, her hand shielding the child's scalp. "Hurry up and close the door. The cold be comin' in." Rocking the tot in her arms, she went into the tiny kitchen. Sprinklings of cat litter on the tattered vinyl flooring crackled under her sandals, and a mountain of crud-plastered dishes filled the sink, a chipped and dented basin. In the den Stacks sat on a red velour couch, the edges of the armrest frayed and stained with a rainbow of spillages from chicken soup to urine. An acidy smell of sour milk fouled the air.

Awake for the past thirty hours, Stacks rubbed his eyelids. Shelly plopped a ceramic sugar bowl on the glass coffee table, and in it was a dusting of cocaine. Stacks coiled his arm around Shelly's caramel-toned thigh and giggled. "All right! All right, baby. I knew you'd come through for your Stacks." He kissed her upper leg, inching closer to her vagina. "I goin' come through for you."

Shelly pushed Stacks's head aside. "Whatchu mean?"

His pulpy lips widened and, teeth missing, his mouth opened to a gaping hole. "Baby, we just done a big, big score, and I'm gonna be comin' into a piece o' change."

"Oh, Stacks, nobody goin' give you nothin'. You been sayin' this since I know you. It never be happenin'."

"It be happenin', baby. You'll see."

"Don't be a fool, Stacks. Stop believin' them white boys. They like to keep everythin' for themselves. And you gotta watch out for those Aitalians. They be bad people."

Stacks didn't care to dwell on this. "Baby, they won't be messing with this nigga." He wrapped his arms around Shelly's buttocks, a pair of basketballs, and lapped at her navel. She hugged his cheeks, and they began snorting the cocaine. At some point, Stacks, ever the lover, lifted Shelly off the couch and carried her to the bedroom, a darkish room with newspapers on the windows. They tumbled in the hay for an hour. Stacks fell asleep, the baby shrilling in the background, and the Ford van—stolen plates and all—stayed illegally parked at the fire hydrant.

By daybreak, law enforcement agencies understood the enormity of the theft, and more and more representation from the NYPD, FBI, the Queens district attorney, Port Authority, New York state troopers, and Brinks detectives were teeming into the Lufthansa cargo hangar.

Dense pewter clouds were spitting out watery snowflakes, and minutes into the inquiry the scene of the robbery underwent a transformation; a cargo shipping plant had turned into a boxing ring. Ranks of investigators from the many police forces were growing uncivilized, hostility mounting by the hour. The sparring for top command of the investigation was brewing antagonism, and blows were about to fly, literally.

NINE

The Northfield Bank Job

J. H. Hanson

The James-Younger gang thought it was just another robbery. The citizens of Northfield, Minnesota, had another idea.

Between August 23 and September 5, a company of strangers made their appearance at different localities in the state of Minnesota, attracting attention by their peculiar bearing, remarkable physique, and decidedly southern phraseology. They would appear sometimes in pairs, and at other times there would be as many as four or five in company. At one time they would be cattle dealers from Texas, and again they were gentlemen in search of unimproved lands for speculative purposes, and then again they were a party of engineers and surveyors prospecting for a new railroad, making enquires about roads, swamps, lakes, and timber lands, carefully consulting maps they had with them and, when opportunity offered, Andreas' State Atlas of Minnesota.

These men visited St. Paul, Minneapolis, St. Peter, Red Wing, St. James, Madelia, Garden City, Lake Crystal, Mankato, Janesville, Cordova, Millersburg, Waterville, and Northfield, putting up at the best hotels, spending their money freely, and creating a general impression of free-handed liberality. But there was a certain air of audacity blended with their *sangfroid* and easy manners that led men to think they were no ordinary persons and aroused speculations as to their true character and vocation. The registers of the hotels honored by these guests bear the names of King, Ward, Huddleston, &c., generally written in one line, but subsequent developments prove these to be merely *noms de guerre.*

They are next seen on the streets on Monday morning when a young man, Chas Robinson, who was acquainted with the notorious Jesse James, went up to one of them and remarked, "How do you do, Jesse? What brings you up this way?"

The man addressed, eyeing the speaker keenly from head to foot, replied, "I guess you have mistaken your man," vaulted into the saddle, and galloped away.

With this incident, the five men who had attracted so much notice, excited so much admiration, and aroused many vague suspicions disappeared from Mankato. The same day five similarly dressed, similarly mounted, and similarly appearing strangers arrived in Janesville, a village on the Winona and St. Peter railroad, in Waseca county, about eighteen miles from Mankato.

As at Mankato they stopped at different hotels, two staying at the Johnson house and two at the Farmers' Home. No one knew where the fifth slept, but on leaving the village on the Tuesday morning they halted some little distance out, and one, taking off his duster, rode back toward the village waving it over his head; he was followed in the maneuver by another when all four rode away. It is thought this was a signal for the fifth man, who, it is supposed, stopped at some house in the neighborhood.

Those who stopped at the Johnson house never made their appearance at the public table until all the rest of the boarders had finished their meals, and during their stay in the town they declined to admit a chambermaid to their room to arrange it. After their departure several packs of playing cards were found in their room torn up and thrown on the floor, and several handfuls of buttons of various sizes were scattered about, showing that the inmates had been indulging in a protracted game of poker. The girls who waited on them at table say they were quiet and polite and never made any trouble.

Cordova is the next place these "gay cavaliers" turn up, all five of them staying at the same hotel, three occupying one room and two another with a commercial traveler, W. W. Barlow of Delavan, Wisconsin, who described them as polite, jocose fellows. They talked considerably of cattle, and from their language and peculiar dialect, Mr. Barlow thought them to be cattle dealers from the south. They left the hotel at seven o'clock in the morning, politely raising their hats as they rode off. Cordova is about eighteen miles almost directly north from Janesville.

The next night, Wednesday, saw these five men housed at Millersburg, about twenty-four miles west and north of Cordova, in Rice County. They left here at an early hour on Tuesday morning and at about ten o'clock appeared in the streets of Northfield, which lies about eleven miles northwest of the latter village.

On the same Wednesday evening, four men who answered the description of some of the bandits stopped at a hotel in Cannon City. The landlord thinks they were Bob Younger, Bill Chadwell, and the two men who finally escaped. He says that the next morning, September 7, while three of the men were at breakfast, one retired to his room and remained a long time with the door locked. After all had departed, the chambermaid discovered a bloody shirt and a portion of a pair of drawers, one leg of the latter being torn off and carried away. The drawers were soiled with blood and matter such as would come from an old inflamed gun wound, and it was evident that the wearer had such a wound on one of his legs. This is considered evidence that the man arrested in Missouri, in October, and supposed to have been one of the James brothers was really him, but the alibi provided by that party appears to be sufficient to prove that it was not.

It will be seen by the foregoing that there were originally nine men engaged in the plot, which gives plausibility to the opinion held by many that the terrible tragedy that followed was the result of a plan conceived by some Minnesota desperadoes who engaged these desperate southern cutthroats to assist in it.

Northfield is a thriving pretty little village, situated pleasantly on both banks of the Cannon River just thirty-nine miles from St. Paul, in Rice County, on the St. Paul and Milwaukee railroad. A neat iron bridge unites the northwest and the southeast sides of the town, and just above the bridge is one of the finest mill races in the state, the water in its incessant flow roaring like the ocean and appearing like a miniature Niagara. There is a large flouring mill on either side of the river belonging to Messrs. Ames & Co. The public buildings are not surpassed in the state for their beauty of design and adaptability of construction, and Carleton College is another institution of which the town may well be proud. With the town placed as it is in the center of a rich farming district, the citizens are considered well-to-do, and the bank transacts a large business.

The five strangers appeared on the streets at an early hour of the morning of September 7 and attracted a great deal of notice from the citizens, some of them recognizing two of the men as a party who visited the village about a week before, stopping at the Dampier House.

At about eleven o'clock, two of these horsemen drew up at Jeft's restaurant on the northeast side of the river and asked for dinner. Jeft told them he had nothing ready but could cook them some eggs and ham. The men told him to do so, ordering four eggs each. Their horses were left standing untied at the back of the premises. After ordering their dinner, the two men went out into the street and after some time returned, when they were joined by three others and all sat down to their meal. They entered into familiar discourse with the proprietor of the house and asked him what was the prospect of the forthcoming presidential election. Jeft's reply was that he took no interest in politics, but one of the men offered to bet him $1,000 that the state would go Democratic. They still chatted on and seemed to be waiting for someone. At length they left and mounted their horses, which were a sorrel, a cream color with silver tail and mane, a black, a bay, and a brown, all fine animals, sleek and clean-limbed and showing indications of blood.

After leaving the restaurant, the five horsemen crossed over the bridge. Two remained in the bridge square, and the other three rode up to Division Street, dismounted, and tied their horses to the posts at the side of the Scriver block. They then sauntered up toward the bridge square and, after talking for some few moments leaning against a dry goods box in front of Lee & Hitchcock's store (Scriver block), walked back toward the bank, which they entered. Three other horsemen then came on the scene and commenced at once to ride up and down the street in dashing style, calling on the citizens who from their doors were watching the eccentric proceeding to get back into their houses. They then began firing pistols in the air with immense rapidity.

Greater confusion could not be imagined than now ensued. Wherever persons were seen on the street, a horseman would dash up to them in full speed and, pointing a long-barreled glittering pistol at their heads, order them to "get in, you G—d— son of a b—." The streets were cleared in a few moments, and stores were closed in quicker time than it takes to tell it.

Although they were taken at a disadvantage, when many of the men were out at work or away chicken hunting, the scare of the Northfield boys was but momentary. Collecting their perturbed thoughts, men rushed about in search of firearms, but this most necessary desideratum for a successful encounter with a body of desperadoes or madmen armed to the teeth was found to be very scarce on this eventful day.

Mr. J. B. Hide, however, succeeded in getting a shotgun with which he blazed away at the marauding scoundrels, or escaped lunatics, for it was not at first exactly understood what the fellows were. Mr. Manning, armed with a breech-loading rifle, came coolly on the field of action, backed by Mr. L. Stacey and Mr. Phillips, while Dr. Wheeler armed himself with an old breech-loading carbine and, placing himself in a room (No. 8) in the third story of the Dampier House, delivered two very effective shots.

The battle was now at its height, and firing was raging in downright earnest. Manning, from the front of the Scriver block, Bates from the clothing store of Mr. Hanauer, and Wheeler from the window directly over the clothing store, unobserved by the daring scoundrels, made it lively for the desperate gang and kept them from passing into Mill Square.

One of the gang was about mounting his horse, and while stooping over the pommel of his saddle with his back toward Wheeler, that gentleman took deliberate aim and fired.

The fellow pitched right over his horse, falling on his head to the earth where he lay gasping for a few moments and soon was everlastingly still.

Manning in the meantime was not idle, and while Wheeler was searching for another cartridge, he advanced from his retreat and, seeing a horseman riding toward him up Division Street, took a steady deliberate aim and fired. The man immediately turned his horse and started off a few rapid paces, but the horse steadied his pace, the man rocked to and fro, and suddenly the horse stopped and the man fell over to the ground. Then another horseman galloped up, sprang from his horse, turned the fallen man over, and took from him his pistols and belt. Then, springing again to his saddle, he rode up the street.

Another scoundrel alighted from his horse and, getting behind it, commenced a rapid fire down the street, seeing which the intrepid and cool Manning, with all the *nonchalance* in the world, raised his unerring rifle and stretched the living barricade lifeless at the bandit's feet. The enraged brigand then ran toward Manning, fearless of the formidable weapon of Bates. Sheltering himself behind some packing cases under the open stairway of Scriver block, he commenced a rapid fusillade, evidently with the intention of keeping Manning from firing up the street at others of the gang.

But Wheeler had succeeded in finding another cartridge and returned to the room from which he delivered his first shot. A young lady, who had remained at the window coolly watching the fight throughout, pointed out to Wheeler the man who was keeping Manning from effectual work.

"Only aim as true as you did before," said the brave girl, "and there will be one the less to fight," and Wheeler fired. Instantly the villain dropped his hand to his thigh, and the girl cried out, "Oh, you aimed too low," thinking the shot had taken effect in the middle third of the right thigh. Wheeler at once left the room in search of another cartridge, which unluckily he was unable to find. The wounded man who had changed his pistol to the left hand and discharged several shots at Manning now turned about and, seeing Bates inside his store with a pistol in his hand and thinking it was from this source he had received his wound, as quick as a lightning flash sent a deadly missive at the unsuspecting Bates.

The ball crashed through the intervening glass of the storefront and burnt a scorching track across the victim's face from ear to nose.

But during this time a bloody and terrible tragedy was being enacted in the bank.

A scene exhibiting a greater amount of reckless daring and brutal ferocity, of intrepid courage and heroic fortitude, ending in a most dastardly tragedy could not be imagined than the one in progress in the bank while the street fight already described was going on.

Just a few moments before the raiders commenced their wild career on the streets, three men rushed into the bank, holding in their hands large pistols, the glittering barrels of which they directed toward the three gentlemen, Mr. Heywood, Mr. Bunker, and Mr. Wilcox, who occupied the desks behind the counter. Springing over the counter, these desperadoes shouted out, "Throw up your hands. We intend to rob the bank."

"Which is the cashier?" one demanded and, instantly approaching Heywood, commanded him to open the safe.

"I am not the cashier" was the reply.

The man then turned to Bunker and made the same demand, but he also denied that he held that important post. The fellow next addressed the bewildered and fear-stricken Wilcox, whose terror prevented him from answering.

The baffled man again turned to Heywood and with oaths and threats endeavored to make him open the safe. When Heywood replied that he could not, the scoundrel fired a pistol close to his ear and said if he did not at once open the safe he would scatter his brains.

The brave Heywood still insisted on his inability to comply.

The ruffian then seized him by the collar and dragging him toward the safe, drew out a long, keen-edged knife, and, poising it over Heywood's throat, threatened to cut it from ear to ear if he did not at once open the safe.

But the brave man, faithful to his trust, stolidly refused, so the robber released his hold of his collar and went into the safe vault.

Now was the opportunity for the faithful Heywood.

"If I can but get that ponderous door closed," thought he, "and spring the bolts on the scoundrel, the villains will be baffled and my integrity saved from suspicion."

It was a supreme moment of dreadful anxiety to him, and such was the intense excitement of his feelings that when he rushed on the door to close it, his strength was unequal to the task, and before he could recover himself to renew the effort, a powerful hand seized him by the throat and threw him back from the vault. At the same time, a ruthless arm struck him to the ground with the butt end of a pistol.

Taking advantage of this struggle between Heywood and the robbers, Bunker sprang to his feet and bounded toward the back entrance of the premises.

But before he reached the door, a sharp report and the crashing of a ball showed him that he had only miraculously escaped from having his brains scattered by one of the bandits. Bounding out of the bank, he ran madly down Water Street, not, however, till another shot from the murderous revolver crunched through his shoulder.

At this point another of the band of ruffians hastily entered the bank and exclaimed, "Clear, boys. The game is up."

The three men instantly jumped on the counter and made tracks for the door.

But one man paused in his headlong retreat and, seeing Heywood reaching for his desk, turned round and, leveling his revolver at the devoted head of the faithful teller, fired. Without a groan, the brave man fell to the floor, his lifeblood staining the desk and seat with its crimson stream.

In the street the baffled and retreating murderers sought their horses, and, vaulting into their saddles, they were soon rushing with frantic haste out of town, heading westward.

It was some few moments before the citizens could sufficiently recover themselves to thoroughly take in the entire situation.

There lay in the open street a few paces from the bank entrance a bandit in all the hideous ghastliness of a bloody death. A few feet from him was stretched the lifeless body of a noble horse, while farther down the street on the opposite side another grim corpse lay in a pool of seething gore.

Windows in all directions were shattered, and door posts showed scars of embedded bullets.

Reluctantly, the assembled citizens approached the bank, and the sight that there met their horror-stricken gaze caused a thrill of indignation to seize on every nerve; strong men turned pale as they clenched their fists and set their teeth, registering an inward oath to wreak vengeance on the miscreant perpetrators of the dastardly outrage.

There lay poor Heywood, the man who dared death and defied three of the most notorious scoundrels who ever "cracked a crib" or broke a skull, who resisted torture and finally gave his lifeblood in defense of his trust. Who was the man to carry the appalling news to the young wife and tell her that he, on whom hung her very life, had left her for all time—that he had been torn from her and hurled into dread eternity by the ruthless hand of the bloody assassin!

Who was stout enough to bear the gore-covered, mangled corpse to the newly desolate and grief-stricken home!

But there were those who were willing to pursue the red-handed murderers.

Some, overcome with indignation, impetuously prepared for the chase, but others, perhaps more determined men, who were willing to follow on to the very death, were not so hasty in their departure but as time proved were prepared to pertinaciously follow up the trail with the tenacity of the bloodhound.

Two of the former, Davis and Hayes, immediately sought for horses, and none being so ready as those of the two dead robbers, seized them, sprang into the saddles, and were soon in hot pursuit.

Both men were well armed with rifles—one an eighteen-shot Winchester with globe sight. At every point they heard of the retreating villains on whom they were gaining rapidly. Dashing through Dundas, Hayes and Davis kept up the pursuit till at last they saw a group of horsemen surrounding a wagon from which they were apparently taking the horses. As the pursuers advanced, one of the horsemen turned from the wagon and, advancing a few steps up the road, ordered the pursuing men to halt.

Davis and Hayes instinctively obeyed, and, strange to relate, these two men who had been so impatient to commence the pursuit, now that they were confronted by the audacious scoundrels, found their courage waning, and they halted.

Nor did they again find their courage return, but they sat there and saw the marauders, after securing one of the farmer's horses, again boldly dash away.

After the robbers had gone, Davis and Hayes leisurely wended their way to Millersburg, where they awaited the coming of the other pursuers, two men standing but little chance against six such desperadoes.

It is true that Davis and Hayes had the advantage of the bandits in arms, but it is doubtful after all if there are many men to be found who would have done differently, confronted as they were by six stalwart fierce knights of the road, well-armed and unscrupulous in shedding human blood, as they had shown at Northfield.

After the departure of Davis and Hayes, about thirty citizens organized into a pursuing party, some mounted on horses, others carried in wagons and buggies, and all set out in full speed along the road the robbers had taken.

Meantime the telegraph was set at work, and messages were sent to all points. Unfortunately, the operator at Dundas was not in his office, and although the call was repeated for an hour, no response was made. Had this gentleman been at his post, the people of Dundas would have been prepared to receive the bandits on their arrival.

It has been expressed as a wonder by many that the gang, before making the raid, did not cut the telegraph wires, but it appears from the confession of one of them that their plan was a much better one. They intended to have destroyed the telegraph instruments before leaving, only the unexpectedly hot attack that was made on them by the plucky boys of Northfield completely demoralized them.

The first indication received at St. Paul of the daring raid was from the following telegram to Mayor Maxfield: "Eight armed men attacked the bank at two o'clock. Fight on street between robbers and citizens. Cashier killed and teller wounded. Send us arms and men to chase robbers. John T. Ames."

This telegram reached St. Paul at about three o'clock in the afternoon. The first train leaving the city for the scene of hostilities, at four o'clock, was the Owatonna Accommodation, on the Milwaukee and St. Paul road. From St. Paul were dispatched Chief of Police King, Detective Brissette, Officers Brosseau and Clark, and Deputy Sheriff Harrison. At Mendota Junction, the party was joined by Mr. Brackett and a posse of police, consisting of Captain Hoy, A. S. Munger, F. C. Shepherd, J. W. Hankinson, and J. West, of Minneapolis, all well-armed with seven shooters and rifles. At Rosemount, Farmington, and Castle Rock, the excitement was immense, many persons at these points getting on the cars and proceeding to Northfield.

The train arrived at the scene of the most daring crime ever perpetrated in the state at 6:20 p.m., the whole platform being crowded with an excited populace.

The police were at once led by the sheriff to an empty store where were lying the inanimate and ghastly forms of the two bandits who had been shot down by the intrepid Northfield citizens. One was found to be six feet four and a half inches in height; his body exhibited a splendid physical development, with arms and limbs of sinewy muscles and skin as fair and soft as a lady's; his face was of rather an elongated oval with sharply cut features; he had high cheek bones, well-arched brow, and deep-set blue eyes. His hair was a very dark reddish auburn, inclined to curl. He wore no hair on his face but was closely shaved and did not appear to be more than twenty-three or twenty-five years of age. He was clothed in a new suit of black clothes, worth about twenty-five or thirty dollars, a new colored shirt, and good boots.

The ball that brought him down entered about three inches in a line with the left nipple and toward the center of the chest and, completely riddling the man, passed out on the same side beneath the shoulder blade. On his person was found the card of the Nicollet House livery stable, St. Peter, on which is printed the distances of the principal cities in this part of the state. He had also on him an advertisement of Hall's safes cut from a local paper. His pockets were well filled with cartridges, and he had round his waist, beneath his coat, a cartridge belt. There has been some dispute as to the identity of the man, but it is now pretty well settled that he is Bill Chadwell *alias* Bill Styles.

There were two men from Cannon Falls who came to view the bodies before the interment with the expectation of identifying one of the latter as a brother-in-law of one of the two. He said if it was his relative, a bullet scar would be found under the left arm. The scar was there, but the man would not say whether the fellow was his relation or not. The man whom the big fellow was thought to be is a former resident of Minneapolis who has a brother-in-law still living there. This Styles left for Texas some time ago. It is said he was a desperately bad man. It is told that his sister received a letter from him a short time before, saying that now he had lucrative employment, and if she wanted money he would send her some. He also wrote in his letter that he would shortly be up this way and would call on her. This sister was adopted by a minister residing at Cannon Falls. A letter recently received from the father of Styles proves beyond doubt the identity of the man. Styles's father now lives at Grand Forks, D.T., and says that his son has for some time lived in Texas. The father expresses no surprise at the untimely end of his son and says he was always a wild, wayward boy with whom he could do nothing.

The other man was five feet eight inches in height but much stouter built than the taller, with hair of the exact color and, like his, inclined to curl. His face was rounder and covered with about two weeks' growth of beard; the eyes, like the other's, were blue.

The clothing was quite new, even to the shirt, which appeared to have been put on that day. He also wore a white linen collar (new) and a white linen handkerchief round his neck. On his feet were striped half hose and good boots but of different make, one boot being finer and lighter than the other.

Gold sleeve buttons, gold pin and gold or filled case watch and chain, with linen ulster duster and new felt hat of fine quality, "John Hancock" make, completed his costume.

Beneath his clothing he wore a money belt of leather, but it was empty. About a dollar and fifty cents had been taken from the two men, but Chief King, in researching this fellow, found four dollars more. The wound was an ugly, jagged bullet hole, very large, with the edges much torn, toward the center of the chest and about four inches below the heart. There were also several small shot wounds on the body of this one and three on the forehead; his hat was also riddled with shot, and it was evident that he had been hit twice from a shotgun, for several of the shot wounds were in the back. From photographs sent to the St. Louis police, the man was at once recognized as Clell Miller.

The empty store in which the two corpses lay is on Mill Square, which is immediately over on the south side of the handsome iron bridge that spans the Cannon River just below the mill race. On the north side of the square is the flouring mill of Ames & Co. On the west is Scriver's block and two or three small stores, among them that in which the bodies lay. On the east side is the office of the Rice County *Journal* and a wagon shop, and on the south is the Dampier House, under which are three stores, the last of which, eastward and just opposite the corner of the Scriver block, is the clothing store of Mr. Hanauer. The Scriver block has also a frontage of eighty feet on Division Street, twenty-two feet of which is occupied by the First National Bank of Northfield, in which one of the saddest and most daring tragedies was perpetrated—the heartless and deliberate murder of a faithful and brave man in the defense of the valuable property under his charge.

There are some four or five wooden buildings below the bank on Fourth Street, and it was in this narrow space, from Mill Square to Fourth Street, that the great fight that startled the whole country took place. Many indications of the fearful contest in bullet holes were found in every direction. Windows were pierced and shattered, and balls must have been thrown around for a time as thick as hail, for the whole encounter took place within the short space of fifteen minutes. The conflict was a sharp and bloody one, and it speaks volumes for the coolness and intrepidity of the citizens of the little provincial town.

From Mr. Bates, who took a prominent part in the encounter, the following was learned: He said at about eleven o'clock his attention was called to four men who came from over the river. They came over the bridge and were mounted on four splendid horses. The men were well-dressed, and Mr. Bates says four nobler-looking fellows he never saw; but there was a reckless, bold swagger about them that seemed to indicate that they would be rough and dangerous fellows to handle. Altogether he did not like the looks of them.

Again, at about two o'clock in the afternoon, as he was standing at the entrance of the store, talking to Mr. C. C. Waldo, commercial traveler from Council Bluffs, he saw the same men ride past—three came up the street from Mill Square and one down the street, meeting within thirty feet of the bank. They dismounted and tied their horses to the hitching posts. Two, he thought, went into the bank, and two came down to the staircase leading up into the upper stories of Lee & Hitchcock's buildings, and here they stood leaning against the banisters talking. Commenting on their fine physique, and on their unusually good mounts, Mr. Bates and Mr. Waldo withdrew to the far end of the store to look over some sample trusses.

They had not long been so occupied when they heard several shots fired in rapid succession, and the thought flashed in the mind of Bates at once that the bank was in danger. Mr. Waldo stated that he cried out, "Those men are going for the town. They mean to rob the bank." Mr. Bates, however, does not recollect saying anything, he became so excited. He remembers, though, rushing to the door and seeing some men riding up from the bank. They came riding toward him with long pistols in their hands and called out, "Get in there, you son of a b—."

Mr. Bates at once seized a shotgun and ran back to the door, but the gun would not go off. He then put down the gun and seized a fine seven shooter that was *not* loaded, and as the men came down again (they were riding to and fro, evidently intent on keeping people from going toward the bank), he, standing behind the doorjambs, called out, "Now I've got you," and pointed the empty pistol as if drawing a bead on them.

They turned their horses suddenly and fired at Mr. Bates, the ball crashing through the plate glass. There were other men at the bank firing down the street. The next he saw was Mr. J. S. Allen running down the street from the bank, and two shots were fired at him.

Mr. Manning, of Mill Square, whose store is adjoining the block in which the bank is, next came on the scene. He ran out of his store with a breech-loading repeating rifle and took a deliberate aim and fired from the corner. Mr. Bates called out, "Jump back now, or they'll get you."

Next Mr. J. B. Hide came up with a double-barreled shotgun and dis-charged the two barrels and retired to reload. Mr. Phillips also took a turn at the scoundrels, and L. Stacy delivered a cool, deliberate aim. Mr. Bates next heard a report over his head and saw one of the desperadoes fall from his horse. The horse made a faltering plunge forward and then suddenly stopped, and the man pitched over with his face to the ground and in a few moments was dead. This shot was fired by Henry Wheeler from an old carbine from out of one of the windows of the Dampier House.

Mr. Manning was still firing, and as he crept to the corner Mr. Waldo called out, "Take good aim before you fire."

Immediately after this shot, one of the horses started up the street, and the rider began to reel and swing to and fro and suddenly fell to the ground just opposite Eldridge's store. Another horseman immediately rode up, dismounted, and spoke to the prostrate man, who was stretched out at full length, supporting himself on his outstretched arms, when he rolled over on his back. Then the other man took from him his cartridge belt and two pistols and, remounting his horse, rode off.

Another horseman, finding Mr. Manning's fire too hot, dismounted from his horse and got on the opposite side of it for protection when an unerring ball from the breech loader brought the horse down, the man running behind some boxes that were piled beneath the staircase before mentioned, and now ensued a lively fusillade between this fellow and Manning, the scoundrel keeping himself well under cover, but a ball from Wheeler's musket struck the fellow in the leg, halfway above the knee.

He at once changed his pistol to the left hand and grasped the wounded limb with the right, still trying to get at Manning. Finding himself getting weak, he turned and limped off up the street, but, seeing Bates with a pistol in his hand, he sent a ball whizzing toward that gentleman, grazing the side of his cheek and the bridge of his nose and burying itself in a collar-box in the store.

Mr. Bates says he feels the ring of that ball in his ear still, and the ball, he says, he will ever keep as a souvenir of the hottest day Northfield ever saw.

The man limped away, and when he got opposite to Mr. Morris's store, he cried out to his retreating companions, "My God, boys, you are not going to leave—I am shot!"

One of the party, riding a sorrel horse with a light tail and mane, turned and took the wounded man up behind him.

Mr. Wilcox, the teller of the bank, stated that he, in company with Mr. Heywood and A. E. Bunker, were in the bank at about two o'clock when three well-dressed, powerful-looking men entered by the door, which was open. They held large revolvers in their hands, and one of them cried out, "Throw up your hands, for we intend to rob the bank, and if you halloo, we will blow your brains out."

They then asked which was the cashier, to which Mr. Heywood replied, "He is not in." They then sprang over the counter and demanded the safe to be opened. Addressing each in turn, they said, "You are the cashier," which each denied.

Seeing Heywood seated at the cashier's desk, one of the ruffians went up to him with his long, narrow-barreled pistol and said, "You are the cashier; now open the safe, you — — son of a b—."

Mr. Heywood said, "It is a time lock and cannot be opened now." One of the men then went into the vault, the door being open. Heywood at once sprang forward and closed the door of the vault, shutting the robber in, when another of the men seized Heywood by the collar, dragged him away from the door, and released the incarcerated robber.

The man who came out of the vault—a slim, dark-complexioned man with a black mustache—then called to the others to seize the silver that was lying loose (about fifteen dollars) and put it in the sack. They did not do this but seized about twelve dollars in scrip and put it into a two-bushel flour sack that they had with them. The dark-complexioned man, who appeared to be the leader, then again attacked Heywood, insisting on his opening the safe, threatening to cut his throat if he did not, and actually drawing a big knife across his throat.

The heroic and faithful teller, however, was not to be deterred from his duty and would rather sacrifice his life than betray his trust. Some few moments—it seemed ages to the bewildered and terror-stricken lookers-on—were spent in Heywood's struggling to break from the murderous villain and gain his liberty.

At length he broke away and, regaining his feet, ran toward the door crying, "Murder!"

The man at once struck him with a pistol and knocked him down and, dragging him to the safe door, commanded him to open it. But the intrepid clerk stolidly refused, so the villain shot at him but did not hit him.

Evidently the shot was intended rather to intimidate him than injure, but the scoundrel had reckoned without his host, for the effect was lost on Heywood.

But upon the discharge of the pistol, Bunker made a start for the back door and ran for dear life, one of the robbers pursuing and firing, the shot taking effect in the shoulder. Bunker, however, reached the street (Water Street) and ran to Dr. Coombs's office.

During the whole of this time, four or five men were riding up and down the street, shooting in every direction and keeping up an incessant fusillade.

One of the men outside came riding up furiously and called for the men to leave the bank. "The game's up," he said, "and we are beaten."

The three men in the bank then sprang over the counter and rushed to the door, and Heywood staggered to the chair, but, as the last one was getting over the counter, with one hand on the cashier's desk, he turned round and deliberately fired. Heywood fell senseless to the floor! The man then sprang on the rail and out at the front door, and he (Wilcox) cleared out of the back door into Manning's hardware store.

Wilcox was not sure whether the ruffian struck Heywood when the latter staggered to the cashier's chair, and he did not stop to see if he was dead when he fell. He said the reason he did not try to get out or help Heywood was that one of the men stood over him with a pistol in his hand.

Mr. Allen said he saw three men cross the bridge and go toward the bank. They were all big, powerful, well-dressed men. One had sandy side-whiskers, shaved chin, and blue eyes. Another wore a black mustache and was a slight but tall man and better dressed than the others. The third man was heavyset with curly brown hair and beard of about one week's growth. They had tied their horses and talked a while when another came up, and he went into the bank. Mr. Allen then waited half a minute, then walked up to the bank to see what was up.

"As I got to the back door," he says, "one man came out and grabbed me by the collar and said 'you son of a b—, don't holler,' drawing a revolver. I got out and made tracks as fast as I could, two shots being fired after me."

Mr. Ben Henry says that he was first attracted to the strangers by seeing the horses tied, and he went up to one and was examining the saddle when one of the men came up and said, "What are you doing here?"

"Looking at this saddle" was the reply. "I want an article like that and thought perhaps I could strike a bargain with the owner."

Drawing a pistol, the fellow cried out, "Now you git!" And he *did* "git," but as he walked away a bullet came hissing by his head and struck a wall close by. Henry deliberately picked up the ball and put it in his pocket but made long strides for home.

It appeared that the object of the men on the street was at first only to keep people back from the bank and not a desire to murder indiscriminately, but when they found that the Northfield people would not scare worth a cent and that real work was before them, they showed all the savage bloodthirsty propensity of their nature, and wherever a face showed itself, whether it was man, woman, or child, the robbers fired murderously at it, crashing in windows in a lively style.

Early Friday morning it was reported in Northfield that Brissette and Hoy had joined their forces at Morristown and had a hot encounter with the gang, which had been reinforced by three others. The police succeeded in killing one man and capturing the wounded man carried from Northfield. The robbers then took to the woods, and the police held them there. This report was proved at a later date to be a complete fabrication, but so excited were the people that every rumor received credence and grew in dimensions as it was handed round by the busy throng of news seekers.

The bank is in a small apartment, about twenty by fifty feet, situated in the Scriver block, folding doors in the center of the front opening into Division Street. It has a counter three feet high, running across to within three feet of the west wall and going back the whole length of the building. This counter is mounted by a thirty-inch glazed rail, leaving a space of two feet in front, where the men jumped over, scratching the counter with their boots. Inside of the center is the safe vault fitted with the Detroit Safe Company's doors, and to the left is the cashier's chair where poor Heywood fell victim to the assassin's hand. A blotting pad lay on the desk stained with the lifeblood of the murdered man.

Poor Heywood was shot through the head, the ball entering at the right temple and passing downward and inward, scattering his brains all about and doubtless depriving him instantaneously of consciousness and putting him completely beyond all suffering, although he breathed for about twenty minutes but did not speak. In addition to the bullet wound, there was a slight scratch on the right side of the neck as from a knife.

Mr. E. E. Bunker was not considered dangerously wounded, the ball passing in at the back of the right shoulder, below the point of the shoulder, passing downward and forward and upward, coming out just above the clavicle, making only a severe flesh wound. This wound, however, was very nearly a fatal one, as the ball passed close to a principal artery, which no doubt, had it been severed by the deadly missive, would have produced death by hemorrhage.

Since the capture at Madelia of the Younger boys, Mr. Bunker has given his recollections of the bank raid, and as it differs in several points from others already given, we embody it in this narrative. It will be seen that the narrative recognizes two of the men who entered the bank as Charley Pitts and Bob Younger.

Mr. Bunker said that himself, Mr. Heywood, and Mr. Wilcox were sitting at their respective desks when they heard a heavy rush from the bank door to the counter. They turned round and saw three men climbing over the counter, with their knees on it and revolvers pointed directly at the three bank officers. A man presumed to be Jesse James, who acted as leader, called out, "Throw up your hands. We are going to rob the bank." James then ran across the room and passed Heywood into the vault, which was open, but seeing the safe door closed, turned back from the entrance and seizing by the collar Heywood, who, from being older than the others and from the position of his desk, was naturally supposed to be the cashier, ordered him to open the safe. Mr. Heywood said it was a time lock, and it could not be opened. The other said that was a damned lie.

Charley Pitts then came up on the other side of Heywood and threatened to kill him if he did not immediately open the safe. One of the others called out, "Let's cut his throat and be done with it." Heywood commenced shouting "murder" and repeated the cry three or four times. They then hustled him about, and James struck him on the head with the butt end of his pistol, knocking him down. He was then dragged toward the vault, where he lay with his head partially in the vault. James then drew the knife across Heywood's neck, who did not say anything, appearing to be partially insensible, when another of them stooped down and fired close to the prostrate man's head, the ball penetrating a tin box containing papers in the vault.

All this time I was on my knees on the floor, with Bob Younger standing guard over me. I had a revolver under the counter, where I stand, which was in full view, and I endeavored gradually to edge over and obtain possession of it, but Bob saw the attempt and, seeing the weapon, put it into his pocket, saying, at the same time, that I could do nothing with this, and it was of no use. He then placed it in his pocket and commenced searching me but did not take anything from me. The pistol was a Smith & Wesson, and we always regarded it as an excellent weapon. Bob turned his head partially around to see what was going on in the other part of the room. I raised my head with the view of giving the alarm to anyone I saw in the street, but my movements were quickly observed by Bob, who pulled me down, saying at the same time that I had better keep quiet, for if I attempted to rise again he would kill me. He then inquired where was the cashier's till, and I pointed to a box containing some nickels and scrip, the former done up in cartridges. He seemed to know very well there was more loose money than that, and he told me he would kill me if I did not show him the till. I did not answer him, and he pulled out a drawer containing stationery, but the drawer having some $2,000 he did not open, supposing, probably, that its contents were the same.

Meantime, while the two men were engaged with Heywood, James told Bob Younger to bring out the sack. Bob took out a green bag and thrust a handful of scrip into it but did not take any of the nickels.

The distance from where I was to the rear of the bank is about twenty-five feet, and the rear door of the two hardware stores adjoin the rear door of the bank. I thought if I could make my way out in this direction, I would have a chance of giving the alarm so that the citizens would come to the rescue. In making this movement, I should have to pass where Mr. Wilcox was sitting, and I made a slight motion for him to move so that I could get past. He saw my motion and shifted his position. The man who stood over me having his attention directed to the proceedings of the others, I started but was immediately followed by Charley Pitts, who fired at me, the ball going through the blinds of the door and lodging in a brick chimney but not striking me. There was a stairway leading down, and Pitts, standing on top of that, fired down on me, I having reached the bottom at the time, then fired again, the ball just striking me below the scapula, passing through the thin portion of it and down, passing out about half an inch below the collar bone, the course traversed being about seven inches, and narrowly missing the subclavian artery, where the wound would have been fatal.

I think it was James that said, while keeping us down, "Don't one of you move; we have fifty men on the street, and you will be killed if you move." The safe was not locked at all, but there was only about $15,000 in it, which they might easily have secured.

Mr. Bunker said he recognized the body killed at Madelia as that of Charley Pitts and also identified Bob Younger by the likeness published herein.

Several citizens of Northfield narrowly escaped with their lives during the encounter. A Norwegian, Nicholas Gustavson by name, was struck with a bullet at the right side of the head, just at the ear, the ball running under the scalp and out at the top of his head. He says when he was struck, and for several minutes after, his whole left side was paralyzed. But after a few minutes of unconsciousness, he was able to reach his boarding house, but the next day he was unable to rise from his bed. It was evident that the skull was fractured and depressing the right lobe of the brain, and if the patient was not opportunely relieved by trepanning the skull, the man must succumb. Subsequent events proved the correctness of this view, for the operation was not performed, and the poor fellow expired on the eleventh—four days after the dreadful tragedy, thus adding another victim to rekindle the fire of indignation in men's minds.

Illustrative of the dangerous nature of the weapons that the lawless ruffians carried, it should have been stated that balls fired from one side of Mill Square struck and completely riddled buildings on the other side of the square, a distance of one hundred and fifty yards.

Friday afternoon the coroner, Dr. Waugh, from Faribault, held an inquest on the bodies of the two scoundrels who met with such a richly deserved end, and the following gentlemen were sworn as a jury: A. H. Rawson, S. L. Bushnell, R. Silk, J. L. McFee, R. Plummer, and C. W. Gross. The jury were not long in arriving at the following verdict: "That the two unknown men came to their deaths by the discharge of firearms in the hands of our citizens in self-defense and in protecting the property of the First National Bank of Northfield."

The same jury, with the coroner, held an inquest over the remains of the lamented victim of the raid. The witnesses who gave evidence were E. Hobbs, ex-policeman J. S. Allen, F. Wilcox, and E. L. Fuller, whose statements were similar to those the same gentlemen made to the writer and recorded elsewhere in these pages. The verdict found was this: "That J. H. Heywood came to his death by a pistol shot fired by an unknown man attempting to rob the First National Bank of Northfield."

The grand jury that had been summoned included twenty-two of the best men in the county, but the prisoner's counsel reduced it to seventeen by challenging a number who had too freely expressed their ideas in regard to the affair. There is no doubt but that by continuing the same line of questioning the grand jury could have all been found wanting, but it was not the intention of the defense to delay the trial by reducing the number below the legal minimum but simply to refer the bills to as few men as possible, feeling that the chance of their finding all the indictments could be materially lessened.

It took the jury but a very short time after they commenced their work to find four true bills against the prisoners, and the evidence given by the witnesses that testified before them was but a recapitulation of what they were entirely familiar with. In the case of the Swede, whom Cole Younger was charged with killing, evidence was given by a man and a woman, both of whom testified that they saw Cole shoot him coolly and deliberately.

On the day after the court convened, the sister and an aunt of the Younger boys arrived in Faribault. The sister, Miss Henrietta Younger, is a very pretty, prepossessing young lady of about seventeen years, and she conducted herself so as to win the esteem of all who met her. Mrs. Fanny Twyman, their aunt, is the wife of a highly respectable physician practicing in Missouri and appears to be a lady of the highest moral character. These ladies passed the greater portion of their time sitting with their relatives, behind the iron bars, reading, talking, and sewing. On Thursday, November 9, the grand jury signified that they had completed their labors as far as the cases of the Younger boys were concerned, and the sheriff was instructed to bring the prisoners to hear the indictments read.

This summons had been expected, and the boys were ready, dressed neatly, and looking wonderfully well after their unaccustomed confinement that had continued for more than a month. They quietly stood up in a row ready to be shackled together. Cole in the middle, Bob at the right, and Jim at the left. The shackles were placed on their feet, Bob being secured by one foot to Cole and Jim by the other. When the handcuffs were placed on Cole, he remarked that it was the first time he had ever worn them. The prisoners showed signs of nervousness, evidently fearing that the crowd outside would think it best to dispose of them without due process of law. However, nothing occurred except some almost inaudible mutterings among the spectators, which were quickly quieted by right-minded citizens. Slowly the procession passed to the temple of justice, the prisoners seeing the sun and breathing the pure air for the first time in thirty days. In advance of them was an armed guard led by the captain of the minutemen, then came the sheriff by the side of his prisoners, the chief of police of Faribault and his lieutenant, and finally another squad of minutemen with their needle guns. On reaching the courthouse, the guards broke to the right and left and allowed none to enter except those known to their captain.

The cortege passed to the courtroom by a rear stairway, and when the prisoners arrived in front of the judge, the courtroom was thoroughly filled with people, all gazing with the greatest curiosity on the three bloody brothers.

The shackles having been removed from the arms and legs of the prisoners, they were ordered to stand up while the indictment charging them with killing Heywood was read to them by the county attorney. As their names were read, the judge asked them if they were indicted by their true names, to which all responded in the affirmative. During the reading, Cole Younger never moved his sharp eye from the face of the attorney; in fact, his gaze was so intense that Mr. Baxter appeared to feel it and to be made somewhat nervous thereby. Bob did not appear to take great interest in the matter, and he gazed coolly about on the crowd.

The sister and aunt of the boys were by their sides during this scene, and they walked with them as they returned to the jail under the same guard that escorted them forth. Until the following Saturday had been taken by the prisoners' counsel to plead to the indictment, and during the interval of three days the subject of how to plead was discussed for many hours. Bob was as independent as ever and declared he would not plead guilty, but the persuasions of sister and aunt finally prevailed, and when taken into court on Saturday in the same manner as before, each responded "guilty" when the question was asked by the clerk. Judge Lord then, without preface or remark, sentenced each to be confined in the state prison, at Stillwater, at hard labor, for the term of his natural life.

After the dread words had been uttered, the sister broke down and fell sobbing and moaning on the breast of her brother Cole.

Thus these bloody bandits escaped the gallows where their many crimes should have been expiated, and in a few days from the time they were sentenced, they were on their way to Stillwater, under a strong guard, but no attempt was made to molest them, although large crowds were collected at each station on the railroads by which they traveled. Sheriff Barton knew well the citizens of his state, and he had no fear that he would be interfered with while discharging his duty. The bandits were accompanied to their final home in this world by their faithful relatives, who left them within the prison walls, taking away as mementoes the clothes that the wicked men had worn. The robbers were immediately set at work painting pails, a labor that called for no dangerous tools to prosecute, and a special guard was set on the renowned villains, as it is not intended that they shall escape to again terrify the world by their wicked deeds.

TEN

Lizzie Borden Took an Ax

Edwin H. Porter

An original look at a notorious crime that shocked the nation.

WHEN THE ASSASSINATION OF ANDREW J. BORDEN AND ABBIE D. BORden, his wife, was announced, not only the people of Fall River and of Massachusetts but the public throughout the country manifested the deepest interest in the affair. The murders soon became the theme of universal comment, both in public and private, and every newspaper reference to the affair was read with eagerness, digested and commented on in a manner unprecedented. The crimes stand out in bold relief as the most atrocious and, at the same time, the most mystifying that the American public had ever before been called on to discuss. The crimes had about them that fascination of uncertainty, horrible though they were, that fixes the attention and holds it continually. Miss Lizzie A. Borden, a daughter of the murdered man, was arrested and charged with the killing. She was a young woman of hitherto spotless reputation and character, and more than that she was educated, refined, and prominently connected with the work of the Christian church in Fall River. Her arrest added more and more to the interest that the public had taken in the matter. She was tried before the Superior Court of Massachusetts and a jury of her peers and found not guilty of the crimes. This event settled beyond question the probability of her guilt, and yet the case lost none of its absorbing interest.

⁓

At high noon on Thursday, August 4, 1892, the cry of murder swept through the city of Fall River like a typhoon on the smooth surface of an eastern sea. It was caught up by a thousand tongues and repeated at every street corner until it reached the utmost confines of the municipality. A double murder, the most atrocious of crimes, committed under the very glare of the midday sun within three minutes' walk of City Hall was the way the story went, and it was true in every particular. Andrew J. Borden and his wife, Abbie D. Borden, had been assassinated in their home at 92 Second Street. The manner in which the deed was done seemed so brutal, so mysterious, and the tragedy itself so unprecedented that people stared with open-mouthed amazement as they listened to the story passing from tongue to tongue. In the excitement of the moment, the murderer had slipped away unobserved, and bloody as his crime had been, he left no trace behind nor clue to his identity. He had wielded an ax or some similar instrument with the skill of a headsman and had butchered in the most horrible manner the bodies of his defenseless victims.

When discovered, the remains of Mr. Borden lay stretched at full length on the sofa in the sitting room of his home, the head literally hacked into fragments and the fresh blood trickling from every wound. Upstairs in the guest chamber lay the body of Mrs. Borden, similarly mangled and butchered with the head reeking in a crimson pool. She had been murdered while in the act of making the bed, and her husband had died as he lay taking his morning nap.

In the house was Miss Lizzie A. Borden, youngest daughter of the slain couple, and Bridget Sullivan, the only servant. They and they alone had been within calling distance of the victims as the fiend or fiends struck the fatal blows. The servant was in the attic, and the daughter was in the barn not more than thirty feet from the back door of the house. This was the condition of things on the premises when the cry went forth that shocked the city and startled the entire country. Neighbors, friends, physicians, police officers, and newspaper reporters gathered at the scene in an incredibly short space of time.

It was soon learned that the daughter Lizzie had been the first to make the horrible discovery. She said that not many minutes before, she had spoken to her father upon his return from the city and that after seeing him comfortably seated on the sofa she had gone out to the barn to remain a very short time. Upon returning she saw his dead body and gave the alarm that brought the servant from the attic. Without thinking of Mrs. Borden, the daughter sent Bridget for help. Mrs. Adelaide B. Churchill, the nearest neighbor; Dr. S. W. Bowen; and Miss Alice Russell were among the first to respond.

Shortly afterward the dead body of Mrs. Borden was discovered, and the unparalleled monstrosity of the crime became apparent. There had been murder most foul, and so far as the developments of the moment indicated, without a motive or a cause. The street in front of the house soon became blocked with a surging mass of humanity, and the excitement grew more and more intense as the meager details of the assassination were learned. Men with blanched faces hurried back and forth through the yard, police officers stood in groups for a moment and talked mysteriously, physicians consulted among themselves, and kind friends ministered to the bereaved daughter and offered her consolation.

Inside the house where the bodies lay, the rooms were in perfect order. Mrs. Borden had smoothed out the last fold in the snow-white counterpane and placed the pillows on the bed with the utmost care of a tidy housewife. Every piece of furniture stood in its accustomed place, and every book and paper was laid away with rigid exactness. Only the blood as it had dashed in isolated spots against the walls and doorjambs, and the reeking bodies themselves, showed that death in its most violent form had stalked through the unpretentious home and left nothing but its bloody work to tell the tale. No one dared go so far as to suggest a motive for the crime.

The house had not been robbed, and the friends of the dead had never heard of such a thing as an enemy possessed of hatred enough to commit so monstrous a deed. As the hours passed, a veil of deepest mystery closed around the scene, and the most strenuous efforts of the authorities to clear the mystery away seemed more and more futile as their work progressed.

Men with cool heads, and with cunning and experience, sought in vain to unearth some facts to indicate who the criminal might be, but their skill was unavailing, and they were baffled at every turn. The author of that hideous slaughter had come and gone as gently as the south wind but had fulfilled his mission as terrifically as a cyclone. No more cunning plan had ever been hatched in a madman's brain, and no more thorough work was ever done by the guillotine.

Mr. Borden and his wife, highly respected residents, were spending their declining years with wealth enough to enjoy all the comforts and luxuries of modern life. Mr. Borden, by years of genuine New England thrift and energy, had gathered a fortune, and his exemplary life had served to add credit to the family name, which had been identified with the development and prosperity of his native state for two hundred years and which has been known to public and private life since the time of William the Conqueror.

His family had the *open sesame* to the best society. The contentment that wealth, influence, and high social standing could bring was possible for his family, if its members chose to have it. But he and his wife had been murdered, and there was no one who cared to come forward and explain why death had so ruthlessly overtaken them. One thing was manifest; an iron will and a heart of flint had directed the arm that struck those unoffending people down in a manner exceeding the savage cruelty of the most bloodthirsty creature—man or beast. The police officers invaded the house and searched in vain for some evidence to assist them in hunting down the murderer. They learned nothing tangible, but they laid the foundation for their future work by carefully scrutinizing the home and its surroundings as well as the bodies. A hint was sent out that a mysterious man had been seen on the doorstep arguing with Mr. Borden only a few days before. Had *he* done the deed? To those who stopped to contemplate the circumstances surrounding the double murder, it was marvelous to reflect how fortune had favored the assassin. Not once in a million times would fate have paved such a way for him. He had to deal with a family of six persons in an unpretentious two-and-a-half-story house, the rooms of which were all connected and in which it would have been a difficult matter to stifle sound. He must catch Mr. Borden alone and either asleep or off his guard and kill him with one fell blow. The faintest outcry would have sounded an alarm.

He must also encounter Mrs. Borden alone and fell her, a heavy woman, noiselessly. To do this he must either make his way from the sitting room on the ground floor to the spare bedroom above the parlor and avoid five persons in the passage, or he must conceal himself in one of the rooms upstairs and make the descent under the same conditions. The murdered woman must not lisp a syllable at the first attack, and her fall must not attract attention. He must then conceal the dripping implement of death and depart in broad daylight by a much-frequented street.

In order to accomplish this, he must take a time when Miss Emma L. Borden, the elder daughter of the murdered man, was on a visit to relatives out of the city; Miss Lizzie A. Borden, the other daughter, must be in the barn and remain there twenty minutes. Less time than that would not suffice. Bridget Sullivan, the servant, must be in the attic asleep on her own bed. Her presence in the pantry or kitchen or any room on the first or second floors would have frustrated the fiend's designs, unless he also killed her so that she would die without a murmur.

In making his escape, there must be no bloodstains on his clothing, for such tell-tale marks might have betrayed him. And so, if the assailant of the aged couple was not familiar with the premises, his luck favored him exactly as described. He made no false move. He could not have proceeded more swiftly nor surely had he lived in the modest edifice for years. At the most he had just twenty minutes in which to complete his work. He must go into the house after Miss Lizzie entered the barn, and he must disappear before she returned. More than that, the sixth member of the family, John V. Morse, must vanish from the house while the work was being done. He could not have been counted on by any criminal, however shrewd, who had planned the tragedy ahead. Mr. Morse came and went at the Borden homestead. He was not engaged in business in Fall River, and there were no stated times when the wretch who did the slaughtering could depend on his absence. Mr. Morse must not loiter about the house or yard after breakfast as was his custom; he must take a car to some other part of the city, and he must not return until his host and hostess have been stretched lifeless. The slightest hitch in these conditions and the murderer would have been balked or detected red-handed on the spot.

Had Miss Emma remained at home, she would have been a stumbling block; had Miss Lizzie left the stable a few moments earlier, she would have seen the murderer as he ran out the side door; had Bridget Sullivan shortened her nap and descended the stairs, she would have heard her mistress drop as the ax fell on her head; had Mr. Morse cut short his visit to friends by as much as ten minutes, the butcher would have dashed into his arms as he ran out at the front gate; had Mr. Borden returned earlier from his morning visit to the post office, he would have caught the assassin murdering his aged wife, or had he uttered a scream at the time he himself was cut down, at least two persons would have rushed to his assistance.

It was a wonderful chain of circumstances that conspired to clear the way for the murderer—so wonderful that its links baffled men's understanding.

City marshal Rufus B. Hilliard received the first intimation that a murder had been committed by telephone message. He was sitting in his office at the Central Police Station when John Cunningham entered a store half a block from the Borden house and gave notice of the affair. He immediately sent officer George Allen to the scene and then by signal informed each member of his force who was on duty at the time. This was at 11:15 in the morning.

Officer Allen was the first policeman to visit the house, and he saw the horribly mutilated body of Mr. Borden as it lay on the sofa. One glance was sufficient to cause the policeman to stand almost rooted to the floor, for he had come unprepared to witness such a sight. Without delay he hurried to the marshal's office and made a personal report of what he had seen.

Almost all the night patrolmen and many of the day men were absent from the city on the day of the killing, on the annual excursion of the Fall River Police Association to Rocky Point, a shore resort near Providence, Rhode Island, and this unusual condition served greatly to handicap the efforts of Marshal Hilliard in his attempt to get possession of a tangible clue to the perpetration of the crimes. The city was but poorly protected by members of the day force, who were doing double duty.

However, within half an hour after the general alarm had been sent out, a half dozen officers from the central part of the city had arrived at the Borden house. They were instructed to make a careful search of the premises. Officer Allen, before he returned to the police station, had stationed Charles S. Sawyer at the door on the north side of the house and had instructed him to allow no one except policemen and physicians to enter the building.

The Borden house, a plain two-and-a-half-story frame structure, stands on the east side of Second Street and is numbered 92. It is but one block away from the main thoroughfare of the busy city of Fall River. Hundreds of vehicles and numberless people pass and repass before the building daily, and yet no person could be found who saw a suspicious move or heard an unaccustomed sound on that fatal forenoon, until Miss Lizzie told how she had called Mrs. Churchill and informed her that a murder had been committed. Mrs. Churchill had been to market and was returning home at about eleven o'clock. She saw Bridget Sullivan, who was also familiarly called "Maggie," running across the street to the residence of Dr. S. W. Bowen, the family physician.

The girl told her that "something awful" had happened, and then Mrs. Churchill went into her own house and in a very short time appeared at the kitchen window, which commands a view of the side door of the Borden residence. She saw Miss Lizzie sitting on the back doorstep with her face buried in her hands and seemingly in great distress. Mrs. Churchill crossed the yard and offered Miss Lizzie a few words of consolation.

Bridget Sullivan, the only living person who admits that she was in the house at the time of the killing, was the first to give the alarm by notifying Mrs. Dr. Bowen. Bridget was in her own room in the attic, where she had gone to wash the windows, and after completing the work had lain down on the bed to rest. While there she heard Miss Lizzie call and from the tone of her voice knew that something was wrong. Bridget came down quickly, and Miss Lizzie said to her, "Father is dead. Go for Dr. Bowen." Bridget obeyed. The physician was not at home, and she returned. Then Miss Lizzie sent her for Miss Alice Russell, who lived two blocks away and who was an intimate friend of the family. Briefly this is what had taken place before the arrival of Officer Allen; and up to that time, no one except the assassin knew that the body of Mrs. Abbie D. Borden lay weltering in its own blood in the guest chamber on the second floor. To those who early visited the house, the vision of Mr. Borden's body as it lay on the sofa, with the lifeblood still warm and flowing from a dozen gaping wounds, was a horror so dreadful that they had no thought of Mrs. Borden. It remained for the neighbor, Mrs. Churchill, and the servant, Bridget, to make this awful discovery.

Bridget was unwilling to go alone in search of Mrs. Borden, so Mrs. Churchill volunteered to bear her company. The two women passed through the front hall and ascended the stairs in the front entry. Reaching a landing halfway up, where their eyes were on a level with the floor, they looked across the hall, through an open door, under the bed, and saw the prostrate form of the dead woman. It lay full on the face, and the arms were folded underneath. Mrs. Churchill turned and retraced her steps to the kitchen. She sighed audibly as she took a chair, and Miss Russell said to her, "What, another?" The reply was, "Yes, Mrs. Borden is killed too." Bridget had followed her back to the kitchen.

The medical examiner arrived at 11:45 and encountered Dr. Bowen and Bridget on his way into the sitting room. He then made a hasty view of the bodies and the house and commenced immediately to make preparations for holding an autopsy.

John Vinnicum Morse, brother of Andrew J. Borden's first wife and uncle of Misses Lizzie and Emma, arrived at the house shortly before noon. He entered the north gate and went directly to a pear tree in the backyard, where he ate two pears and then returned to the side door and entered; then Miss Lizzie told him that Mr. and Mrs. Borden had been murdered. Mr. Morse had slept in the guest chamber, where Mrs. Borden's body was found, on the previous night and had, after eating his breakfast that morning, left the house to visit a relative who resided on Weybosset Street in Fall River, about a mile from the Borden house. It was remembered that Mr. Borden fastened the screen on the side door after Mr. Morse passed out at 9:20 in the morning and bade his guest return in time for dinner.

Miss Lizzie sat at the foot of the back stairs and near the side door when Mrs. Churchill arrived. She had called her neighbor and informed her that Mr. Borden had been "stabbed or killed." Then she went into the kitchen and remained a few minutes. Here she was seen by a number of policemen, physicians, and others who had been admitted to the house before noon. She told Mrs. Churchill that she had been absent from the sitting room a few minutes and that she spent the time in the barn, where she had gone to get a piece of iron.

So confused was the servant girl that she could tell no coherent story of the condition of things about the house during the forenoon. She did say that during the morning, Mrs. Borden had instructed her to wash the windows from the outside of the house. This she had done. After receiving this order from her mistress, Bridget did not see her alive again. She finished her work before ten o'clock and while in the sitting room heard

Mr. Borden trying to get in at the front door. He had returned from the city. She opened the front door and let Mr. Borden in and then went upstairs. This was the last she saw of him until Miss Lizzie called her when the body was found.

When the police officers arrived, they began to search the house for the weapon, and Bridget showed them into the cellar. Here they found four hatchets, one of which had the appearance of having been washed after recent use. At this time little attention was paid to this particular hatchet, but all the hatchets were taken to the police station.

Shortly after twelve o'clock, special officer Philip Harrington arrived at the house, as had other policemen. He joined in the search for evidence that would lead to the arrest of the murderer or to the discovery of the weapon. After viewing the bodies, he went to Miss Lizzie, who was in her own room talking with Miss Alice Russell. He asked her if she knew anything about the crime, and she replied, "No." It was then that she detailed to him the story of her visit to the barn, and he cautioned her to be careful and to give him all the information in her possession.

"Perhaps tomorrow," said the officer, "you will have a clearer frame of mind."

"No, sir," responded Miss Lizzie with a gentle courtesy. "I can tell you all I know now just as well as at any other time."

The conversation was prolonged, and during the entire time Miss Lizzie controlled her emotions wonderfully for a young lady who had so recently been called on to witness the blood of her father and stepmother flowing from dozens of hideous wounds. When the officer left her, he went to the city marshal and related his experience. The public was not informed that then and there suspicions were aroused in the minds of the police that the daughter knew more of the circumstances of the tragedy than she cared to tell, but nevertheless this was true.

All through that eventful day, the police searched the house, cellar, yard, and barn but found nothing to confirm any suspicions that they might have entertained as to who was guilty of the crimes.

Investigators found the house in perfect order. The front and cellar doors were locked, and every window sash was down. Even the victims as they lay showed no signs of a struggle, and the blood that spurted as the weapon fell had not bespattered the rooms and furniture as it generally does under circumstances such as these that surrounded the butchery of the Bordens. They found two persons in the house living and two dead, and the living could throw no light on the darkness that clouded the stark forms of the dead.

Medical Examiner Dolan and a corps of physicians held an autopsy on the bodies in the afternoon and found that thirteen blows had rained down on the head of the unsuspecting Mr. Borden and that no fewer than eighteen had descended on the skull of Mrs. Borden. The cuts were deep and long, and any one of them would have produced instant death.

This was the baffling condition of things that beset Marshal Hilliard and his officers after the scene had been hurriedly gone over. Out of this chaos of bloody crime and bewildering uncertainty, the police were expected to bring light and order. It was a herculean task, yet they went to work with an energy prompted by duty and spurred to greater efforts by the public demand that justice overtake the author of the foul deeds.

On the afternoon following the massacre, Medical Examiner Dolan and his associates conducted the autopsies. The bodies had been removed to the sitting room. The physicians found thirteen wounds on the head of Mr. Borden, which were clean cut and evidently made by some very sharp instrument. The largest was four and a half inches long and two inches wide. Many of them penetrated the skull, and one severed the eyeball and jaw bone. Mrs. Borden's body was even more severely dealt with. The head was chopped into ribbons of flesh and the skull broken in several places. A deep wound was discovered between the shoulder blades and had the appearance of having been made by a hatchet, the blade penetrating fully three inches deep.

The pool of blood in which Mrs. Borden's head lay was coagulated, while the life-giving element of Mr. Borden's body was fresh and oozing from the wounds. It was evident that the woman had been dead two hours before the assassin slaughtered the old man. The autopsy was partially finished and the bodies delivered into the hands of undertaker Winward, who prepared them for burial.

The police were more than ever active during the afternoon. City Marshal Hilliard and State Detective George Seaver of Taunton visited the house, made personal inquiry of the inmates, and viewed the bodies and their surroundings. The search for evidence was continued until night with little or no satisfactory result, so far as the public knew.

Dr. Bowen would recall, "Members of the family had been sick recently. Mrs. Borden came to me Wednesday morning and said that she was very much frightened, for she thought she had been poisoned. She and Mr. Borden had vomited all night, and she feared the poison had been from the baker's bread or the milk. Miss Lizzie and Bridget had been sick with the same symptoms, and it was their belief that an enemy had attempted to kill the whole family."

The police, upon investigation, found that Dr. Bowen's story that the Bordens had been ill was true in every particular, and they naturally went to work in order to find, if possible, the person who administered the poison. Special officers Harrington and Doherty were assigned to this task, and before midnight they had made a startling discovery—so astounding, in fact, that they hardly believed their senses. They started out late in the afternoon to visit the various drugstores of the city and to make inquiry as to who bought or offered to buy poison. They worked without success until they came to D. R. Smith's pharmacy, at the corner of South Main and Columbia Streets. Eli Bence, the clerk, informed them that on Wednesday before the murder, a young woman had come into his store and asked to buy a small bottle of hydrocyanic acid.

Suspicions are cruel, and, if unfounded, they burn like hot iron; but in a murder mystery, where every link may strengthen the chain, they rise up at a thousand points and cannot be ignored. She wanted poison to kill the moths that were eating her sealskin cloak. If a person wished to kill and avoid detection, and that person were wise, hydrocyanic acid would be first choice among all deadly drugs. It is a diluted form of prussic acid, and it does its work surely. It is not necessary to use it in bulk; homeopathic doses are all sufficient. It is absorbed by the nervous system and leaves no traces, and it produces none of the premortem symptoms peculiar to most violent poisons. There is no vomiting, no spasm or convulsions, no contraction of the muscles—hydrocyanic acid simply takes hold of the heart and stops its beating. It may not have been used in this case, and at this time the detectives did not claim that it was. Mr. Bence told the young woman that he did not sell so deadly a poison except on a doctor's certificate, and she went away empty-handed.

This woman Mr. Bence and others positively identified as Miss Lizzie Borden.

When the clerk told his story to the officers, they took him to the Borden house. This was about ten o'clock on the night following the murder. He was placed in a position to see Miss Lizzie, and when he came out he was more certain than before that she was the lady who called for the prussic acid. This, then, was a possible clue and the first and only one that the police had secured.

There arose countless suggestions during the afternoon that the police were called on to consider. John V. Morse developed into a seemingly very important factor before the day had passed, and special officer Medley was detailed to look up the facts concerning his whereabouts during that day. Mr. Morse had told the newspaper reporters of his visit in the morning to the house of a relative, Mrs. Emery at 4 Weybosset Street. Thither went the policeman accompanied by the writer to investigate. The Emerys were found at home, and Mrs. Emery said that Mr. Morse had visited her house that morning, arriving there before ten o'clock and remaining until 11:20. A niece of Mr. Morse was present, and she also declared that her uncle had left the house at the time stated. The testimony of these two witnesses would set at rest forever the theory that John V. Morse was within a mile of the Borden house when the old people were done to death. But these facts were not then generally known, and there were many persons who believed that he knew more concerning the killing than he cared to relate.

The city marshal sent a detail of police to guard the Borden house soon after the murder was reported, and instructions were given out that every member of the household be shadowed. Officer John Devine was designated to keep Mr. Morse in sight, and every movement that he made was carefully watched. He was allowed to come and go at will, but whenever he appeared on the street a great crowd gathered. On one evening in particular, when the excitement was at the highest tension, Mr. Morse set out for the post office. Before he had completed his journey, a mob numbering a thousand people was at his heels, and fears were entertained that he would be roughly handled. Officer Devine was in the shadow of Mr. Morse and saw him safely back to the Borden house.

Miss Lizzie Andrew Borden was thirty-two years old at the time of her father's death. Her mother died when she was two years of age, and she was cared for in her early childhood by her elder sister. A few years before the murder, she joined the Central Congregational Church and was oftentimes an active member of that society. She was reared under conditions that could have made life a luxury had she and her parents turned their attention to society. The most aristocratic drawing rooms of the city would have welcomed the daughters of Andrew J. Borden. But Miss Lizzie seemed to care but little for society. She preferred to move in a limited circle of friends and never sought to enlarge the number of her acquaintances. She avoided strangers and persons with whom she was not familiar. She was born in the old Borden homestead on Ferry Street in Fall River and received her education in the public schools, graduating from the high school early in life. Her classmates say that she was rather eccentric in her manner of life and of a retiring disposition. She never attended college, although her father was amply able to give her the best education that the schools of the country could furnish.

At the mission of the Central Church on Pleasant Street, Fall River, she taught a class of young people and there formed the acquaintance of the Reverend Edwin A. Buck, who was her constant companion and spiritual adviser during the great affliction that came to her in after life. Besides her active church work, she was a member of the Fruit and Flower Mission and other charitable organizations as well as the Woman's Christian Temperance Union.

In all these she was considered a valuable and conscientious worker. In the summer of 1890, she joined a party of young ladies who made the tour of Europe, but aside from this she never traveled extensively.

Miss Emma L. Borden was the eldest child, being thirty-seven at the time of her father's murder. She had been less active in church matters than Miss Lizzie and had not traveled outside the bounds of New England. Her education, disposition, and manner of life were somewhat similar to those of her sister. At the time of the murders, she was visiting friends in Fairhaven, Massachusetts, and arrived home on the evening of August 4 in response to a telegram sent by Dr. Bowen.

John V. Morse was sixty-nine years of age at the time of the murders. He is a native of New England, his early home being at Dartmouth, Massachusetts. At the age of twenty-five, he went west and located at Hastings, Iowa, where he engaged in farming and built up a comfortable fortune. For twenty years he was separated from his friends in Massachusetts, and during that time, by honesty and frugality, made himself a respected and influential citizen of his adopted state. Besides his farming interest, he was engaged in other enterprises that brought in a goodly sum of money. After his years of work in the west, he came back to New England, arriving at Warren, Rhode Island, in April 1888. He remained a short time in Warren and then removed to Dartmouth, which place he called his permanent home. After his return he made frequent visits to the home of the Bordens in Fall River and was on the most intimate terms with all the members of the family.

Hiram C. Harrington, a brother-in-law of Andrew J. Borden, having married Mr. Borden's only sister, Luanna, and a blacksmith by trade, threw some light on the manner in which the Bordens lived, which was highly interesting and important for the police to know. He said in an interview the day after the murder, "I have become acquainted with a good deal of the family history during years past. Mr. Borden was an exceedingly hard man concerning money matters, determined and stubborn, and when once he gets an idea nothing could change him. As for the motive for this crime, it was money, unquestionably money. If Mr. Borden died, he would have left something over five hundred thousand dollars, and in my opinion that estate furnishes the only motive and a sufficient one for the double murder. Last evening I had a long interview with Miss Lizzie, who has refused to see anyone else. I questioned her carefully as to her story of the crime. She was very composed, showed no signs of any emotion, nor were there any traces of grief on her countenance. That did not surprise me, as she is not naturally emotional. I asked her what she knew of her father's death, and after telling of the unimportant events of the early morning, she said her father came home at ten thirty. She was in the kitchen at the time, she said, but went into the sitting room when her father arrived.

"She was very solicitous concerning him and assisted to remove his coat and put on his dressing gown and inquired about his health. She told me that she helped him to get a comfortable reclining place on the sofa and asked him if he did not wish the blinds closed to keep out the sun so that he could have a nice nap. She pressed him to allow her to place an afghan over his body, but he said he did not need it. Then she asked him tenderly several times if he was perfectly comfortable, if there was anything she could do for him, and upon receiving assurance to the negative, she withdrew.

"I then questioned her very carefully as to the time she left the house, and she told me positively that it was about ten forty-five. She said she saw her father on the lounge as she passed out. On leaving the house, she says she went directly to the barn to obtain some lead. She informed me that it was her intention to go to Marion on a vacation, and she wanted the lead in the barn loft to make some sinkers. She was a very enthusiastic angler. I went over the ground several times, and she repeated the same story. She told me that it was hard to place the exact time she was in the barn, as she was cutting the lead into sizable sinkers, but thought she was absent about twenty minutes. Then she thought again and said it might have been thirty minutes. She entered the house and went directly to the sitting room, as she says she was anxious concerning her father's health. 'I discovered him dead,' she said, 'and cried for Bridget, who was upstairs in her room.' 'Did you go and look for your stepmother?' I asked. 'Who found her?' But she did not reply.

"I pressed her for some idea of the motive and the author of the act, and, after she had thought a moment, she said calmly, 'A year ago last spring, our house was broken into while Father and Mother were at Swansea, and a large amount of money stolen, together with diamonds. You never heard of it because Father did not want it mentioned, so as to give the detectives a chance to recover the property. That may have some connection with the murder. Then I have seen strange men around the house. A few months ago, I was coming through the backyard, and as I approached the side door, I saw a man there examining the door and premises. I did not mention it to anyone. The other day I saw the same man hanging about the house, evidently watching us. I became frightened and told my parents about it. I also wrote to my sister at Fairhaven about it.'

"Miss Borden then gave it as her opinion that the strange man had a direct connection with the murder, but she could not see why the house was not robbed and did not know of anyone who would desire revenge on her father.

"Yes, there were family dissentions, although it has been always kept very quiet. For nearly ten years, there have been constant disputes between the daughters and their father and stepmother. It arose, of course, with regard to the stepmother. Mr. Borden gave her some bank stock, and the girls thought they ought to be treated as evenly as the mother. I guess Mr. Borden did try to do it, for he deeded to the daughters, Emma L. and Lizzie A., the homestead on Ferry Street, an estate of one hundred and twenty rods of land, with a house and barn, all valued at three thousand dollars. This was in 1887. The trouble about money matters did not diminish, nor the acerbity of the family ruptures lessen, and Mr. Borden gave each girl ten shares in the Crystal Spring Bleachery Company, which he paid one hundred dollars a share for. They sold them soon after for less than forty dollars a share. He also gave them some bank stock at various times, allowing them, of course, the entire income from them. In addition to this, he gave them a weekly stipend amounting to two hundred dollars a year.

"In spite of all this, the dispute about their not being allowed enough went on with equal bitterness. Lizzie did most of the demonstrative contention, as Emma is very quiet and unassuming and would feel very deeply any disparaging or angry word from her father. Lizzie, on the contrary, was haughty and domineering with the stubborn will of her father and bound to contest for her rights.

"There were many animated interviews between father and daughter on this point. Lizzie is of a repellant disposition, and, after an unsuccessful passage with her father, would become sulky and refuse to speak to him for days at a time."

Friday morning came and with it little but mystery to add to the awful tragedy. The police had guarded the house all night. Marshal Hilliard had been active to an unusual degree, but the solution of the great murder mystery seemed to be as far distant as at any time since the discovery of the bodies. It was stated early Friday morning that arrests would be made during the day, but they were not.

Miss Lizzie Borden was suspected, but there was no evidence against her. It would have been a serious matter to arrest a person for such a terrible crime as this double murder, especially when it is considered that the one suspected occupied a high social position in the community. Besides, she had a spotless reputation, not one word of criticism had passed on her before this time, and, furthermore, she was an heiress to a fortune of not less than $300,000.

The officers of the law must have more evidence, and with this idea in view they again visited the house for the purpose of a more thorough search. On the afternoon before, the report had gone out that Miss Lizzie had refused the officers permission to search her room. This was promptly denied. However, they were not satisfied, and the ground was carefully gone over again. Five officers spent over three hours ransacking rooms, bureaus, beds, boxes, trunks, and everything else where it was thought that anything that they would like to find might be hidden.

Not a thing was discovered that afforded the slightest clue to the perpetrator of the bold and blood-curdling crimes.

The search party went to the house shortly after three o'clock and did not leave until nearly six o'clock. There were a number of people in the house beside the two daughters, the servant, and John V. Morse. The squad of police surrounding the house were given instructions not to let anyone enter or leave while the search was in progress, and they obeyed their orders to the letter.

Attorney Andrew J. Jennings of Fall River was also present. He had been retained by the Misses Borden to look after their interests but made no attempt to interfere in any way with the search party. Mr. Morse offered his services to the officers, but they were declined with thanks. The police were satisfied after an hour's work on the first floor and cellar, then they passed to the second floor. Miss Lizzie was in her room when they approached the door. She opened her trunk and said, "Is there anything I can do or show you, gentlemen?" She was told that nothing further was expected of her.

They spent another hour ransacking the rooms on this floor, but their efforts were unrewarded. Then the yard and barn were again searched but with the same result. Nothing was found and nothing was taken from the premises, if the words of a policeman at the time were to be depended on.

After the party left, one of the officers in conversation dwelt particularly on the demeanor of Miss Lizzie at the time of the search. He said, "I was surprised at the way she carried herself, and I must say that I admire her nerve. I did not think that a woman could have so much. She did not appear to be in the least bit excited or worried. I have wondered why she did not faint upon her discovery of the dead body of her father. Most women would have done so, for a more horrible sight I never saw, and I have walked over a battlefield where thousands lay mangled and dead. She is a woman of remarkable nerve and self-control, and her sister, Emma, is very much of the same disposition, although not so strong."

After so thorough a search of the house, it was expected that some startling developments would be made, but the public was doomed to disappointment. Contrary to the expectations of all, it was announced that absolutely nothing had been discovered that would lead to a clue or assist in any way in clearing up the great mystery.

There was one thing of importance that the police did accomplish on the second day after the murder. The time of the taking off of Mr. Borden was fixed at between 10:50 and 11:03, and it was assumed that Mrs. Borden was killed before that time.

On the morning after the tragedy, the following notice was sent to the newspapers: "Five thousand dollars reward. The above reward will be paid to anyone who may secure the arrest and conviction of the person or persons who occasioned the death of Andrew J. Borden and his wife. Signed, Emma L. Borden and Lizzie A. Borden."

Here was an incentive calculated to invigorate the work of those who were bent on solving the great mystery. But the police officers did not stop to read this announcement. It was as plain as a pike staff that they were not devoting their entire time and energies toward hunting up farmhands, mysterious Portuguese, and Westport horse traders. Yet it is an unquestionable fact that City Marshal Hilliard left no stone unturned to follow every clue of this kind to its end. They all ended in smoke.

The hatchets that had been found in the cellar had been sent for critical examination, and the public awaited with almost breathless anxiety the making of his report. On it depended much that would assist in clearing up the case. After the bodies had been placed in the receiving vault at Oak Grove, Mr. Morse concluded to bury the clothing that the victims wore at the time of death. He employed men to do the work. Under orders, the clothing was interred in the yard behind the barn. Just after this incident, Mr. Morse locked the barn door with two Boston reporters on the inside, and when they demanded their release, he found considerable fault with the liberties people were taking on the premises. He was reminded that a reward of $5,000 had been offered and that therefore everybody was intensely interested.

Within a few hours after the murder was reported, a detail of police was sent to guard the house. This policy was kept up for more than a week, and as early as Friday morning the officers on guard had instructions to keep the Misses Borden, John V. Morse, and Bridget Sullivan under the strictest surveillance and not allow any of them to leave the city. If they left the premises, they were followed.

On Saturday the case took on an unexpected phase. Superintendent O. M. Hanscom of the Boston office of the Pinkerton Detective Agency appeared on the scene. He was not employed by the mayor of Fall River nor the marshal of police, and it soon became noised abroad that he was present in the interests of the Misses Borden with the avowed intention of clearing up the mystery. In company with Mr. Jennings, he visited the Borden house and was in consultation with members of the family for about two hours.

Detective Hanscom remained in Fall River nearly two days and then disappeared as mysteriously as he came. It was the universal opinion at the time that the Pinkertons would unearth the assassin in a short while, but the public was never informed as to the reasons why they withdrew from the case. It was believed, however, that there was a rupture between Marshal Hilliard's men and the Pinkertons. This may or may not have been the cause of their sudden disappearance.

Marshal Hilliard and his officers, after two days' and two nights' work, concluded that the case was of so much importance that it was advisable to call District Attorney Hosea M. Knowlton, of New Bedford, Massachusetts, into their counsels, and accordingly he arrived from his home in New Bedford on Saturday morning. A short consultation was held at police headquarters and then adjourned until the afternoon. The district attorney, Marshal Hilliard, State Officer Seaver, Mayor Coughlin, and Dr. Dolan met according to agreement in one of the parlors of the Mellen house.

The marshal took all the evidence that he had collected in the shape of notes, papers, and other documents bearing on the case into the room where the five men were closeted, and they commenced at the beginning.

At the close of the conference held earlier in the afternoon, the district attorney had advised the officers to proceed with the utmost caution, and he was extremely conservative in the conclusions that he found. At that time he had not been made acquainted with all the details. At the Mellen house consultation, the same caution was observed. The quintet were working on one of the most remarkable criminal cases in history and were obliged to proceed slowly. The marshal began at the beginning and continued to the end. He was assisted in his explanation by the mayor and the medical examiner.

Mr. Seaver listened. There were details almost without end, and all of them were picked to pieces and viewed in every conceivable light. Considerable new evidence was introduced, then the testimony of officers not present was submitted, which showed that Miss Lizzie Borden might have been mistaken in one important particular.

The marshal informed the district attorney that the murder had occurred between 10:50 and 11:13 on Thursday morning. The time was as accurate as they could get it, and they had spared no pains to fix it.

The alarm had been given by Miss Lizzie Borden, the daughter of the murdered man, when she returned from the barn. At the moment of the discovery, she did not know that her stepmother was also dead, though she explained afterward that she thought her mother had left the house. It was but a short distance from the barn to the house. Nobody had been found who had seen anybody leaving the yard of the Borden house or entering it, although a number of people, who were named, were sitting by their windows close by.

It was also true that nobody had seen Miss Borden enter or leave the barn. She had explained that she went to the stable to procure some lead for a fish line, which she was going to use at Warren. Here there was a stumbling block that puzzled the district attorney and his assistants. On the day of the murder, Miss Lizzie had explained that she went to the loft of the barn for the lead, and an officer who was examining the premises also went to the loft. It was covered with dust, and there were no tracks to prove that any person had been there for weeks.

He took particular notice of the fact and reported back that he had walked about on the dust-covered floor on purpose to discover whether or not his own feet left any tracks. He said that they did and thought it singular that anybody could have visited the floor a short time before him and make no impression on the dust. The lower floor of the stable told no such tale, as it was evident that it had been used more frequently and the dust had not accumulated there.

The district attorney was much pleased with the work of the police and that an inquest would be held immediately before Judge Josiah C. Blaisdell of the Second District Court of Bristol, which is the Fall River local court.

The report that an inquest was to be held in the Second District Court before Judge J. C. Blaisdell was sufficient to draw the crowds.

Up to the time of opening the inquest, there had been nothing but circumstantial evidence found whereon to base a suspicion of guilt, and the fact that District Attorney Knowlton and Attorney General Albert E. Pillsbury, a distinguished and acute lawyer, had been called into the case showed that the authorities needed the wise counsel of the foremost legal talent in Massachusetts before taking the all-important step of making an arrest. If, after a thorough sifting of this circumstantial evidence, it was discovered that the theory of the state was wrong, then the guard would be called away from the Borden house and the authorities would be compelled to start on a new trail. The police were free to admit that there was but one theory, one clue, and if it proved unsuccessful, they had no other to take its place.

Officer Doherty was sent to the Borden house to bring Bridget Sullivan to the police station to appear as the first witness at the inquest.

He had some difficulty at the house because the impression had gone forth that he intended to arrest the servant girl. For a time there were tears and lamentation, but finally the officer made it understood that the only intention was to have the young woman talk to the district attorney.

On the way to the station, Miss Sullivan's tears came forth again. She told the office that she had given all information in her power to the police and that she knew nothing more than what she had stated. Talking about the family relations, she remarked that things didn't go in the house as they should and that she wanted to leave and had threatened to do so several times in the past two years. "But Mrs. Borden," she declared, "was a lovely woman, and I remained there because she wanted me to. Now that she is gone, however, I will stay there no longer than I have to and will leave just as soon as the police will allow me."

Bridget also said that the strain of remaining in the place was intense. All the women there who were members of the household—the Borden girls and Miss Sullivan—were almost ready to give way to nervous prostration. Awaiting her presence were District Attorney Knowlton, State Officer Seaver, Marshal Hilliard, and Medical Examiner Dolan, and soon after they were joined by Mayor Coughlin.

A report that an inquest was underway quickly spread but received prompt denial by the marshal. When asked the meaning of the gathering, he said it was an inquiry and the officers were searching for information. The domestic was in the presence of the officials for several hours and was subject to a searching cross-examination, every detail of the tragedy being gone over exhaustively. After this informed conference in the marshal's office, the party adjourned to the district courtroom, which is situated on the second floor in the building. There were present Judge Blaisdell; District Attorney Knowlton; City Marshal Hilliard; District Officers Seaver and Rhodes; Medical Examiner Dolan; the district attorney's stenographer, Miss Annie White; and a couple of police officials who were among the first called to the house of the Bordens.

Bridget Sullivan was in deep distress and, if she had not already cried her eyes out, would probably have been very much agitated. On the contrary, while tremulous in voice and now and then crying a little, she was calm enough to receive the interrogatories without exhibiting much emotion and answered them comprehensively.

The first question put to her was in regard to her whereabouts all through the morning of Thursday up to the time of the murder. She answered that she had been doing her regular work in the kitchen on the first floor. She had washed the breakfast dishes. She saw Miss Lizzie pass through the kitchen after breakfast time, and the young lady might have passed through again. Bridget continued that she had finished up her work downstairs and resumed window washing on the third floor, which she had begun the preceding day. She might have seen Mrs. Borden as she went upstairs. She could hardly remember. Mr. Borden had already left the house.

The witness went up into the third floor and, while washing windows, talked down to the sidewalk with a friend. She went on with the windows and might have made considerable noise as she raised and lowered them. She heard no noise inside the house in the meantime.

By-and-by she heard Miss Lizzie call her. She answered at once and went downstairs to the first floor, not thinking of looking about on the second floor, where Mrs. Borden was found dead shortly afterward, because there was nothing to make her look around as she obeyed Miss Lizzie's call. She found Mr. Borden dead and Lizzie at the door of the room.

City Marshal Hilliard had served the summons on Miss Lizzie at the house, and she arrived at the station about two o'clock. About this time attorney Andrew J. Jennings appeared at the city marshal's office and applied for permission to be present at the inquest in order to look after the interests of the witnesses, but he was refused. The counsel argued at length against being excluded, but the court would not yield, and he was compelled to withdraw.

All afternoon Miss Lizzie was kept on the witness stand and testified to what she knew of the killing of her father and stepmother. At the close of the day, District Attorney Knowlton gave out a bulletin stating that two witnesses had been examined. As the inquest was held behind doors closed and doubly guarded by the police, there was no way of finding out what had transpired within.

Although the inquest was held in secret, the day was marked by numerous happenings that lent interest to the already famous case. The attorney general who had been in consultation with the local authorities left the city in the afternoon, but before going he took occasion to say to an assembly of newspapermen that the case was not so mysterious as had been reported and bantered with them concerning their clues.

Perhaps his conversation was a bit of sarcasm. He was informed that the murder was mysterious enough to baffle the police and that five days had elapsed and there had been no arrest. Somebody took the pains to further inform him that the evidence was purely circumstantial.

"You newspapermen know, or ought to know," said Mr. Pillsbury, "that you may not be in a position to pronounce on the case. There may be some things that you have not heard of and that may have an important bearing."

The reply was to the effect that the head men who had been working on the case had conceded at noon that day that they had no other evidence and that they ought to be pretty good authority. "Police officers do not always tell what they know" was the parting shot of the attorney general as he withdrew.

At five o'clock Bridget Sullivan left the police station in the company of Officer Doherty and passed down Court Square. She was dressed in a green gown with hat to match and appeared to be nervous and excited. Nobody knew her, however, and she attracted no attention whatever. She went to the Borden house for a bundle and, still accompanied by Officer Doherty, walked to 95 Division Street, where her cousin, Patrick Harrington, lives and where she passed the night. She was allowed to go on her own recognizance and seemed to be much relieved to get away from the Borden house.

The government impressed her with the necessity of saying nothing about the proceedings at the inquest, and she was warned not to talk with anybody regarding her testimony.

Professor Wood, of Cambridge, arrived on the four o'clock train Monday afternoon but was not called to testify at the inquest on Tuesday. He was questioned regarding the nature of his visit and stated that he had come to Fall River to see what there was for him to do. "Have you examined any ax, professor?" was asked. Professor Wood hesitated a moment, then said, "I have seen an ax."

"Will you make an examination down here?"

"I do not expect to. I could not very well bring down my laboratory."

At six o'clock Miss Lizzie Borden, accompanied by her friend Mrs. George Brigham and Marshal Hilliard, entered a carriage and drove to Miss Borden's home. The excitement was not over for the day, but the district attorney's bulletin made it plain that the authorities would make no further move that night. When the inquest adjourned, the situation in a nutshell was this: The authorities were evidently convinced that they could rely on Bridget Sullivan, and she was released from custody. She had been in custody since Thursday noon. Miss Lizzie Borden had been partially examined, and the police had completed their work on the case, so far as the collection of evidence was concerned.

As was natural, the newspapers throughout the country began at about this stage of the proceedings to take sides on the question of the wisdom exhibited by the police. The editorial quoted below is from the *Springfield Republican* and is a fair sample of the opinions of those who saw the investigation from a distance. It read:

All through the investigations carried on by the Fall River police, a lack of ability has been shown seldom equalled, and causes they assign for connecting the daughter with the murder are on a par with their other exhibitions of lack of wisdom. Because someone, unknown to them and too smart for them to catch, butchered two people in the daytime on a principal street of the city, using brute force, far in excess of that possessed by this girl, they conclude that there is probable reason to believe that she is the murderess. Because they found no one walking along the street with his hands and clothes reeking with blood, they conclude that it is probable, after swinging the ax with the precision and effect of a butcher, she washed the blood from her hands and clothes.

Wednesday morning the inquest was resumed. At its close the district attorney issued the following bulletin: "Inquest continued at 10 today. Witnesses examined were Lizzie Borden, Dr. S. W. Bowen, Adelaide B.

Churchill, Hiram C. Harrington, John V. Morse, and Emma Borden. Nothing developed for publication."

Among those present, in addition to the prosecuting officials, was Professor Wood of Harvard, to whom the stomachs of the murdered couple had been sent for analysis. After an hour's stay in the police station, a carriage was ordered by the marshal, and, upon its arrival, Professor Wood entered. Next a trunk was brought out under the charge of Medical Examiner Dolan and placed on the carriage. The latter bade Professor Wood good-bye, and the Cambridge man was driven to the station. It was promptly presumed that included in the contents of the trunk were the ax and articles requiring analysis, and an inquiry covering these points was directed to Dr. Dolan. He declined to affirm or deny anything and informed the newspaper representatives in a jocular vein that all the clues and secrets of the case were carefully secreted in the trunk.

All this time public interest was centered on the fact of Miss Lizzie's presence in the courtroom, and it was felt that the most important hours of the investigation were dragging along. If the young woman, toward whom such suspicion had been directed, should come forth and retire to her home, little more could be expected in this direction.

Certainly, after the searching examination, which all knew she was undergoing, any further questioning could but be useless, and there were those in the gathered crowds in the vicinity of Court Square who openly proclaimed their earnest convictions that with the exit of Lizzie Borden from the station house the cloud of suspicions that had hovered about her must be dispelled, with the accompanying practical admission by the authorities that they were unable to connect her with the commission of the crime.

This statement was based on the widespread knowledge that the police had been moving with the greatest caution in their investigation on the thoroughly understood line.

The members of the Borden family held a high position, their wealth was great, and, apart from the fact that their interests were being guarded by one of the ablest attorneys in the city, it was known that influential friends of the family had deemed it wise to request the marshal to move with the utmost care before taking active steps toward the arrest of any member of that household.

Perhaps the accusation that, had certain suspected persons been possessed of less wealth and influence, they would long ere this have been apprehended was unjust to the hardworking police, but the fact was patent to everybody that the extreme care in this particular case reached far beyond the usual, particularly as all the time every movement of the Borden girls was only made under the surveillance of a police officer.

During the afternoon carpenter Maurice Daly, the marshal, and Officer Harrington appeared at the Borden house. The first mentioned had a kit of carpenter's tools in his hand, and the three men entered the house. After half an hour, they came out and were noticed carrying three bundles. These contained parts of the woodwork about the doors and windows that showed blood spots.

Thursday was the last day of the inquest, and in its evening hours a veritable sensation was produced. The same impenetrable secrecy was maintained all day long, and no one knew what progress was being made behind the grim stone walls of the Central Police Station wherein Judge Blaisdell and the chosen few sat in solemn conclave.

Crowds surged about the doors, and a double guard of patrolmen were doing duty in the hallways. The forenoon session developed nothing so far as the public was concerned. In the afternoon, Eli Bence, the drug clerk; Fred Hart, another clerk; and Frank Kilroy, who saw Mr. Borden on the morning of the tragedy, strolled into the guard room and were shown upstairs. Later, Bridget Sullivan, escorted by two officers, walked up the alley.

She attracted no attention and appeared to be at her ease. The fact that Bridget walked from her temporary residence at 95 Division Street to the police station, a distance of more than a mile in the heat of an August day, while other female witnesses rode in a hack from the Borden house, a distance of less than an eighth of a mile, caused some comment.

About three o'clock in the afternoon, the closed carriage that had become almost as familiar a sight as the police patrol rattled over the rough pavement. Half a dozen men were in sight, and in a twinkling two hundred men, women, and children swarmed around the coach.

The city marshal gave an order, Steward Geagan cracked a whip, officers hustled the crowd back, and Mrs. George S. Brigham alighted. She was followed by Misses Emma and Lizzie Borden. Then Officer Doherty disappeared with the hack and returned with another witness. The same crowd collected, but no one tried to drive it back. The excitement subsided. It was growing tiresome in Fall River.

The reaction had set in; the community was losing its patience. For two days it had been informed that the end was near and that the die was about to be cast, but at three o'clock the bulletin boards announced that no action had been taken and no verdict had been rendered, and the crowds muttered and grumbled. They wanted something done; their interest in clues and theories and suspicious characters had about died out. More than that, they were no longer satisfied with reports of the proceedings at the inquest detailed step by step.

They demanded the grand finale that would bring the drama to a close or ring the curtain up on a new scene, but it seemed as if the grand finale had been indefinitely postponed. The hour dragged along, and the gray walls of the courthouse in the square kept their secrets, if they had any to keep. It was the same story over and over again. Witnesses known to be connected with the case appeared and disappeared, officers were sent hither and thither, and various rumors were afloat regarding the probable outcome.

From the time that the carriage rolled up to the entrance to the Central Police Station at 4:30 p.m. and Lizzie Borden, Emma Borden, and Mrs. George Brigham dismounted under the watchful eye of Marshal Hilliard, people commenced to congregate about the streets contiguous to the station house. By that intuitive perception by which the general public becomes aware of all important proceedings looking toward the capture or apprehension of criminals in noted cases, it was recognized that the most important movements of the long investigation had been entered on and that their passing was fraught with the greatest import to all directly concerned in the case as well as the public, restless under the week's delay in clearing the way for the arrest of the murderer.

There was nothing remarkable in the appearance of the party, Miss Emma Borden being evidently the most agitated. The excitement grew as the hour passed and there was no movement from the courtroom. In the meanwhile information arrived that an expert safe opener had arrived from Boston and had been driven hurriedly to the Borden house on Second Street.

Investigation showed the truth of this story and the further fact that he had commenced work on the safe in which Andrew J. Borden kept his books and papers. This safe was found locked at the time of the tragedy, and the secret of the combination died with the murdered man. The expert believed he could easily open the safe, but he found the combination most intricate, and he worked away without apparent result.

At five o'clock Marshal Hilliard and District Attorney Knowlton came from the courtroom and entered a carriage. Soon the marshal returned, but the district attorney was absent for nearly an hour, and it was reported that he had visited the Borden house and had learned that the safe opener had not completed his work. Outside the courtroom, the stalwart officers kept guard, and at the foot of the stairs in the station house, the large force of newspaper representatives was on guard.

The subordinate officers who had been working on the case expressed their convictions that the long-delayed arrest was about to be made and that Lizzie Borden would not depart from the station with the remaining members of the household.

Soon Bridget Sullivan emerged and, escorted by a police officer, walked slowly down the street. The gravity of the situation was apparent, for the natural sternness of some of the officials, including the marshal, was increased to such an extent as to warrant the inference that something of importance in connection with the case was about to happen.

Soon the inquisition was apparently ended. Then Lizzie Borden, her sister, and Mrs. Brigham were escorted across the entry from the courtroom to the matron's room, which is situated on the same floor. An officer came out and soon returned with supper for the party. Miss Lizzie Borden threw herself on the lounge in the room, and the repast was disturbed but little.

Across the room there was grave work, and the decision of the authorities to arrest Lizzie Borden was arrived at after a consultation lasting but ten minutes. The services of the clerk were called into requisition. The warrant was quickly drawn, and the result of the long examinations and the week's work of the government was in the hands of the police force of Fall River. At this time the news was among the reporters, but none were certain enough of the fact to dispatch the intelligence to the journals they represented.

The excitement became general, and men, women, and children stood about the street and waited. Soon Marshal Hilliard came out accompanied by Mr. Knowlton, and as they entered a carriage a telephone message informed Andrew J. Jennings, attorney for the family, that the two men were about to pay him a visit at his residence. This information obtained but little publicity, and not a few in the assembled crowds believed that Mr. Knowlton was being driven to the Boston train. The marshal and the district attorney proceeded to Mr. Jennings's residence and informed that gentleman that the government had decided on the arrest of Lizzie Borden, and, recognizing that his presence at the station would be desirable, had deemed it wise to notify him of the decision arrived at and the contemplated action. The officials returned to the courtroom and were followed in a few moments by the attorney. George Brigham also came to the station and entered the presence of the women in the matron's quarters.

There was a moment's preparation, then Lizzie Borden was informed that she was held by the government on the charge of having murdered her father. Marshal Hilliard and Detective Seaver entered the room, the former holding in his hand a sheet of paper—the warrant for Lizzie Borden's arrest—and, after requesting Mrs. Brigham to leave the room, addressing the prostrate woman in the gentlest possible manner, said, "I have here a warrant for your arrest—issued by the judge of the district court. I shall read it to you if you desire, but you have the right to waive the reading of it."

He looked at lawyer Jennings as he completed the latter part of the statement, and that gentleman turned toward Lizzie and said, "Waive the reading." The first and only time during the scene that the accused woman uttered a word was in response to the direction of her attorney.

Turning slightly in her position, she flashed a look at the marshal, one of those queer glances that nobody has attempted to describe, except by saying that they are a part and parcel of Lizzie Borden, and replied, "You need not read it."

The information had amost depressing effect on all the others present, particularly on Miss Emma Borden, who was greatly affected. On the face of the prisoner there was a pallor, and while her eyes were moist with tears, there was little evidence of emotion in the almost stolid countenance.

The remaining members of the party then prepared to depart, and the effects of the arrest became apparent on the prisoner. She still displayed all the characteristics of her peculiarly unemotional nature, and though almost prostrated, she did not shed a tear.

A carriage was ordered, and Miss Emma Borden and Mr. and Mrs. Brigham prepared to leave. As they emerged from the station into the view of the curious crowds, the women, particularly Miss Emma, looked about with almost a pathetic glance. The people crowded forward, and the police pushed them back. Miss Borden appeared to be suffering intensely, and all the external evidences of agitation were visible on her countenance. Mrs. Brigham was more composed but was evidently deeply concerned. The party entered the carriage and were driven rapidly toward Second Street.

Lizzie A. Borden was accused of the murder of her father, Andrew J. Borden. The warrant made no reference to the killing of Abbie D. Borden. That night the prisoner was overcome by the great mental strain to which she had been subjected for nearly a week, and, when all had departed except the kindly matron, the burden proved heavier than she could bear. She gave way to her feelings and sobbed as if her heart would break. Then she gave up to a violent fit of vomiting, and the efforts of the matrons to stop it were unavailing. Dr. Bowen was sent for, and he succeeded in relieving her physical sufferings. The prisoner was not confined in a cell room of the lockup downstairs.

Judge Blaisdell, District Attorney Knowlton, and Marshal Hilliard are men of experience, good sense, and reliable judgment, and no other three men on earth regretted the step they had taken more than they. But from their point of view it was duty, not sentiment, that guided their actions. No other prisoner arrested in Bristol County had been accorded the delicate and patient consideration that Marshal Hilliard bestowed on

Miss Lizzie Borden. No cell doors closed on her until after an open, fair, and impartial trial before a competent judge and, defended by her chosen legal counsel, she was adjudged "probably guilty."

Miss Lizzie A. Borden was to be arraigned in the Second District Court on Friday morning. By nine o'clock a crowd of people thronged the streets and stood in a drenching rain to await the opening of the door of the room in which the court held its sittings. It was not a well-dressed crowd, nor was there anybody in it from the acquaintance circle of the Borden family in Fall River. Soon after nine o'clock, a hack rolled up to the side door, and Emma Borden and John V. Morse alighted and went up the stairs. They were not admitted at once to the matron's room. Reverend E. A. Buck was already present and was, at the time, engaged in conversation with the prisoner. Judge Blaisdell passed up the stairs, while Miss Emma was waiting to see her sister, and entered the courtroom. Mr. Jennings, the counsel, also arrived.

The district attorney was already in the courtroom, and soon the marshal brought in his large book of complaints and took his seat at the desk. The door of the matron's room opened, and Mr. Jennings, Miss Emma Borden, and Mr. Morse met the prisoner. All retired within the room. A few moments later, Mr. Jennings came out and entered the courtroom. He at once secured a blank sheet of legal cap and began to write. The city marshal approached him, and Mr. Jennings nodded an assent to an inquiry if the prisoner could now be brought in.

Lizzie Borden entered the room immediately after on the arm of Reverend Mr. Buck. She was dressed in a dark blue suit, and her hat was black with red flowers on the front. She was escorted to a chair. The prisoner was not crying, but her features were far from firm. She has a face and chin betokening strength of character but a rather sensitive mouth, and on this occasion the sensitiveness of the lips especially betrayed her. She was constantly moving her lips as she sat in the courtroom in a way to show that she was not altogether unemotional.

Clerk Leonard called the case of the commonwealth of Massachusetts against Lizzie Borden, on complaint of murder. Mr. Jennings, who was still writing, asked for a little more time. He soon arose and went over to the prisoner. He spoke to her, and then she arose and went to his desk. He read what he had been writing to her, then gave her a pen. She signed the paper.

Mr. Jennings then addressed the court, saying, "Your honor, before the prisoner pleads she wishes to present the following." He then read as follows: "Bristol ss. Second District Court. Commonwealth versus Lizzie A. Borden. Complaint for homicide. Defendant's plea.

"And now comes the defendant in the above entitled complaint and before pleading thereto says that the Honorable Josiah C. Blaisdell, the presiding justice of the Second District Court of Bristol, before which said complaint is returnable, has been and believes is still engaged as the presiding magistrate at an inquest on the death of said Andrew J. Borden, the person whom it is alleged in said complaint the defendant killed, and has received and heard and is still engaged in receiving and hearing evidence in relation to said killing and to said defendant's connection therewith, which is not and has not been allowed to hear or know the report of, whereof she says that said Honorable Josiah C. Blaisdell is disqualified to hear this complaint, and she objects to his so doing, and all of this she is ready to verify.

"Lizzie A. Borden, by her attorney, Andrew J. Jennings, (her signature) Lizzie A. Borden. Sworn to this the twelfth day of August, A.D., 1892, before me, Andrew J. Jennings, justice of the peace."

When Mr. Jennings concluded, the district attorney arose and asked the court if this paper was to delay the prisoner's plea. The court said it was not and ordered the clerk to read the warrant.

"You needn't read it," said Mr. Jennings. "The prisoner pleads not guilty."

The text of the warrant, however, was as follows:

Commonwealth of Massachusetts,

To Augustus B. Leonard, clerk of the Second District Court of Bristol, in the county Bristol, and justice of the peace:

Rufus B. Hilliard, city marshal of Fall River, in said county, in behalf of said commonwealth, on oath, complains that Lizzie A. Borden of Fall River, in the county of Bristol, at Fall River, aforesaid, in the county aforesaid, on the fourth day of August, in the year of

*our Lord 1892, in and upon one Andrew J. Borden, feloniously, will-
fully, and of her malice aforethought, did make assault and that the
said Lizzie A. Borden, then and there with a certain weapon, to wit,
a hatchet, in and upon the head of the said Andrew J. Borden, then
and there feloniously, willfully, and of her malice aforethought, did
strike, giving unto the said Andrew J. Borden, then and there, with
the hatchet aforesaid, by the stroke aforesaid, in manner aforesaid, in
and upon the head of the said Andrew J. Borden, one mortal wound,
of which said mortal wound the said Andrew J. Borden then and
there instantly died. And so the complainant aforesaid, upon his oath
aforesaid, further complains and says that the said Lizzie A. Borden,
the said Andrew J. Borden, in manner and form aforesaid, then and
there feloniously, willfully, and of her malice aforethought did kill and
murder.*
(Signed) R. B. Hilliard.

"The prisoner must plead in person," said Judge Blaisdell. At a sign
from City Marshal Hilliard, the prisoner arose in her seat.

"What is your plea?" asked the clerk.

"Not guilty," said the girl, and then, having said this indistinctly and
the clerk repeating his question, she answered the same thing in a louder
voice with a very clearly cut emphasis on the word "not."

Sources

Jon Seidel. "Murderess Row," from *Second City Sinners, True Crime from Historic Chicago's Deadly Streets*. Guilford, CT: Lyons Press, 2010.

Thomas Furlong. "The Preller Murder Case," from *Fifty Years a Detective*. St. Louis: CE Barnett, 1912.

Jason Ryan. "They Took Everything," from *Hell Bent, One Man's Crusade to Crush the Hawaiian Mob*. Guilford, CT: Lyons Press, 2014.

J. North Conway. "King of Thieves," from *King of Heists, The Sensational Bank Robbery of 1878 That Shocked America*. Guilford, CT: Lyons Press, 2009.

Cleveland Moffett. "The Rock Island Express," from *True Detective Stories from the Archives of the Pinkertons*. New York: G. W. Dillingham, 1893.

Dick North. "The Mad Trapper of Rat River," from *The Mad Trapper of Rat River*. Guilford, CT: Lyons Press, 2005.

Nicholas J. C. Pistor. "The Ax Murders of Saxtown," from *The Ax Murders of Saxtown, The Unsolved Crime That Terrorized a Town and Shocked a Nation*. Guilford, CT: Lyons Press, 2014.

Henry Hill and Daniel Simone. "The Lufthansa Heist," from *The Lufthansa Heist*. Guilford, CT: Lyons Press, 2015.

J. H. Hanson. "The Northfield Bank Job," from *The Northfield Tragedy*. St. Paul, MN: John Jay Lemon, 1876.

Edwin H. Porter. "Lizzie Borden Took an Ax," from *The Fall River Tragedy: A History of the Borden Murders*. Fall River, MA: George R. H. Buffington, 1893.